INTERNATIONAL JOBS
Where They Are and How to Get Them
Fourth Edition

ERIC KOCHER

ADDISON-WESLEY PUBLISHING COMPANY

Reading, Massachusetts   Menlo Park, California   New York
Don Mills, Ontario   Wokingham, England   Amsterdam   Bonn
Sydney   Singapore   Tokyo   Madrid   San Juan
Paris   Seoul   Milan   Mexico City   Taipei

Library of Congress Cataloging-in-Publication Data

Kocher, Eric, 1912–
   International jobs: where they are and how to get them / Eric Kocher. — 4th ed.
     p. cm.
   Includes bibliographical references and index.
   ISBN 0-201-62222-X
   1. Employment in foreign countries—Handbooks, manuals, etc.
   2. Americans—Employment—Foreign countries—Handbooks, manuals, etc.
   I. Title.
   HF5549.5.E45K63   1993
   331.7'02—dc20   93-8766
                                                                       CIP

Cover design by Skolos/Wedell, Inc.
Text design by Anna George
Set in 10-point Palatino by CopyRight, Inc.

4 5 6 7-MA-97969594
Fourth printing, July 1994

To all students everywhere — and their parents — who cast a longing eye on international work; and to Peggy, who was once a student herself and still has that glint in her eye.

CONTENTS

ACKNOWLEDGMENTS

This handbook would not have been written without the contribution of students. In a sense they have written it for me, because the problems they have posed in their search for international careers — and the various courses of action we have discussed — provide the material that appears in the following pages.

An older group, Foreign Service Officers leaving the Department of State for other international jobs, must also be thanked. Many of the job leads developed in my work with this group have found their way into this handbook.

Special thanks must go to Sarah Ashton, Education Specialist and holder of an M.A. in International Affairs at Columbia University, who has shown unusual efficiency and imagination in her research for this fourth edition. I am also indebted to Dr. Steven Noble, recently vice president of the Association of Management Consultant Firms, and now Executive Director, Human Resource Planning Society, who gave me many helpful suggestions for the section on management consultants. I would also be remiss not to make special mention of Gordon Paulsen, eminent lawyer, friend, and neighbor, who helped me understand the complexities of international law.

In addition to her editing skills, I am indebted to Sharon Broll, my editor, for offering creative suggestions to update the contents of the Publishing Section and for generally shepherding the shape and contents of the book to optimum effectiveness.

INTRODUCTION

With the recent disintegration of the Soviet Union and the tilt to democracy of Eastern Europe, this is an especially good time to consider an international career.

Even before these changes, and during the fourteen years since *International Jobs* was first published, the world has been drawing closer together. Fourteen years ago, the recognition that we are all living interdependently in "one world" came primarily from the nuclear threat. Since then, additional threats have accumulated — acid rain, hazardous waste, overpopulation, the greenhouse effect.

The drive to world unity has not always been fueled by threats, however. The ease and speed of communications and transportation have increased, and with them have come the possibility of new jobs never before envisioned. A New York insurance company, for example, processes its claims in Ireland more cheaply than if these claims were processed in New York. And the interval between receipt and payment of claims is no more lengthy than before. High technology, though it has its detractors, is reemphasizing our dependence on each other. And as the world draws more closely together, more jobs become international.

This handbook is for everyone interested in an international career, whether an undergraduate at college or a graduate student. If you are already at work full time but wish to explore opportunities in the international field, it will help you in shifting jobs and/or careers.

The purpose of this handbook is to broaden your knowledge of international career opportunities so that you can find the job you want. Its contents are divided into two parts: Part I is concerned with career planning and job strategy; Part II, with the international job market.

In Part I, we take up job-hunting problems chronologically, as you will probably experience them. First you have to plan your career in the international field (Chapter One). Then you will want to tailor your curriculum to one or more possible careers (Chapter Two). If you are a student looking for summer work overseas, or if you are the spouse of an American working abroad and decide to get a job yourself, you will need information on work permits and any special problems related to work in a foreign country (Chapter Three). On any job hunt — whether for summer or full-time employment — you must present yourself in the strongest and most favorable light using three main tools: job letters, résumés, and interviews (Chapter Four).

Even with the most effective job strategy in the world, you will not get far unless you know your target. This subject — the job opportunities available in each international field — is so crucial it constitutes a special section of the handbook, Part II.

The handbook recognizes that some of you may know specifically what kind of international career you want; others may not yet have defined your goal any more closely than "doing something international."

No matter which group you are in, the following breakdown of international career opportunities, which is the focus of Part II, will be of interest to you:

The New World of the 1990s (Chapter Five)

Federal Government (Chapter Six)

United Nations (Chapter Seven)

Businesses and Banks (Chapter Eight)

Nonprofit Organizations (Chapter Nine)

Journalism, Broadcasting, and Publishing (Chapter Ten)

Teaching (Chapter Eleven)

Law (Chapter Twelve)

The names and addresses of organizations in each field, as well as a brief description of their functions, are listed. (Always check the addresses given before sending out a letter or résumé; organizations sometimes move.) Further, the handbook describes the qualifications for each type of job.

If you know which career or careers interest you, you will want to look closely at the detailed opportunities available in these fields. If you are not attracted to any particular career, you may wish to browse through Chapters Five through Twelve. Perhaps exposure to the organizations and jobs in each international field may dissipate the uncertainty and inspire you to experiment with one particular career.

part one

INTERNATIONAL CAREER PLANNING AND JOB STRATEGY

1

FIRST QUESTIONS

Despite an occasional longing for isolationism, the United States seems firmly committed to internationalism. This orientation is shared by the government and the private sector alike. As a result, job opportunities in the international field cover a broad spectrum: federal government, business, communications, banking, nonprofit organizations and foundations, and of course the whole United Nations system.

This diversity of fields affords unparalleled opportunities for those of you who know what you want to do in the international framework and who prepare yourselves accordingly. A career decision, however, needs focus and definition if you want it to work for you. "Doing something international" is usually only the first stage in a decision. Your goals must be further narrowed to help you compete effectively with others who are also entering the international market.

Do you want to be a Foreign Service officer working on one of the embassies of the Department of State? Do you wish to be an intelligence analyst for the federal government? Or a branch bank manager in some remote — or cosmopolitan — part of the globe? How about a U.N. employee working on developmental problems of Third World countries? Or a foreign correspondent in Rome, Paris, London — or Ouagadougou or Tegucigalpa — for one of the press services?

All of these are acceptable and reasonable career goals. But don't be so rigidly committed to one that everything else is excluded. If, for example, you want to work in the U.N. Development Programme, don't overlook similar job opportunities in the Agency for International Development (AID) or development work in foundations. If your aim is to be a *New York Times* correspondent in Moscow, consider also working as an overseas press officer for the federal government's United States Information Agency (USIA).

The first question, then, is "What is it I really want to do in the international field?" Your answer will probably be narrower than "doing something international" but broader than "working at the UNDP office in Bangladesh." If you are really lucky, you may be able to achieve a very specific objective such as the latter, but the odds are against you, so it is generally preferable to keep yourself flexible — within limits. As you go through this handbook you will find that a career objective need not be nailed down to one specific job. There are related jobs that will use your background just as fully and probably give you equal satisfaction.

After you have decided what you really want to do in the international field, you will come upon another major question needing equal attention: "How available are jobs in the field or fields I have chosen?" Then further questions will have to be looked at: "How do I prepare myself so that my academic credentials are strong enough to attract employers? What limiting factors (such as location and salary) exist in my job search? Are there special considerations — because of the international aspect — that enter into my job strategy?" These are some of the questions that will be discussed in this handbook.

WHAT EXACTLY IS AN INTERNATIONAL JOB?

"International" does not necessarily mean "abroad." You can have an international career working in the international division of a corporation in New York and seldom, if ever, go overseas. You can work in the Department of State in Washington and spend your whole career on foreign policy problems without leaving the country. The usual international career, however, consists of varying degrees of work at headquarters and in the field.

HOW DO YOU FIND OUT WHAT YOU WANT TO DO?

A specific job objective (or objectives) is the foundation on which the edifice of job-hunting techniques is built. If you don't know what you're looking for, the search becomes aimless, each action taken without relation to a central focus.

Still, there are no absolute truths in career guidance, and exceptions to the above do exist. None of the international careers available may attract you sufficiently to orient your curriculum toward such an objective, narrow or broad. Accordingly, you may decide — either consciously or through failure to make a choice — to "hang loose" and "see what comes up." In other words, you stick with "doing something international," which is usually only the first step in a career decision.

International drifting does not necessarily mean disaster or an unsatisfactory professional life. It *does* mean that the initial job hunt may be more difficult; it can also mean that the level you reach on the organizational ladder may not be as high as that of some of your colleagues. If you are prepared to accept these risks because of your own emotional predispositions, don't allow yourself to be pushed into a career in which you have little interest.

If you don't know what you want to do but prefer not to drift, you will be seeking two kinds of knowledge. One is self-knowledge, an awareness of your skills, capabilities, and emotional needs; the other is knowledge about the world of work.

Self-knowledge lies beyond the scope of this handbook and may be explored through psychological and testing centers as well as self-evaluation. Knowledge of the kind of international work available is more tangible. A large part of this handbook is concerned with providing information on this subject. But you will also want to inform yourself about various international careers in a number of other ways.

College Placement Offices

If you are still in school, you should consult your placement office during each stage leading to your career decision. A knowledgeable placement officer can be enormously helpful in expanding your job horizons. He or she will not make a career decision for you but can act as a sounding board for your questions and doubts.

Available Literature

There are many books and brochures giving information on international careers. The U.N. organizations, various federal agencies, and nonprofit organizations all have informational literature available for the asking. Banks and businesses have annual reports and recruiting brochures, also readily available. Glamorized as much of this material may be, it will give you helpful information on organizational functions, availability of jobs, and career development.

Especially useful is the *Encyclopedia of Career and Vocational Guidance.** It is in two parts: *Planning Your Career* and *Careers and Occupations*. If, for example, you wish to explore a mild attraction for banking without much knowledge of the field, go through the material on banking in these volumes. In the first

*Garden City, NY: Doubleday. Out of print, but the 1987 edition is available in most large reference libraries.

volume you will find information on the nature of banking, opportunties in the field, educational preparation for a career, and areas of employment. The second part discusses specific bank jobs, such as the functions of a lending officer or credit analyst. Each job category lists information on qualifications needed, methods of entering the field, advancement opportunities, employment outlook, earnings, and conditions of work. By going over this material and visualizing yourself in a number of roles, you will make progress in determining their suitability for you and yours for them. The various departments of labor in the federal and state governments also have much useful reference material on occupations and job functions. Much of this material will round out your knowledge and clarify questions arising from your study of the *Encyclopedia*.

If you are interested in federal government work, try to get the *Career America Literature*.* This lists the brochures used in nationwide recruiting by each federal agency. For example, under "Department of State" we find listed a brochure *Foreign Service Careers*, which can be obtained easily from that department.

Directories of businesses, banks, nonprofit organizations, publishers, and consultants (see the Bibliography) are available in your city or college library.

Friends, Relatives, and Alumni

It is said that 85 percent of all jobs are obtained through contacts. Even if the correct figure is only 60 or 70 percent, that percentage is still too high for you to ignore this most important source of jobs. Do you have friends or relatives working in organizations with international interests? If so, go see them. Get names of alumni in specific international occupations from your school and ask them about their work. Knowledgeable people are better sources of career information than printed material, which sometimes raises more questions than it answers. Talk to your contacts at length. Find out how they prepared for their careers, how they obtained their jobs, what their career development has been. In particular, get information about what they do on a daily basis. A detailed description of their functions may provoke boredom, curiosity, or enthusiasm in you; whatever the reaction, this information provides one more indication of your suitability for that field of work.

The Outlook for Each Occupation

If you have read the available literature on one or more careers and talked to friends, relatives, and alumni you should by now have a great deal of useful

*Obtainable from the U.S. Government Printing Office, Washington, DC.

information. You may be quite turned off by one or more of these careers — or perhaps your interest has grown and you are eager for further exploration.

Suppose you are favorably disposed toward one of these international occupations. What sort of future does it have? Is it in a growing industry or a shrinking one? What will it look like in 1998 — or 2010? The *Occupational Outlook Handbook** is helpful in answering these questions. If you consult the *Handbook*, you will find that increases in employment (not necessarily international) are expected in the fields of population, ecology, conservation, energy, pollution control, technology, and in service industries (such as leisure activities and hospital care). Concerning federal government employment, the number of professional and administrative personnel will probably increase in the next decade, whereas the number of clerical workers will most likely decrease.

Mobility Between Careers

Even after informing yourself thoroughly about a career, you may still hestitate to make a decision. You're pretty sure but not absolutely sure. Further, you fear that any decision will commit you to a specific career for the rest of your life.

Recognize that there will almost always be a degree of uncertainty in any career choice you make. It is the rare individual who will be absolutely certain. It is only when you are actually at work that you will really know the atmosphere, the people, the details of the job, and all those other fine, intangible points that sometimes make the difference between liking and not liking the work.

When you have reached the stage of 80 or 90 percent certainty, perhaps it is time to relax. No choice is irrevocable or totally binding. If you start in on an international banking career, for example, and later wish to slip over into government, the skills and experience you have learned will strengthen your credentials for work with the Treasury Department, the Export-Import Bank, and other government agencies dealing with matters of international finance.

If, to take an outside example, you should decide to switch from banking to a career in the theatre, you'll have less immediate mobility. The choice of quite a different career may mean returning to school or otherwise gaining credentials to make you attractive to an employer in that field.

Fortunately, mobility between careers these days is higher — and more acceptable — than it was some years ago. Employers are now usually more tolerant of individuals who move from one career to another. Instead of change being viewed as the action of an insecure or even neurotic individual, it is often considered as adding richness and depth to an applicant's background and personality.

*Washington, DC: U.S. Department of Labor or Government Printing Office, updated yearly.

Tax Exemption and Other Perquisites

The salary of a job may or may not be important to you. But if a high salary is among your top priorities, you should be aware that working overseas usually brings special financial rewards. Although the base pay may be the same as in the States, there are perquisites attached to overseas jobs which may double or even triple your stated salary. Among them is a cost-of-living allowance if you are stationed in a country where the cost of living exceeds that in the United States. If you are posted to a country where guerrillas are fighting near the capital, there may be a differential in salary to compensate for the danger. Free housing may be provided, as well as a special representation allowance for entertaining, if that is an important part of the job. You may also be reimbursed for the expense involved in sending your children back to school in the United States.

But the greatest addition to overseas salary is provided by Public Law 97-34 whereby much or all income earned overseas (except by government employees) is exempt from U.S. income taxes. Since 1986 the exemption has been set at the first $70,000 of overseas earnings.

HOW CAN YOU GAIN EXPERIENCE?

Summer Jobs

Expose yourself whenever possible to various kinds of international work. One way is to look for summer and part-time jobs.

There are more summer jobs in the federal goverment than elsewhere because the government has a policy of attracting young talent. Therefore, each agency is encouraged to provide a certain number of jobs for beginning professionals during the summer.

These jobs are listed in *Summer Jobs — Opportunities in the Federal Government*, a brochure available in December or January of each year. Go through the job listings and you will find many opportunities for those with a background in economics (sometimes international economics), public administration, and business administration. This booklet can also usually be found in a college placement office or at the local job information center of the Office of Personnel Management. Get it as soon as it is issued because deadlines for submitting applications are sometimes as early as January.

Summer exposure to government work is not only remunerative, it also provides illumination on the pressures, peculiarities, and pleasures of government career. In almost all cases, Standard Form 171 (Personal Qualifications Statement), available in college placement offices or at the local Job Information Center, is needed to apply for these summer jobs. Exams are not usually required.

If your career aims lie in nongovernment directions, you may have a harder time getting a paid summer job with international content. Some years ago many large businesses and banks with international interests had regular summer programs that employed graduate students working toward these careers. Now, however, the size of these programs has been whittled down to the selection of a very few highly qualified and talented students.

Another drawback: If you are specializing in international business or banking within your M.A. in international relations, you will find yourself competing with M.B.A. students for the few summer jobs available. The M.B.A.s may have the edge in getting business jobs because they will have had more technical business courses and need less training to become productive in a short-term assignment. On the other hand, you may have the edge in getting the bank jobs, if the international earnings of the bank you are applying to are a substantial proportion of total earnings. More on this later.

The experience of summer work abroad can be one of the strongest items on your résumé; it is also one of the most difficult to get. Hardly any organizations — whether they are businesses, banks, nonprofit organizations, government, or the United Nations — will pay your transportation abroad for a job lasting only two or three months. In addition, there is the considerable problem of work permits (see Chapter Three). If you can get overseas on your own, however, your chances improve considerably. Contact the foreign branches of American or international organizations for possible short-term work; these include U.S. embassies and consulates, U.N. offices, businesses, and local Citibank and other bank branches in whatever country you happen to be.

Finally, the Council on International Educational Exchange (205 East 42nd St., New York, NY 10017) publishes a brochure, *Work Abroad*, describing short-term (summer or one semester) work opportunities in Great Britain, Ireland, France, Costa Rica, New Zealand, Germany, and Jamaica. In 1991 more than 6,000 students from more than 1,000 colleges and universities took advantage of the council's Work Abroad program.

Internships

If you can't find a paid job, a useful alternative is to volunteer as an intern and accumulate experience that will help you get the paid job you want later. In fact, internship and paid summer work can sometimes be the same, since a stipend may occasionally come with the internship.

Here are some organizations that usually use interns each summer, and sometimes during the academic semester as well. Where a stipend is paid, that fact is noted.

United Nations

Secretariat

Obtain from the address below an internship application form. When filled out, send it with a statement indicating several types of work in which you are interested and for which you are qualified; e.g., international economics, Middle East research, social studies, or youth programs. Look at Chapter Seven for additional information. Write to:

> Professional Staffing Services
> Office of Human Resources Management
> United Nations
> One U.N. Plaza
> New York, NY 10017

World Association of Former United Nations Interns and Fellows

As its name suggests, this nonprofit, nongovernment organization is an alumni group for U.N. interns. It is sometimes able to arrange internships at the United Nations. WAFUNIF is undertaking a major project to establish a computerized directory listing all U.N. internships, fellowships, and related training activities. Its office is staffed with volunteers. Contact the association at 2 U.N. Plaza, 11th floor, or write to:

> WAFUNIF
> P.O. Box 3241
> Grand Central Station
> New York, NY 10163

U.N. Department of Public Information

This office has two kinds of internship each summer, one in New York and one in Geneva. Applicants should have an M.A. or be close to getting one. The program in New York is held in June and July; in Geneva, in July and August. No stipends are paid for either program. Chapter Seven has additional information. Write to:

> United Nations Department of Public Information
> United Nations Secretariat
> United Nations
> New York, NY 10017

U.N. Development Programme

Summer internships exist both at headquarters in New York and in field offices overseas. A background in economics, economic development, and/or developing areas, as well as languages, is needed. Write to:

> Summer Internship Programme
> Division of Personnel
> United Nations Development Programme
> One U.N. Plaza
> New York, NY 10017

U.N. Educational, Scientific, and Cultural Organization

An occasional internship is available in this organization for those with educational, scientific, and/or cultural credentials. Write to:

> UNESCO
> 7 Place de Fontenoy
> F-75700 Paris, France

> or

> UNESCO
> U.N. Secretariat
> New York, NY 10017

In addition, consult *The Directory of International Internships*, a compilation of internships with the United Nations, its specialized agencies, and nongovernmental organizations. It costs $20.00, and is available from:

> Placement Services
> Room 113
> Student Services Building
> Michigan State University
> East Lansing, MI 48824

Federal Government

Department of State

The State Department's intern programs offer highly qualified college and university juniors, seniors, and graduate students an opportunity to gain firsthand knowledge of the foreign affairs process. There are two types of student interns: paid summer interns and unpaid work-study interns who serve for one semester or quarter during the year. Most opportunities are located in Washington, DC; however, a limited number of internships are available at U.S. embassies and consulates abroad. The deadline for summer applications under both types of programs is usually November 1 of the previous year. Contact:

> Intern Coordinator
> Recruitment Division
> Department of State
> P.O. Box 12209
> Rosslyn Station
> Arlington, VA 22209

In addition, the Department of State participates in the Presidential Management Intern Program, which is administered by the U.S. Office of Personnel Management. For more information, see "Executive Branch: Domestic-Oriented Agencies" (Chapter Six).

United States Information Agency (USIA)

The USIA offers a limited number of salaried internships for university students through its summer-hire program. Write to:

> Employment Branch
> U.S. Information Agency
> 301 Fourth St., SW
> Washington, DC 20547

Voice of America (VOA)

This agency offers a limited number of two-year paid broadcasting internships that can lead to a career in journalism. Student volunteer internships, available throughout the year, enable participants to earn college credit. Contact:

> Office of Personnel
> Voice of America
> Suite 1543
> 330 Independence Ave., SW
> Washington, DC 20547

Agency for International Development (AID)

AID offers internships based on the needs of its various offices. Generally, students are recruited in the areas of public health, accounting, finance, agriculture, and international relations. All positions are located in Washington, DC, and are available during both the academic year and the summer.

Although most of these internships are on a voluntary basis, a limited number of paid internships are available during the summer, generally for undergrads.

To apply, send a transcript of grades, a Standard Form 171 (Personal Qualifications Statement), and a letter of endorsement from your school to:

Student Program Coordinator
Office of Personnel Management
Agency for International Development
2401 E St., NW
Washington, DC 20523

Domestic Agencies

The Civil Service Reform Act of 1978 authorized federal agencies to establish programs for student volunteers at nonpay status. As a result, most federal agencies now accept student interns. Write to the international division of the agency in which you are interested.

Also, the American Political Science Association (1527 New Hampshire Ave., NW, Washington, DC 20036) publishes *Storming Washington: An Intern Guide.*

Banks

Citibank

Each year Citibank hires several hundred summer interns, either graduate students or undergrads one year from graduation. Internships are available both in New York and in various branches abroad. Obviously, you should have an accounting and finance background, although economics may be used as a substitute if you can show motivation for a banking career. Write to:

Summer Intern Program
Citibank
575 Lexington Ave.
New York, NY 10043

Business

Mobil Oil

Internships both in New York and overseas have been available. Students with an engineering background and those working for an M.B.A. are preferred, but internships are sometimes available for those with a marketing background plus the language of the country of assignment. Write to:

Internships
Mobil Oil
3225 Gallows Rd.
Fairfax, VA 22037

Nonprofit Organizations

Most nonprofit organizations welcome volunteer workers. Approach those organizations that interest you (see Chapter Nine).

Communications

Newsweek

For those with a journalism background plus some area knowledge and research interests, this is a good place to try. Write to:

>International Division
>*Newsweek*
>444 Madison Ave.
>New York, NY 10022

Associated Press

Again, this is for those with a journalism background and motivation for a journalism career. Each summer AP has a 13-week minority program for black and Hispanic college students who have completed junior or senior year or are in graduate school. Write to:

>Associated Press
>50 Rockefeller Plaza
>New York, NY 10020

United Press International

UPI usually requires a journalism background. Write to:

>United Press International
>1400 I Street, NW
>Washington, DC 20005

Newspapers

The Dow Jones Newspaper Fund offers a limited number of internships each summer for college students. Write to:

>Dow Jones Newspaper Fund
>P.O. Box 300
>Princeton, NJ 08540

Note: Don't limit yourself to the few examples cited above. Many other organizations in these fields have summer and/or short-term internships. The *National*

Directory of Internships lists opportunities in nonprofit organizations, the U.N., and the Peace Corps. It is put out by the National Society for Internships and Experiential Education, 3509 Haworth Dr., Suite 207, Raleigh, NC 27069. The directory is updated every other year.

If you are interested in a particular organization, don't hesitate to approach an appropriate official of that organization, whether or not it has a formal internship program. Internships can sometimes be worked out if you take the initiative and propose a project of benefit to the company as well as to yourself.

Academic Work

You can also expose yourself to an occupation through academic work. If, for example, you have been looking into a journalism career but are still plagued with uncertainties, take a course or two in international communications. It won't be long before you get an idea of your competence in the field as well as another indication of how comfortable you might feel as a practicing journalist.

If you decide that taking a course for credit is too much of an investment in time because of your career uncertainties, the next best thing is to audit a course. Listen to the lectures and class discussions. Auditing won't be as helpful as doing all the class work, but it will take a minimum of time while throwing some light on your interest in the subject matter.

Visit Job Sites

Another way to savor a career, albeit superficially, is to visit the job site. If, for example, you think you might be interested in a banking career, visit a bank just to sense what goes on. Enter without any thought of depositing or withdrawing money. Observe the comings and goings of people, the faces of tellers, the activities of all those enterprising people sitting behind the "vice president" signs on their desks. Get the "mood" of the place. Is this the right atmosphere for making your own special impact on the professional world, whether your aims are for money, prestige, self-expression, security, helping people, or a combination of all of these and more?

Unfortunately, this type of impression and information gathering cannot always be practiced. In the foreign-oriented agencies of the federal government — e.g., the Department of State or the CIA — you will probably find yourself in deep trouble if you tell the guards at the entrance that you "just want to look around."

WHAT ARE THE RIGHT QUALIFICATIONS?

Is Knowledge of Language and Culture Important?

This question can be divided into two parts: getting a job and doing a job. The answer is not always the same for both.

Getting a Job

Language is helpful but is usually not a determining factor in being hired. For the Foreign Service of the Department of State, language ability is respected but is not required among your qualifications — initially. If you have no foreign language capability, you will be placed immediately in a rigorous language training program.

For the United Nations, French and Spanish are important, but equally important is knowledge of economics, economic development, and area studies. For businesses with large international markets, knowledge of languages is highly desirable, but just as desirable is a background in technical business subjects: accounting, finance, marketing.

Language, then, is an extra added attraction in getting a job — one more arrow for your job-hunting bow — but it is not usually what you get hired for.

Doing a Job

In jobs requiring close contact with foreigners who may not know English, language assumes increasing importance. To be sure, there are always interpreters, but the presence of a third person creates a distance between you and your foreign contact.

Furthermore, understanding foreigners does not depend only on a knowledge of language, important as that is, but also on a knowledge of culture — the customs and traditions of a people that make them distinctive from the people of another country. Without this understanding of culture, you may find yourself confusing and, even worse, antagonizing others when you wish to offer them friendship.

In Bulgaria, for example, an up-and-down movement of the head means no and a sideways shake means yes. Moslems consider the left hand unclean, and it therefore should not be used in passing food and drink. In Thailand, crossing your legs so that one foot points directly at your guest is an insult.

There is more at stake than personal relations if you are ignorant of foreign cultures. Lack of this awareness — whether you are in the Foreign Service, business or banking, nonprofit organizations, journalism, publishing, teaching, or law — may not only affect your personal relations with foreigners but may also decrease the effectiveness of the work you are doing overseas.

Foreign Service officers receive an indoctrination course in the culture of the country to which they are assigned. Many corporations with large foreign operations, including IBM, General Motors, and CPC International, give similar instruction.

If you are not working for an organization that offers courses in languages and customs to their employees going abroad, you will be thrown on your own resources in your effort to understand a foreign culture. In that case, read extensively on the history and sociology of the country you intend to visit. Talk to people who have lived in the area. Take a course or two at a college that will help you understand multicultural differences. Whatever your reason for going to a foreign country — to sell a product, to understand people and culture, to research, or even for pleasure — you will be more successful in achieving your goal if you are sensitive to the meaning of the customs you will be encountering in your daily life abroad.

B.A.? M.A.? Ph.D.?

Two of the most-asked questions are "How far will a B.A. get me?" and "Do I need a Ph.D.?"

A B.A. won't get you very far, but it's not worthless. In some careers, such as the Foreign Service of the Department of State, no degree at all is needed. If you can pass the written Foreign Service exam with your accumulated knowledge, you have the same chance of eventual entry as the Ph.D. In government jobs, depending on a Civil Service rating (see Chapter Six), a B.A. will qualify you for some lower-level jobs. The same applies to business and banking. In some small nonprofit organizations a B.A. is quite adequate, and if you apply with a Ph.D. you may well be told that you are overqualified.

As for the second question — "Do I need a Ph.D.?" — the answer again must be hedged. In essence, the value of the doctorate depends on the kind of job you are seeking.

If you are after a teaching job at any level over junior or community college, the Ph.D. is necessary. If you wish to go into profound research (e.g., in international relations, regional studies, or international economics), the Ph.D. will be exceedingly helpful. If you are after a career in international banking, business, or journalism, the Ph.D. is irrelevant or may even be considered a liability — unless you have a persuasive answer to the question "Why did you take a doctorate instead of courses in accounting, finance, marketing, or journalism?" The old skepticism toward "eggheads" is liable to be encountered by a Ph.D.

trying to break into these fields — plus honest doubts about your motivation for this kind of career.

A further warning: Don't take the Ph.D. just because the extra two or three years will postpone the fears and frustrations of job hunting. The economic climate some years from now may be better — or worse. So why postpone the inevitable unless the extra degree will help you toward your international job objective? In other words, know your motivation for taking a Ph.D. Know how you will use it and what it will do for you.

In general, an M.A. is an optimum degree for most international jobs.

Should I Go to a School of International Affairs?

If the optimum degree for many positions is an M.A. in international affairs, the optimum way of getting it is through a school of international affairs. There are several that deserve your particular attention:

Columbia University's School of International and Public Affairs, New York City

Georgetown University's School of Foreign Service, Washington, DC

Johns Hopkins' School of Advanced International Studies, Washington, DC

Princeton University's Woodrow Wilson School of Public and International Affairs, Princeton, New Jersey

Tufts University's Fletcher School of Law and Diplomacy, Medford, Massachusetts

American Graduate School of International Management (sometimes referred to as Thunderbird), Glendale, Arizona

Monterey Institute of International Studies, Monterey, California (if you are particularly interested in languages)

International Business Program of the University of South Carolina, Columbia, South Carolina (for those particularly interested in international business)

A degree from any of these schools will bring you closer to the international job you want, not only because of their excellent international curricula but also because of the prestige enjoyed by each school in organizations with international jobs.

Some, and occasionally all, of the following career-oriented programs are offered in these schools:

Career conversations. Representatives of various international organizations come to the campus each week to discuss careers in their fields.

Career workshop. Material covered includes available job opportunities in the international field, academic and professional qualifications for entry jobs in each occupation, and job strategy, including résumés and interviewing techniques.

Career day. Alumni representing each major international occupation visit the campus for in-depth discussions of careers in each international field.

Trip to Washington. An annual trip to Washington is organized for those interested in exploring a career with the federal government.

Field work. An internship can be arranged with an international organization. Students doing field work perform a substantive project of value to the organization. Reimbursement is not always received, but academic credit may be given toward the degree. Time spent on the job may vary from one or two days a week during the academic semester to five days a week during the summer. Field work programs abroad during the summer may be available at U.S. embassies, at UNESCO headquarters, in field offices of the U.N. Development Programme, and in foreign branches of banks, businesses, and the wire services.

For further information on these and other basal schools of international affairs, contact the Association of Professional Schools of International Affairs at 2400 N St., NW, Washington, DC 20037. Phone (202) 862-3750.

In Chapter Two we will assume that you are now finishing your academic work and are unsure how and where to use the skills you have acquired. What international jobs are available for someone with your background? Suppose that you have a major in international economics, Russian studies, or even in that most amorphous of specializations, foreign policy. Who will find your credentials of particular interest? Where do you apply?

2

MAKING YOUR ACADEMIC STUDIES WORK FOR YOU

So far we have discussed the problems inherent in planning an international career. Now it is time to focus in more detail on the vital connection between your academic work and the attainment of your career goals.

CAREER OBJECTIVES AND ACADEMIC COURSES

In planning your curriculum, you ideally should work backward from your career objective. Your starting point should be "What do I want to do *after* I have my graduate or undergraduate degree?" Try to answer this question before you finish—and preferably before you *start*—your international studies.

Once you know what you want to do with your degree, the other necessary decisions fall into place: first, the choice of a major or specialization within international affairs, and second, the selection of courses within this concentration. By knowing where you want your academic work to lead, you will be able to choose the courses best suited to helping you reach your goal.

In some cases, the choice of a specialization is an obvious one. If you eventually want to be a foreign correspondent, you will take a specialization in international media and communications. If you want a career in international banking, you will take courses in international finance and banking; and if you want your future to be in international business, you will specialize either in that or in international marketing or international finance, depending on which track you wish to follow.

However, if you wish to enter the Foreign Service of the State Department, your choice of specialization is less obvious. You can approach your goal either through area studies or international economics, or a generalized background in international affairs and foreign policy. This plan also works with the other career objectives listed.

The above progression—starting with a career choice and working backward to specialization and courses—represents the ideal. Further, it avoids the fatal embarassment of deciding during your last semester before graduation that you want to go, say, into international journalism only to discover that you have never taken any of the required courses for jobs in that field.

IF YOUR CAREER OBJECTIVE IS:	YOUR SPECIALIZATION SHOULD BE:
International banking	International finance and banking
International business	International business
International communications (journalism, broadcasting, publishing)	International media and communications
U.S. government Foreign affairs agencies (State Department, AID, USIA, etc.)	International economics, economic development or world resources, area studies, foreign policy
International divisions of domestic agencies (Departments of Commerce, Labor, etc.)	International economics
U.N. agencies	International economics, economic development, world resources, preferably combined with area studies and French or Spanish
Nonprofit organizations	International economics, economic development, world resources, or area studies, depending on the nature and orientation of the organization

A GENERAL VS. SPECIALIZED BACKGROUND

But suppose, despite all logic, you have worked forward. You have taken international courses in college or grad school without knowing what kind of work you want. Graduation comes along, and anxiety, if not actual panic, takes over. You still don't know what you want to do. What organizations will find your academic work attractive? Where do you apply for a job?

Let us take three types of academic backgrounds in international affairs—(1) a major in international economics, (2) a major in area studies (Chinese, Russian, Middle Eastern, African, Latin American, and so on), and (3) a generalized background of international courses without specific focus—and trace their acceptability in the federal government, the U.N. structure, nonprofit organizations, businesses and banks, and media organizations.

International Economics

This is one of the most valuable and job-worthy majors or specializations that you can offer. There are more jobs available for economists, particularly in the U.S. government, than for those with most other international skills. International problems at one time considered purely political now are seen as having important economic components. Accordingly, job opportunities for those with an economic background extend to almost all international occupations.

U.S. Government

Both the foreign-oriented and the domestic agencies of the government value those with an economic major or specialization (see Chapter Six).

U.N. Organizations

Most U.N. vacancies require economic skills. Try particularly the United Nations Secretariat, the Development Programme, the Population Fund, the International Children's Emergency Fund (UNICEF), and the United Nations Institute for Training and Research (see Chapter Seven).

Businesses and Banks

Even though most corporations are seeking skills in finance, accounting, and marketing, some of them find economics an acceptable substitute (see Chapter Eight).

Nonprofit Organizations

Many of these, except for those oriented toward academic exchanges or cultural matters, need economic-minded individuals (see Chapter Nine).

Media

Writing and reporting skills are of paramount importance in these organizations, but even here a knowledge of economics that can be expressed in simple, popular language can be put to good use (see Chapter Ten).

Area Studies

You may have taken Russian, Chinese, or other area studies with the thought of teaching after getting a graduate degree. When faced with the difficulty of finding a teaching job, you have perhaps decided to explore research or non-teaching jobs. When, then, can you put your area specialization to good use?

If you have taken mostly political courses in your area, you may find yourself at a disadvantage in the job market; the purely political problem is a rarity. Accordingly, you may be required to show some expertise in economics, marketing, or journalism, depending on the kind of job for which you are applying. This means that with an appropriate second major or subspecialization you will increase your chances of being tapped for a vacancy.

U.S. Government

Area studies with a political orientation will limit your attractiveness. Try the Department of State, the Central Intelligence Agency, the National Security Agency, or the Library of Congress. With economics, however, your chances improve, and you can get a favorable reception in a broad range of agencies, both foreign-oriented and domestic (see Chapter Six).

U.N. Organizations

If you have area studies without economics, your main chance is to apply to the U.N. Secretariat, where some political research is undertaken. Area studies with economics, however, will give you a hearing in many other U.N. organizations (see Chapter Seven).

Businesses and Banks

Sole emphasis on the political side of area studies will not get you very far. Finance, marketing, and accounting are still considered the optimum background for an applicant, although exceptions occasionally occur. An export-import firm about to start trade with China may find political knowledge of China plus fluency in the language of sufficient importance to overcome deficiencies on the business side. The same consideration may apply in the case of a bank starting a branch in Moscow or a Japanese bank opening a branch in New York. But these are rare opportunities. It would be wise to broaden your background with economics, marketing, finance, and accounting if you hope for serious consideration in these organizations (see Chapter Eight).

Nonprofit Organizations

A politically oriented area background will be best received in those organizations geared to that area, such as the Center for Inter-American Relations (for those with a Latin American background), or the Citizen Exchange Council (for those with Russian studies). Again, your chances increase if you add a sub-specialization or minor to your concentration—economics, administration, or cultural studies, for example (see Chapter Nine).

Media

The political specialist with an area background should look to research periodicals, such as *Time, Newsweek,* and *Facts on File.* Otherwise, an area knowledge without journalism studies will not get you far. A rare exception may be the sudden need of a wire service for an area and language specialist in one of its overseas offices (see Chapter Ten).

If I Have Two Specializations, Should Both Be Played Up in Applications?

This depends on the job for which you are applying. In some cases, your chances increase because of the two specializations offered. In other cases, only one background is relevant. If, for example, you have a dual background in Latin American studies and economics, both count heavily if you apply to the Agency for International Development. If, however, you apply for a job in the Center for Inter-American Relations, your Latin American background is probably going to be all important and economics of little relevance. In still other cases, it may be that your economics will be the more attractive specialization and your Latin American studies of subsidiary or no importance. In other words, know the type of job for which you are applying, so that the appropriate part of your background can be emphasized on your résumé and in your interview.

Note: If you were not born in the United States, you probably do not have to prove your credentials as an expert in the part of the world you come from. Therefore, unless you have overriding reasons for taking an academic major in the area of your birth, it would be helpful to have some specialization in which your credentials must be proved, such as in business, economics, or journalism.

Generalized International Background

You are in the danger zone if you have no specific major or concentration in the international field. Most organizations with international interests have become more specialized over the years, and they now look for specific skills when they recruit new employees.

What do you do if you have taken a hodgepodge of international courses? You have no area specialization; you have insufficient economics to claim a concentration; you have no marketing, accounting, finance, and certainly no journalism. Your chances are distinctly limited, but they are not nonexistent. Try the following arenas:

U.S. Government

Even though most government agencies have a constant need for economists or area-trained people, openings do exist occasionally for administrators and those classed loosely as "foreign affairs/international relations specialists" (see Chapter Six).

Nonprofit Organizations

Unless these organizations have area interests (for example, the Asia Society) or are active in development (the Ford Foundation or the Overseas Development Council), they sometimes prefer to fill vacancies with people who have a generalized international background (see Chapter Nine).

MYTHS AND REALITIES

The relationship of academic work to career goals is full of the kind of myths that, unfortunately, most students do not uncover until it is too late. So perhaps the best way to summarize this chapter is to list some of these myths, as well as their corresponding realities.

MYTH	REALITY
Courses on the United Nations and international organizations are helpful in getting a U.N. job.	The United Nations primarily wants economics, economic development, area studies, and languages.
An economics specialty is necessary for a business or banking job.	Only in rare cases. Normally business employers want an international business major; banks want finance and banking majors.

MYTH	REALITY
Students aiming for a career in international business or international banking will get jobs in those fields if they take courses in economics of the firm, business in a changing economy, statistics, industrial management, and industrial relations, instead of marketing, finance, or accounting.	Business employers usually look for marketing and accounting; banks usually require accounting and finance.
Foreign-born students should specialize in studies of the area from which they come; e.g., African students should major in African studies as a help on the job hunt.	Employers assume that the foreign-born have intimate knowledge of their part of the world; academic studies in that area are therefore usually not needed.
General courses in foreign policy are helpful on the job hunt.	Except for the Foreign Service and some nonprofit organizations, these courses rarely help.

3

HOW TO GET A JOB WHEN YOU LIVE OVERSEAS

Getting a job in the United States is plagued with well-known difficulties. Getting a job overseas is plagued with the same difficulties plus a few more unique to the foreign milieu. For one thing, most countries — including the United States — insist that their nationals receive priority in the local job market. This means that a foreigner usually must have a work permit, which is not easy to get. Often the foreigner has to find a job before the permit is issued. The employer in turn is given the sometimes difficult task of showing that the job opening cannot be filled satisfactorily by a native of that country. Long-winded forms of justification must often be completed by the employer, who will clearly not relish the bother unless the foreigner to be employed has qualifications vastly superior to the local competition.

START THE HUNT AT HOME

How, then, can you maximize your chances for getting a job when overseas? One way is to start the job hunt *before* you leave the United States. If you are able to find a job abroad while you are still here, it sometimes simplifies the problem of legalizing your work status. With a job promise under your belt, you may receive a work permit or at least diminish the procedural hassles in getting yourself legalized.

Immediately, however, you run up against a different set of difficulties. Before you are offered a job, you usually must have an interview. If you're in the United States, how do you arrange this interview with an employer who may be 12,000 miles away? Sometimes foreign employers may be visiting the United States and interviews can be arranged, but this is rare. Usually there is no touring representative of the company at hand and the only way to get an interview is to pack your bags and travel overseas.

Fortunately, there is sometimes a small loophole out of this almost impossible situation. In countries that have close economic ties with the United States, many important jobs — and even some that are less important — require a knowledge of English. This is especially true in Japan. As a result, there are many language institutes in that country filled with Japanese from all walks of life learning English. This in turn has created a demand for English-language teachers. Japanese journals in America often carry ads for this type of work. The qualified applicant can write to several of these Japanese institutes and might perhaps be offered a job without an interview. Once the job is obtained, a work visa is readily forthcoming from the Japanese Embassy in Washington or the Japanese Consulate General in New York. This is an exceptional situation, admittedly. But you will probably have to search out many exceptional situations before you land a job overseas. (If you are interested in teaching English in a Japanese or Chinese school or college, rather than in a language institute, the procedure is somewhat different. Consult Chapter Eleven.)

Another unusual way to minimize permit problems is to get a job with a foreign organization in the United States, such as a British bank. If, after working there awhile, you ask for a transfer to England, your supervisor may be able to arrange it; if not, perhaps you can at least get introductions to officers at headquarters in London.

Also, before you leave the United States, explore possibilities with the headquarters of American banks and businesses that have a branch in the country you expect to visit. You won't have your transportation paid — and you won't be sure of a job — but you may be able to carry with you an introduction from headquarters to the branch manager in the country where you will be going.

To get lists of American companies with foreign branches, go to the reference desk of any large library and ask for the *Directory of American Firms Operating in Foreign Countries*, compiled by Juvenal Angel and published by Simon & Schuster.

Another interesting prospect exists for those of you who have a journalism background and are interested in writing. Arrange, if you can, to submit articles from abroad to the wire services — Associated Press, United Press International — or to large metropolitan or small-town dailies in the United States. There will be no guarantee that your articles will be accepted, but if they are, you will be paid. Another advantage of being a "stringer" is that you will not be hamstrung by permit problems.

Before going abroad, get names and addresses of alumni from your school who are living or working in the countries where you expect to be. The old alum network is a potent force in leading you directly or indirectly to a job.

ACTIONS ABROAD

Suppose that you find yourself abroad, perhaps as the spouse of someone working for an American firm, and then decide you want to work full time. Immediately you come up against a Catch 22: You won't be able to get a job unless you have a work visa, but in some cases (again let us use the example of Japan) you won't be able to get the visa unless you apply for it *outside* Japan. This results in a rather ludicrous series of events. First you have to latch on to a job in Japan; then you must leave the country for, say, Korea, where you will apply for a work visa from the Japanese Embassy; and finally, when you get it, you return to Japan endowed with the legal wherewithal for work. The procedure is the same whether your employer is Japanese or American. There are exceptions, however. If you are a student in Japan or the spouse of someone working in Japan and you want to work part time, permission can often be obtained from the Japanese authorities without your leaving the country.

Americans abroad often take jobs illegally, hoping that the authorities will not catch up with them. This may work if employers cooperate in the conspiracy and if the job is temporary or part time, but the risks usually outweigh the gains.

PROCEDURES: TWO CASES

Since the employment situation varies from one country to another, we will examine the policies of other nations, primarily England and France. Both are meccas for tourists and students, some of whom, infatuated with the foreign ambience, impulsively decide to take a year off, stay abroad, and, of course, work.

Nonstudents

A work permit is required in England and, as might be expected, is extremely difficult for nonstudent foreigners to obtain. You have to be outside England to get it, and the proposed employer has to prove to the government that no British citizen has the appropriate qualifications for the job under consideration. If, for example, the job requires excellence in Urdu, Arabic, Chinese, Japanese, Russian, Serbo-Croatian, and Malay, and you happen to be fluent in all seven languages, it may not be hard to beat the British competition and get the work permit and the job. However, if you apply for ordinary clerical work in an office, neither permit nor job will probably be forthcoming.

In France, if you are not a student, getting a work permit and a job has been termed impossible in official government quarters. Even though nothing is really impossible, getting legal jobs for nonstudent foreigners comes perilously close to it. Chances are you will be in France under a tourist visa, and work permits are not issued for that category. The sole possibility seems to be black-market job (some part-time or casual work for which the employer is willing not only to hire you but also to conceal your presence from the authorities). An American we know, unable to find work legally, learned that a château on the outskirts of Paris was about to be renovated by its owners. He persuaded them to hire him both for his skills in carpentry and for his willingness to teach them English.

There are always jobs to be found — in France and elsewhere — by those with initiative and without preconceived ideas of the level or type of work they are willing to accept. But if you have trouble, don't go rushing to the nearest American embassy or consulate general with your work permit problems. The most they can do is direct you to the appropriate foreign authorities or, in some cases, inform you of regulations and procedures for obtaining the permit.

Students

The prospects for students are brighter, especially in Great Britain, Ireland, France, Germany, Costa Rica, New Zealand, and sometimes Australia (depending on the school you are attending). In these countries the Council on International Education Exchange (CIEE) in New York can be of help. For a fee of $125 you can get a work authorization as well as information on housing and general literature on living and working abroad. The length of the authorization varies from one country to another: up to three months for France and longer for other countries. No guarantee of a job goes with the authorization, but with one in hand you obviously have a better chance of connecting with a job.

For additional information on work opportunities in other countries, you may find it useful to consult the *Whole World Handbook*, which can be obtained from the CIEE for $12.95. Of some help also is the brochure *Student Travel Catalog: The Q's and A's of Work, Study, and Travel Abroad*, available for the asking from the CIEE. Write to:

> Council on International Educational Exchange
> 205 East 42nd St.
> New York, NY 10017

Since the difficulties and procedures for getting permits to work abroad vary among nations, get detailed information on the problems you will face before you leave the United States — from the particular embassies (in Washington) or consulates (usually in New York) of the countries where you want to work. If you are a student, be sure to mention that fact, since you will probably find fewer obstacles in your path toward summer or part-time employment.

SPECIAL SITUATIONS

International Association of Economic and Management Students (AIESEC)

This association offers a worldwide program of work traineeships. Students are placed in positions in industry abroad, usually for the summer but sometimes for a year or more. They receive a stipend to cover living and incidental expenses. Several thousand students are placed annually in traineeships in 74 participating countries in Europe, Africa, Latin America, and Asia. In order to qualify for an internship, students must join a local chapter and become an active member. Write to:

> AIESEC
> International Association of
>   Economic and Management Students
> 15 West 50th St.
> 20th Floor
> New York, NY 10020
> (212) 757-3774

International Association for the Exchange of Students for Technical Experience/United States (IAESTE/US)

This organization has a program for students of engineering, architecture, mathematics, and the sciences to obtain on-the-job training with employers in 46 countries. Traineeships usually last from two to three months during the summer. Some longer-term placements are possible by special arrangement. Trainees receive a maintenance allowance and pay their own costs of travel. Write to:

> International Association for the Exchange of Students
>   for Technical Experience/United States
> Park View Building, Suite 320
> 10480 Little Patuxent Parkway
> Columbia, MD 21044

Central Placement Office of Germany

The Zentralstelle für Arbeitsvermittlung (ZAV) in Frankfurt has a special job placement service — free of charge — for students of several countries, including the United States. Most of the jobs are available only to women, but a limited number of opportunities exist for men. Jobs are usually for the summer, last a minimum of two months, and ordinarily are in hotels and restaurants. Write to:

> The Zentralstelle für Arbeitsvermittlung
> Feuerbachstrasse 42
> D-6000 Frankfurt/Main 1
> Germany

ADDITIONAL TIPS

1. Consult the classified ads of major newspapers, such as the London *Times*, *Le Figaro* (Paris), *Die Welt* (Hamburg), *Messagero* (Milan).
2. If you are in Belgium and have translating and/or interpreting skills, contact the EEC (European Economic Community). Write to:

> Commission of European Community
> Rue de la Loi 200
> 1049 Brussels, Belgium

3. In France, the Alliance Française (101 boulevard Raspail, F-75270 Paris) sometimes has information on summer jobs in Paris.
4. In Japan, if you have a good knowledge of Japanese, contact:

> Japanese-American Conservation Institute
> 21 Yosuya 1-CHOME
> Shinjuku-KU, Tokyo 160

and

> Y.B.U. English Center
> 15-3 Taishida 2-CHOME
> Setagoya-KU, Tokyo 15

There is also an English-language division of the Japanese National TV Network, where knowledge of English and Japanese is potentially useful.

4

ATTACK AND COUNTERATTACK: GETTING THE JOB

Now that you have identified an international career that interests you, and (if still in school) tailored your curriculum to reflect your interest in this career, you come to the two final stages of the job search.

THE FINAL STAGES

The first stage is uncovering the many kinds of international opportunities available. These opportunities are so diverse and numerous that Part II of this handbook is given over entirely to listing the organizations in which jobs may be available, as well as the necessary qualifications.

The second of these stages is planning your campaign. Until now you have been preparing yourself — through self-analysis, studies, research — for the attack. At this point the tempo increases considerably. Now you must use all the training and knowledge you have accumulated to impress a number of employers with your qualifications so that you get the job you want.

No matter what field you have in mind — banking, law, government — the strategy you use to reach your goal consists of three simple tools: (1) a letter of application, (2) one or more résumés, and (3) a few techniques for the interview. These three — letter, résumé, and interviewing techniques — are common to all job strategies, whether your interests are in domestic or international areas. You will almost never get a job without an interview, and you will ordinarily not get an interview without first submitting a letter and résumé. The trick, then, is to make your letter interesting enough to lead to a reading of your résumé, which in turn should be impressive enough to lead to an interview.

Many books, some of them listed in the bibliography, have been written on letters, résumés, and interviewing techniques. Here we shall dwell primarily on those aspects of strategy that are different for the international arena.

Before you start sending out résumés and letters, you will have to make three fundamental decisions:

1. Do You Want to Work Abroad or at International Headquarters in the United States?

The decision may be based on personal desire or on family considerations, but the question will have to be faced and the answer known before you start the job hunt. If, for example, you have a spouse who is unwilling to live abroad, you may have to eliminate the Foreign Service and some Citibank jobs from your goals — unless you are prepared for a separation or divorce. Likewise, if you have an ailing parent you may have to adjust your target to accommodate family needs.

2. When Should You Start Looking for Work?

The lead time for international jobs is often longer than for other types of work. In government jobs the time between initial application and a job offer may be as long as 18 months because the security check itself may take up to six months. Jobs in the U.N. system may take up to a year because of the many levels of approval needed.

For government and U.N. jobs, then, begin the application process at least a year before you want to start working. With other types of international work, count on a lead time of four or five months.

3. To Whom Should Letters and Résumés Be Sent?

If you have no contact in an organization, you may automatically assume that you should apply to the Personnel Section (often called Human Resources Section). It's an easy solution, but resist it. *It is preferable to apply to the head of the section in which you want to work.* If the organization has an International Division, sending your letter and résumé to the head of that division will net you an advantage because your international training will be more highly valued and understood when examined by someone knowledgeable in the field. Of course, it takes time to research the organization and to determine whether there is an International Division, and if so, the name and title of the person in charge. But sometimes the effort pays off.

A student with a major in Asian studies and international economics once sent his résumé to the personnel section of a large corporation. Personnel rejected him offhand. Undeterred, he applied directly to the Asian Department of the corporation and had no difficulty in making contact with a high official of that department. An interview followed. A month later a job developed, and he was subsequently hired. Admittedly, this type of success does not always happen, but it does happen frequently enough to warrant the extra research required to identify those involved in the international work of an organization.

The following is a rough guide to optimum contact points in each of the international occupations covered in this handbook:

Government

Foreign-oriented agencies: Personnel or Human Resources Section (these agencies have exams and panels to screen applications, so there is little point in trying to bypass Personnel)
Domestic-oriented agencies: International Division (Civil Service rating needed)

U.N. Agencies

Head of divisions in which you are interested; otherwise, Personnel or Human Resource Section

Nonprofit Organizations

Large foundations: International Division
Small foundations: President or Chief Executive Officer
Other nonprofit organizations: President or Executive Officer

Businesses

Large businesses and multinationals: International Division
Small businesses, including export-import: President or Chief Executive Officer

Banks

International Division, if there is one; otherwise, Personnel or Human Resources Section

Communications

International Division, if there is one; otherwise, Publisher, Marketing Chief, or Personnel or Human Resources Section

LETTERS

Four examples of letters used in the application process follow:

1. Letter in response to a job vacancy notice, at school or in the classified ads
2. Letter for foreign nationals and Americans with regional specializations
3. Letter when you don't know whether any job exists
4. Follow-up letter (after the interview)

These are sample letters. They are not meant to be followed slavishly, and in fact you would be doing yourself a disservice if you did so. They are included here only to expose you to various styles of letter writing and to set your mind working on constructing the kind of letter you think will present your credentials in the strongest and most favorable light. Above all, letters should reflect your personality and style.

However, there are certain characteristics of letters that seem to have a positive impact on many employers:

1. Keep the letter brief — no longer than one page.
2. Emphasize achievements and accomplishments rather than duties.
3. Start with the most impressive achievement in your background.
4. Refer to your résumé (which should be attached).
5. Request an interview.
6. Make it easy for the employer by pointing out those parts of your background that are pertinent to the job for which you are applying.
7. Above all, write the letter from the employer's point of view: not "I want to do so and so," but "I have certain qualifications that will help you...."

Note: Proofread your letters and résumés before sending them out. Most employers who find errors in your spelling and grammar will stop reading and automatically throw the résumé or letter in the wastebasket.

1. LETTER IN RESPONSE TO A JOB VACANCY NOTICE AT SCHOOL OR IN THE CLASSIFIED ADS

33 Loudoun Street
Yonkers, NY 10705
April 13, 1993

Mr. Thomas Sawyer
Continental Can Company
800 Connecticut Avenue
Norwalk, CT 06856

Dear Mr. Sawyer:

Your recent contact with Columbia University [*or* Your recent ad in the *New York Times* about a job opening] suggests that research on the Middle East is an increasingly important concern of Continental Can Company.

As the attached résumé indicates, I have been specializing in Middle East research for the last few years. Among subjects I have researched are:

1. The effect of the Arab boycott on U.S. policy
2. Jordan's relations with Syria, Egypt, and Israel
3. The internationalization of Jerusalem
4. Divisive forces in OPEC

Readers of my reports have commended me for new insights into these subjects. In all cases, I have used original sources through my reading knowledge of Arabic and Hebrew.

I expect to be graduating from Columbia University in June 1993 with the degree of Master of International Affairs and a specialization in Middle East studies.

At your convenience, I would enjoy meeting with you to review my background in relation to your research needs.

Sincerely,

Jeanette Gomez

2. LETTER FOR FOREIGN NATIONALS OR AMERICANS WITH REGIONAL SPECALIZATIONS

1834 Beacon Street
Brookline, MA 02146
11 May 1993

Ms. Alma Potter
Director, Market Analysis
Doyle, Johnson, and O'Reilly
Prudential Center
Boston, MA 02199

Dear Ms. Potter:

As a native of Venezuela, I have unique knowledge of Latin America and its potential as a market for American products.

If your company intends to expand its markets in Latin America and needs someone with a specialized knowledge of the area, you may be interested in the details of my background:

1. I have a resident visa and can stay in the United States for an unlimited time.
2. I am fluent in the two languages of Latin America, Spanish and Portuguese.
3. I graduated from the University of Caracas with a major in International Relations, where I ranked in the top 5 percent of my class. I subsequently obtained an M.B.A. from New York University.
4. I worked for two years as an Assistant Economist with the Ministry of Economic Affairs in Caracas.
5. I was elected leader of a delegation of Venezuelan exchange students. In the United States I lived for two years with different American families.

I should be glad to discuss with you my potential usefulness to your organization in the specialized markets of Latin America.

Sincerely,

Jorge Cabezudo

3. LETTER WHEN YOU DON'T KNOW WHETHER ANY JOB EXISTS
SAMPLE OPENING PARAGRAPHS

Where You Have a Contact

1. I'm acquainted with your friend George Smith, who has phoned about me. He suggested that I meet with you briefly to get your advice on possible employment opportunities.

or

2. Several months ago, a group of us from the Sloan School visited the Department of Commerce and were impressed with your emphasis on the need for economics in the federal government.

Where You Have No Contact

1. As a researcher in Middle East problems, I have concentrated on bringing new insights into Arab-Israeli relations.

   You may be looking for someone with specialized research skills. If so, you may be interested in some of the analyses I have made:

or

2. As a summer employee of the Coca-Cola Company, I helped influence the expansion plans of that organization in the Latin American area.

   You may be looking for a trainee in your marketing department. If so, you may be interested in some of the other things I have done:

4. FOLLOW-UP LETTER (AFTER THE INTERVIEW)

927 Follen #4
Seabrook, TX 77012
August 17, 1993

Mr. George A. Sims
Research Coordinator
Cooper Industries
First City National Bank Building
Houston, TX 77002

Dear Mr. Sims:

Thank you for the opportunity of meeting you yesterday to discuss a research opening with Cooper Industries.

In talking over your research needs, I was struck by the increasing importance of an in-depth knowledge of the Middle East, not only to your organization, but to the people of this country. With this in mind, it may be useful to recapitulate some of my research work in the field:

1. Effect of the Arab boycott on U.S. policy
2. Libya's relations with Syria, Egypt, and Israel
3. Divisive forces in OPEC
4. Effect of a possible oil find in Jordan on U.S. policy

My background in research has, I believe, given me the necessary skills to make an effective contribution to the work of your corporation. The job opportunity we discussed sounds extremely rewarding.

Sincerely,

Lawrence Golden

To conclude this section, here are two fascinating letters that were actually used in applying for jobs. The first was written by Franz Schubert when he applied for the post of Assistant Conductor at the Imperial Court of Vienna in 1826. The second letter is a petition from Leonardo da Vinci to the Duke of Milan, written in 1482, for a job that seems to have been a combination of chief engineer, Minister of Defense, and artist in residence.

Your Majesty!
Most gracious Emperor!

With the deepest submission the undersigned humbly begs Your Majesty graciously to bestow upon him the vacant position of Vice-Kapellmeister to the Court, and supports his application with the following qualifications:

1. The undersigned was born in Vienna, is the son of a schoolteacher, and is 29 years of age.
2. He enjoyed the privilege of being for five years a Court Chorister at the Imperial and Royal College School.
3. He received a complete course of instruction in composition from the late Chief Kapellmeister to the Court, Herr Anton Salieri, and is fully qualified, therefore, to fill any post as Kapellmeister.
4. His name is well known, not only in Vienna but throughout Germany, as a composer of songs and instrumental music.
5. He has also written and arranged five Masses for both smaller and larger orchestras, and these have already been performed in various churches in Vienna.
6. Finally, he is at the present time without employment, and hopes in the security of a permanent position to be able to realize at last those high musical aspirations which he has ever kept before him.

Should Your Majesty be graciously pleased to grant this request, the undersigned would strive to the utmost to give full satisfaction. Your majesty's most obedient humble servant,

Franz Schubert

Your Excellency:

Having, most illustrious lord, seen and considered the experiments of all those who pose as masters in the art of inventing instruments of war, and finding that their inventions differ in no way from those in common use, I am emboldened, without prejudice to anyone, to solicit an appointment of acquainting Your Excellency with certain of my secrets.

1. I can construct bridges which are very light and strong and very portable, with which to pursue and defeat the enemy; and others more solid, which resist fire or assault, yet are easily removed and placed in position; and I can also burn and destroy those of the enemy.

2. In case of a siege I can cut off water from the trenches and make pontoons and scaling ladders and other similar contrivances.

3. If by reason of the elevation or the strength of its position a place cannot be bombarded, I can demolish every fortress if its foundations have not been set on stone.

4. I can also make a kind of cannon which is light and easy of transport, with which to hurl small stones like hail, and of which the smoke causes great terror to the enemy, so that they will suffer heavy loss and confusion.

5. I can noiselessly construct to any prescribed point subterranean passages either straight or winding, passing if necessary underneath trenches of a river.

6. I can make armored wagons carrying artillery, which shall break through the most serried ranks of the enemy, and so open a safe passage for his infantry.

7. If occasion should arise, I can construct cannon and mortars and light ordinance in shape both ornamental and useful and different from those in common use.

8. When it is impossible to use cannon I can supply in their stead catapults, mangonels, trabocchi, and other instruments of admirable efficiency not in general use — in short, as the occasion requires I can supply infinite means of attack and defense.

9. And if the fight should take place upon the sea, I can construct many engines most suitable either for attack or defense and ships which can resist the fire of the heaviest cannon, and powders or weapons.

10. In time of peace, I believe that I can give you as complete satisfaction as anyone else in the construction of buildings both public and private, and in conducting water from one place to another.

I can further execute sculpture in marble, bronze, clay; also in painting I can do as much as anyone else, whoever he may be.

Moreover, I would undertake the commission of the bronze horse, which shall endue with immortal glory and eternal honor the auspicious memory of your father and of the illustrious house of Sforza.

And if any of the aforesaid things should seem to anyone impossible or impracticable, I offer myself as ready to make trial of them in your park or in whatever place shall please Your Excellency, to whom I commend myself with all possible humility.

Leonardo da Vinci

As you might suspect, Leonardo, with his emphasis on achievements and his eye on the duke's needs, got the job. Schubert's letter — bland and unexciting — was not even acknowledged by his most gracious emperor.

RÉSUMÉS

A résumé usually accompanies your letter of application; the two are closely related. You may have one letter of application to be used in all employment situations, or you may have several letters, depending on your résumé. The kind of résumé used depends in turn on the number of your career objectives and how closely defined they are.

If You Have One or More Job Objectives

How does your strategy change if, for example, you have one job objective or three objectives? If you know you are going into international banking and that's all that concerns you, your job strategy is relatively simple. Not only is your target well defined and easily identifiable, but the search itself will be facilitated. You will ordinarily have one résumé that has a job objective of "international banking" or something similar. You need then have only one letter of application, which will also be geared to banking. The two together — letter and résumé will suffice very well if your focus stays with the international banking world.

Suppose, however, you have had a specialization in international economics and there are three kinds of jobs you would like to explore: research with the government or a nonprofit organization; banking; and writing economic articles for a newspaper. With three such varying objectives you would probably do well to have three résumés, each with a different focus. The three objectives might be stated roughly as follows: (1) economic research; (2) international banking; and (3) economic writing in the communications field. Each résumé would be constructed differently to emphasize those parts of your education and experience that are pertinent to the job for which you are applying. Sending a résumé with the second objective to a nonprofit organization, or a résumé with the third objective to a bank or research organization, would all but destroy your chances of getting an interview. Accordingly, these three résumés should be matched with three different letters, each geared to the specific objective mentioned in the accompanying résumé.

If You Have No Job Objectives

Now let us examine your job strategy if you have no job objective whatever. You have taken many courses in international affairs but have majored in nothing more specific than world affairs or foreign policy. In other words, through inability or unwillingness you have not narrowed your career objective beyond "doing something international." Since it would be rather foolhardy to mention "something international" as an objective on your résumé, what do you do?

In one sense your job is easier; in another sense, harder. You will probably end up with one résumé, a rather bland one, since it lacks a job objective and, therefore, a particular target. If you send out this résumé, you will have to write a special letter adapted to the particular job for which you are applying. In other words, a "something international" background often means one résumé and innumerable letters. Again, there is nothing wrong with this once you are aware of the results of the choices you make all along the job-hunting route.

On the following pages you will find examples of five different types of résumés to fit varying situations. Analyze each one and you will notice certain key questions it raises about the motivation and background of the applicant.

RÉSUMÉ #1: WITHOUT THE EDUCATION AND EXPERIENCE TO SUPPORT YOUR CAREER OBJECTIVE

Trudy Schmidt
1415 Nostrand Avenue
Brooklyn, NY 11211
(718) 423-3406

Objective:	Career in travel industry
Qualifications:	Extensive foreign travel: Four European trips since 1986 Residence abroad: Six months in West Germany Languages: German, French Have facility for getting along with people and helping them with travel problems as needed

Skills:

Escorting, Hosting	Have frequently invited foreigners to meet Americans in my home. Have also escorted foreign friends throughout New York state.
Planning, Administration	Planned European trip for four friends and myself. Based on success of this trip, was asked following year by parents of one of my friends to plan European trip for them.
Learning	Lived in Hamburg with family that knew no English. My German, at first mediocre, soon became fluent.
Negotiations	In Berlin, bargained with shopkeepers until I succeeded in obtaining complete glass menagerie at reasonable prices.
Friendliness	Frequently have met Europeans at public places, e.g., restaurants, theaters, opera, and several times was invited to their homes.
Education:	Duke University, B.A. in History 1988 in top 10% of class
Employment:	Research Associate, Conference Board, 1990–92 New York Research Assistant, Conference Board, 1988–90 New York Other: Waitress at summer resort hotel (Wyoming) Taxi Driver (through experimentation learned routes and hours that produced most business)
References:	Available on request

Schmidt wants a job in the travel industry, but as far as education and experience are concerned, there is little to recommend her. She has therefore turned to a type of résumé that draws on the skills she has used in private life.

**RÉSUMÉ #2: WITH THE EDUCATION AND EXPERIENCE TO SUPPORT
YOUR CAREER OBJECTIVE, VERSION A**

JAMES SMITHEY
817 West End Avenue
New York, NY 10025
(212) 480-2234

OBJECTIVE

Research with specialized knowledge of Latin American area

HIGHLIGHTS OF EXPERIENCE

Research

At IBM, helped make estimates of IBM business in Ecuador for 1993–97. These
estimates influenced expansion plans of IBM in that country.

At Center for Inter-American Relations, evaluated coverage of Latin American
countries in American press. Procedures I recommended to increase coverage
were accepted.

Latin America

At Institute of Latin American Affairs at Columbia University, specialized in
political and economic problems of area.

At University of Texas:
— spent junior year abroad at University of Santiago, Chile
— as President of Latin American Club, arranged conferences on United
Nations and international problems

EMPLOYMENT CHRONOLOGY

Spring 1991	IBM World Trade, New York. Research Intern
1986–90	International Student Services, New York. Program Officer
Summer 1985	Center for Inter-American Relations, New York. Program Assistant

EDUCATION

1993 — Master of International Affairs, School of International and Public Affairs, Columbia University
Specialization: Latin American Studies. Was commended for writing paper giving new insights into effect of Castro on eight Latin American countries.
1986 — B.A., University of Texas

ACTIVITIES

Memberships: Student representative on Committee on Instruction, School of International and Public Affairs
Recommendation that field work program be expanded was accepted.

Languages: Spanish (excellent); Portuguese (good)

REFERENCES

Available on request

Smithey did not go into Latin American work after getting his B.A., even though as an undergrad he had done several things in that field. An employer now will ask: "Why did you go to graduate school? Weren't you able to get what you want with a B.A., or is your Latin American job objective one that you only recently decided on?"

**RÉSUMÉ #3: WITH THE EDUCATION AND EXPERIENCE TO SUPPORT
YOUR CAREER OBJECTIVE, VERSION B**

Pedro Vasquez
1020 Amsterdam Avenue
New York, NY 10025
(212) 963-1071

OBJECTIVE   Career in international banking

EDUCATION   Master of International Affairs, School of International and
                     Public Affairs, Columbia University   1993

                     Specializations:
                     International Finance and Banking (courses taken at
                         Columbia School of Business)
                     Latin American Studies

                     Financed tuition and expenses through work as
                         security guard
                     B.A., University of Wisconsin   1991
                     Major: Political Science

WORK   Bank of America, New York. Intern, Trainee
EXPERIENCE   Program   Jan.–May 1992
                     (Developed internship myself without aid from School
                     of International and Public Affairs)

                     CITICORP, New York. Intern   Sept.–Dec. 1991
                     Worked on Sovereign Risk analysis for Latin American
                     area. As a result of my analysis, CITICORP was able to
                     increase profits in Peru and Venezuela.

                     Summer Employment: Warehouseman, shipping clerk,
                     housepainter

MEMBERSHIPS & ACTIVITIES	School of International and Public Affairs 　Study Group on Professionalism 　　Represented School on committee composed of rep- 　　resentatives of Columbia, Princeton, Johns Hopkins, 　　Georgetown, and Tufts. My recommendation that 　　curriculum of schools of international affairs be more 　　heavily oriented toward job market was accepted. 　International Fellows Program.
HONORS & AWARDS	Dean's List of Honor Students, University of Wisconsin
LANGUAGES	Spanish (excellent), Portuguese (fair)
TRAVEL	Argentina, Brazil, Chile, Paraguay, Colombia, Spain, England, France, Scotland, Italy, and continental United States
REFERENCES	Available on request

This is a straightforward résumé that does not pose any particular problems of why, when, or where.

**RÉSUMÉ #4: WITH THE EDUCATION AND EXPERIENCE TO SUPPORT
YOUR CAREER OBJECTIVE, VERSION C**

H. Ramanathan
1312 Netherland Avenue
Riverdale, NY 10471
(212) 980-4623

PERSONAL	U.S. citizen
JOB OBJECTIVE	Product management in company with international interests
EDUCATION	COLUMBIA UNIVERSITY — School of International and Public Affairs

COLUMBIA UNIVERSITY — School of International and Public
   Affairs
Master of International Affairs degree   1993
Concentration in International Marketing — top 10% of
   class (courses taken at Columbia School of Business)

Business Manager, *Journal of International Affairs*
   Increased subscriptions by 20%
Financed 100% of education costs through loans and work

UNIVERSITY OF OKLAHOMA
Bachelor of Arts degree   1989
Major in History

Treasurer, Student Association; Varsity Soccer;
   Member: AIESEC; College Band
Financed 40% of expenses through part-time work

WORK
EXPERIENCE   CORNING GLASS WORKS, CORNING, NEW YORK   1989–91

   Marketing Analyst

Recommended product line modifications that increased
   profits of reporting units by 15% annually
Changed procedures so that subsidiaries were able to
   accelerate marketing reports to head office in half
   usual time

GULF OIL COMPANY, HOUSTON, TEXAS   1988

Summer Sales Trainee

Sold 175% of quota and, as a result, received special commendation and monetary award

OTHER SUMMER AND PART-TIME JOBS
Waiter, bank clerk, bookkeeper, taxi driver

INTERESTS   Playwriting (one-act play produced at University of Oklahoma), Swimming, Tennis, Stamp Collecting

LANGUAGES   Hindi (fluent), French (good), Spanish (good)

REFERENCES   Available on request

Ramanathan went into business but apparently decided he was not getting as far or going as fast as he wanted. Question: With all the glowing accounts of his performance at Corning Glass Works and Gulf Oil, why didn't he make it? Why did he have to go to graduate school? Be prepared to address obvious holes in your résumé.

RÉSUMÉ #5: WITHOUT A SPECIFIC CAREER OBJECTIVE

Wallace Brown
29 Loudoun Street
Yonkers, New York 10705
(914) 963-1070

EDUCATION	Columbia University — School of International and Public Affairs 1993
	Master of International Affairs degree
	Specialization:
	East Asian Studies
	University of Taipei, Taiwan 1989–90
	Courses taken in Chinese language, culture, history, and Buddhism
	Lived with Taiwanese family and received room and board in exchange for tutoring family in English
	B.A., University of Wisconsin 1989
	Major: History
	Financed tuition and expenses through summer work and position as Head Resident, graduate residence hall, University of Wisconsin
WORK EXPERIENCE	Foreign Policy Association, New York. Intern Jan.–May 1992
	Helped evaluate *Great Decisions* program
	U.S. Embassy, Singapore. Intern Summer 1992
	Won transportation award from School of International and Public Affairs
	Commended by Ambassador for new insights revealed by my study on Singapore-Malaysian cultural relations
	Other Summer Employment: Warehouseman, shipping clerk, housepainter, taxi driver
MEMBERSHIPS & ACTIVITIES	School of International and Public Affairs
	Committee on Instruction
	Recommendation that new International Energy course be added to School's curriculum was accepted
	University of Wisconsin Football Team
HONORS & AWARDS	Phi Beta Kappa, University of Wisconsin
	Dean's List of Honor Students, University of Wisconsin
LANGUAGES	Modern Mandarin Chinese (excellent), Classical Chinese (excellent)
TRAVEL	Taiwan, Western Europe, continental United States
REFERENCES	Available on request

Brown has progressed from an objective of "something international" to "something Chinese," but then what? Since he does not know, he ends up with this bland curriculum vitae, which would probably have to be accompanied by a different letter for each job lead he explores.

In all of these résumés you will find certain characteristics that often make a positive impact on employers:

1. *They each fit on one standard page.* Since the purpose of a résumé is to get an interview, don't overload it with details. Include just enough information on each item to hook the employer so that, out of the many applicants for the job, you will be among the favored few to be interviewed.
2. *They emphasize achievements and accomplishments rather than duties.* Not "Subscription manager of the *Journal,*" but "As subscription manager of the *Journal,* increased circulation by 60 percent." Not "Conducted career workshop," but "Organized career workshop that helped students get jobs they wanted."
3. *They utilize an outline format.* No long narrative paragraphs.
4. *They usually show a job objective.* If you decide to include your objective, word it simply. Not "Want position of responsibility that will utilize my background and experience," but "International banking" or "Research with emphasis on the Middle East." Everyone wants a position of responsibility and to utilize his or her background and experience. Why make the employer wade through all these useless words?
5. *They facilitate evaluation by the prospective employer.* This is particularly true of Version A, which extracts those parts of education and experience most pertinent to the job applied for.
6. *They list the most important things first.* If experience is most impressive, it should come first; if education, it should come first.
7. *They show dates on the same vertical line.* Usually it is desirable to put dates to the right of each item of education and experience (employers are more likely to first want information on events and only afterward the dates when they occurred), but if you judge that dates have special importance, then put them to the left.
8. *They list education and experience chronologically, working backward from the most recent.*
9. *They mention summer employment.* Even manual work has features in common with professional jobs: discipline, punctuality, ability to work with people. All types of summer work will strengthen your qualifications on the job hunt.
10. *They are phrased from the employer's point of view.* Keep in mind, "Are the words I'm using getting across to the employer the ways I can help do the job he or she is supposed to do?"

11. *They do not give references.* No names or addresses should be listed. Some organizations may contact references if listed, and ask for letters of recommendation even if there is no job opening in sight. This means you will soon wear out the people whose recommendations you want. Give the names and addresses of your references only when an employer is seriously negotiating with you about a job you know actually exists.

There is no perfect résumé any more than there is one perfect way to Nirvana. This means that you should expose yourself to a variety of formats, then make your own decisions on the style that presents your credentials in the strongest, most favorable light.

INTERVIEWING TECHNIQUES

We now come to the last stage of the job hunt — and perhaps the most important. You may have been brilliant all along the way: the self-knowledge you have poured into the job hunt; your early decision of a career objective and the superb choice of majors and courses to support this objective; the extensive research you have undertaken to identify your targets; the hours you've sweated over your letter(s) and résumé(s).

All this effort has borne fruit. You have impressed an employer who has the exact job you are after and you have been asked to come in for an interview. This is the moment that counts. The whole job-hunting structure you have diligently built up over the years has brought you within striking distance of the job you want. If you blow the interview, however, the job will slip down the drain.

How can you take steps to avoid this disaster?

Interviewing for a job is essentially a game of skill and wits. It is as much an art as a science. Much of the result will depend on the chemical reaction between personalities and there's not much you can do about that. Further, much of the result will be based on psychological and mood factors, for instance, the employer's frame of mind — and yours, for that matter. These factors also may be outside your control.

But even if interviewing is as much an art as a science, there are still certain tips that may be helpful. Twelve of these that seem to have stood the test of time follow.

Twelve Interviewing Tips

1. *Know the company.* Read all available literature on it. Consult annual reports, brochures, and the directories listed in the bibliographies. This knowledge will increase your confidence during the interview.

2. *Prepare questions you wish to ask the interviewer.* These should be based on your research of the organization's functions, plans, and problems. Don't ask obvious questions, such as "Did you make a profit last year?"

3. *Know the points about yourself you wish to make.* The insertion of this material into the discussion is a skill that comes with practice. Don't wait until the last moment, when you are at the door saying good-bye, then suddenly blurt out, "By the way, I forgot to mention that I'm president of the student association. Oh yes, I'm also . . . "

4. *Evaluate your strengths and weaknesses before the interview.* You may be asked about them. Sometimes a weakness can be presented as a strength, e.g., being highly demanding of yourself and other people.

5. *Expect the unexpected.* Some interviewers may insist on doing all the talking; others may lean back, close their eyes, and murmur, "What are all the things I should know about you?" leaving you an open field for the next 25 minutes. Fortunately, most interviews approximate conversations, with questions and answers on both sides.

6. *Be familiar with the parts of an interview.* Most are divided into roughly five parts:
   a. Amenities and platitudes ("How are you?" "What a lovely view from your window.");
   b. Discussion of your qualifications, background, and career plans ("Why do you want an international career?" "How far along in your career do you expect to be in ten years?");
   c. Discussion of requirements of the job opening;
   d. Attempt to relate (b) to (c); and
   e. Summation and final instructions ("Fill out this form," "Call me in two weeks").

   The order may vary. Sometimes (c) precedes (b). Sometimes (d) may not be voiced; if it isn't, the attempt to relate your qualifications to the requirements of the job will certainly be churning around the interviewer's mind.

7. *Keep this question in mind throughout the interview: Why would someone want to hire me for this job?* Remember the employer's point of view and base your case on how you can be useful to the employer. The latter will be less interested in whether the job gives you an emotional thrill or advances your career objectives.

8. *Be prepared to explain your motivation.* "Why do you want to work in international economics?" or "Why are you applying to our particular firm?" are common types of questions. If you are honestly enthusiastic about the job, don't hestitate to express your enthusiasm. Everyone likes to feel popular.

9. *Don't raise questions about salary, vacations, or pensions during your first interview.* If asked about salary, indicate that it is negotiable. If pressured to name

a specific figure (an unfair tactic but all too common), know the salary range of the type of job for which you are applying and set your figure accordingly.

10. *Always tell the truth.* As someone once said, "You will have less to remember."

11. *Stress accomplishments and achievements, rather than duties and responsibilities, in any past employment.* ("As circulation manager of the school magazine, I increased subscriptions by 50 percent.") You are not being immodest. You are making it easier for the employer, who, when faced with a hundred résumés, has time for only six or eight interviews and wishes to see only the outstanding applicants.

12. *Keep the initiative, if possible, for future contacts.* ("Shall I call you in two weeks to see how my candidacy is coming along?") Certainly don't sit by the phone waiting for employers to call, unless they have specifically stated they will contact you within a definite time frame. Be pleasantly surprised if they do contact you at the appointed time. If they don't, give them a few days' leeway, then phone to determine the status of your candidacy and express continuing enthusiasm for the job.

Above all, be yourself — not what you think the employer wants, and certainly not a stereotype. Let the interview reflect your personality just as your letters and résumés have. If in a banking interview you find yourself giving an interpretation of what you think a banker should be, you might want to consider whether banking is really the career you're after. And if you are taking the oral exam for the Foreign Service, you don't have to pretend to agree with all aspects of U.S. policy. If, for example, you disagree with U.S. policy in Nicaragua, give reasons for your disagreement ("I understand the reasons why the State Department has recommended so and so, but I wonder whether certain factors were given adequate weight."). In all probability, the oral panel has become fed up with the platitudes they've heard from other candidates and will respect a fresh and original point of view, once your reasoning indicates you are not living on Cloud Nine.

Some organizations — particularly businesses and banks — have special forms on which an interviewer evaluates each candidate. Here are two examples.

Bank A rates candidates on the following factors:

1. Introductory material
   Oral communications skill
   Self-confidence
   Appearance
   Social effectiveness

2. Education
> Ability to reason logically
> Level of overall academic accomplishment
> Ability to apply academic background
> Apparent maturity of judgment
3. Work experience
> Apparent motivation to succeed
> Significance of summer work to career goal
> Prior leadership roles
> Ability to work with others
4. Self-direction
> Overall management potential
> Maturity of career objectives
> Commitment to banking

Bank B rates candidates on the following factors:

1. Interpersonal/social skills
> Ease in working with clients and associates
> Effectiveness of communication skills
> Ability to develop and maintain client confidence
2. Judgment/analytical skills
> Ability to reason logically
> Planning and organizational skills
> Affinity for numbers
3. Motivation/internal drive
> Realistic career objectives
> Achievement orientation
> Commitment to banking

Every factor in each bank's assessment is given a numerical rating. The ratings are added and candidates with a high total are invited back for further interviews. Below a certain numerical level, no invitation to return is tendered.

You may well wonder how some of the above factors, such as "achievement orientation" or "overall management potential," are evaluated. Obviously, personal impressions and reactions play a large part in some evaluations.

Most important, you should note that academic standing is one factor among many in Bank A's assessment; in Bank B's, grades are not directly evaluated at all, although they are taken into consideration under "judgment/analytical skills" and "motivation/internal drive."

Many organizations look for the "rounded individual," preferably one who has a number of extracurricular interests, social presence, and at least average intelligence.

Academic standing and grades are more important if the job under discussion is in research, requiring intellectual capacities. Other jobs may put a premium on social effectiveness or leadership abilities.

The first interviews may well be grueling, but as you gain experience the encounter with employers should resemble a game. You will be trying to impress the interviewer that you are the right person for the job; the interviewer will be trying to assess your qualifications and personality in relation to the job available. Even if it's not Ping-Pong, it can still be fun.

Good luck!

part two

THE INTERNATIONAL
JOB MARKET

5

THE NEW WORLD OF THE 1990s

Over the past few years many powerful countries have undergone tremendous political and economic changes — changes that have affected the entire world. Economic problems, nationalism, and political enmities have caused the splintering and disintegration of the former Soviet Union, as well as portions of Eastern Europe. Yet at the same time, the creation of a number of regional free-trade pacts, and the increasing ease and speed of communications and transportation, have made it not only easier, but more necessary, for countries to work together.

Of importance to international job seekers are the new free-trade agreements that are now or shortly expected to be in effect. These include the North American Free Trade Agreement (United States, Canada, and Mexico), the Andean Pact (Colombia, Ecuador, Bolivia, Peru, and Venezuela), and the Association of Southeast Asian Nations Free Trade Area (Thailand, Malaysia, Philippines, Brunei, and Singapore).

Of even greater potential importance is the development of the European Community (Belgium, Great Britain, Denmark, France, Germany, Greece, Netherlands, Ireland, Italy, Luxembourg, Portugal, and Spain). In 1991, these countries adopted the treaty of European Unity, a blueprint for turning the European Community into a major world power by committing all 12 nations to adopt common foreign and security policies. By mid-1993, the laws necessary for free trade of manufactured goods had been approved by all 12 countries. Agreements are now being worked out on services (banking, insurance, transportation) and agricultural trade. Finally, a single currency is to be negotiated before the end of the century.

Poland, Hungary, and other Eastern Europe countries are negotiating an "Association Agreement" to make them half members of the Community. At present, there are no plans to bring Russia into the club. With its large oil reserves, however, it would not be surprising for the Europeans to find a way to work some of the former Soviet states into their trading alliance.

At one time, it was feared in the United States that the European Community might exclude American goods. Yet American exports to the Community have more than doubled recently, while imports from the Community have risen only 27 percent.

Particular attention focuses on the North American Free Trade Agreement, since it is the only new pact to which the United States is likely to belong. How will it affect the employment of Americans in both the United States and abroad? The score is not yet in, but from preliminary analysis, it appears that the results will be mixed. Because U.S. tariffs are already low, the Agreement does more to increase U.S. exports to Mexico than vice versa. According to the *New York Times*, the Agreement is expected to create about 300,000 new jobs in U.S. export industries, while eliminating about 100,000 jobs in industries displaced by imports.

At the time of this writing, none of the trade pacts mentioned above has headquarters to which job applications and résumés can be sent (except for the European Community, 200 Rue de la Loi, Brussels, Belgium 1049). For information on other trade pacts, contact the International Trade Administration, Department of Commerce [14th St. between E St. and Constitution Ave., N.W., Washington, DC 20230 (202) 377-3808] as well as the Office of the U.S. Trade Representative [600 17th St., N.W., Washington, DC 20506 (202) 395-3230].

Ironically, even as many countries are benefiting from membership in trade agreements, and as the European Community is turning Europe into the world's single largest capitalist market, other countries are splitting up — Czechoslovakia into separate Czech and Slovak states, Yugoslavia into a number of still undecided entities, and, of course, the former Soviet Union, now a number of separate countries and independent Baltic states, all of them restlessly trying to become viable countries. While the political upheaval has been traumatic, some businesses view it from another perspective. Increasing interest in international sales comes particularly from companies like Pepsico and Coca-Cola that have already developed their American markets to the maximum extent and must now find new markets in other countries. And sometimes they are being met more than halfway. In order to encourage imports, the Russian government has for the time being removed import tariffs from most consumer products, including cars. At the same time, Russian taxes on subsidiaries of American companies have been decreased. Read the daily papers in order to follow the impact of employment of Americans resulting from the various trade agreements as well as from the splintering of countries in Eastern Europe and the former Soviet Union.

Following are some examples of recent American business initiatives in the former Soviet Union, Eastern Europe, and in a few other countries. Note that all of these arrangements are in various stages of flux, and things change quickly. But if you are interested in any of these developments, and if you have the necessary background and skills to contribute to their implementation, by all means apply to the company involved.

For addresses, refer to any of the following volumes usually available in large reference libraries: Dun and Bradstreet's (*Million Dollar Directory*, and, for smaller companies, *Middle Market Directory*); *Standard and Poor's Register of Corporations*; and *Moody's Manual*.

RUSSIA AND UKRAINE

RJ Reynolds Tobacco International and the Ukraine government announced a joint venture: RJ Tobacco will take a 70 percent stake in a cigarette factory in Lvov in western Ukraine and a similar stake in the city of Kremenchug. RJ Reynolds does not yet plan to manufacture any of its American brands, e.g., Camel, in the Russian plants in which it has invested, but with an eye to the future, they have been advertising Camels on the side of trolley cars in Moscow.

York International will build a manufacturing plant for milk refrigeration units in Russia. The Commerce Department in Washington believes that the refrigeration units will eliminate 80 percent of the milk spoilage in Russia annually.

Conoco plans to spend up to $3 billion to develop multiple oil fields in Russia.

Mobil Oil has established a "high level unit" to negotiate oil deals directly with officials in Russia. Mobil estimates that the chances for big oil discoveries in the former Soviet Union are "extremely large."

A contract to develop a huge gas field off the coast of Sakhalin island was signed by the Russian government with the **Marathon Oil Company** and **McDermott International**.

The **Boeing Company** will establish a research center in the Moscow area in order to gain a foothold in Russia's long closed aerospace industry.

Phillip Morris will build a factory in the Saint Petersburg area for the production of Marlboro and other cigarettes. Construction is expected to begin in 1993.

Pittsburg Brewing Company will sell one of its beers in Russia after reaching a $5 million deal with a new holding company, BFB Inc.

Rockwell International has signed an agreement to pursue space ventures with a Russian aerospace company, *NPO Energia*. The latter will develop hardware to allow American space shuttle vehicles to dock with Russia's air space station. Rockwell has also announced a deal to develop the avionics system for a Russian airliner.

Pepsico signed a joint-venture deal to produce plastic bottles in the republic of Byelorussia, formerly part of the Soviet Union. Pepsico also operates several Pizza Huts in Moscow. Altogether, it operates 16 bottling plants in Russia.

Smaller deals have been negotiated by **Benton Oil and Gas** (Ventura, CA) in Uzbekistan (gold); **American International Group** in Russia (insurance); and **Unocal** (Los Angeles) in Azerbaijan (oil). **Pennzoil** has obtained exclusive rights from Azerbaijan to develop the Guneshi field in the southern Caspian Sea; **Huntsman Chemical** (Salt Lake City) in the Ukraine (petrochemicals); and **Magnatek** (Los Angeles) in Russia (electrical equipment).

AT&T has expanded its joint venture in Ukraine to include Germany's telephone company. The venture plans to modernize the phone system in the former Soviet republic.

AT&T and **Corning, Inc.** announced separate agreements in which each company will hire more than 100 Russian scientists in the field of fiber-optic research.

General Electric has reached an agreement with Kyrgyzstan to build a hydroelectric dam in the former Soviet republic in central Asia. The new dam will be the first stage of a plan that includes the construction of two more dams nearby.

Note: American individuals or companies interested in investing in, or exploring employment possibilities with, units of the former Soviet Union may wish to contact the following address for information on the economic situation in any of the nations formerly part of the Soviet Union as well as forecasts of socio-economic development in Russia:

> Russian Perspective Foundation — International Center
>   for Scientific and Technical Information
> Maronovsky St. 26
> Moscow 117049 Russia

EASTERN EUROPE

IBM Enterprise Corp. (with headquarters at the University of North Carolina in Chapel Hill) has made arrangements for business students from Cornell, University of Michigan, University of Pennsylvania, Columbia, New York University, Dartmouth, and the University of California to work in Eastern Europe. In 1992 there were 180 applicants with only 50 places available.

IBM expects double-digit sales growth in Eastern Europe over the next few years. Current sales in Bulgaria, Czechoslovakia, Hungary, Poland, Romania, and the former Yugoslavia are about $300 million each year.

Pepsico has opened a Kentucky Fried Chicken restaurant in Budapest, the first of a number under a franchise agreement with Hemingway Holding A.G. of Budapest. KFC is also considering locations in Czechoslovakia, Poland, Russia, and the Ukraine.

Microsoft Corp. will be the first software company to open wholly owned subsidiaries in Russia, Poland, Czechoslovakia, and Hungary. Four of Microsoft's best-selling programs will be translated into the languages of these four nations.

Coca-Cola has become the biggest foreign investor in Bulgaria after creating a joint-venture company in Sofia. Coca-Cola Bottlers Sofia Ltd. brings together Bulgaria's Central Co-operative Union, the Leventia Group subsidiary Clarina Holdings, and the Coca-Cola Export Corporation.

CPC International entered the Czech food market by buying 77 percent of Zabreh, a mayonnaise and tartar sauce maker. CPC also operates in Poland, Hungary, and what was East Germany.

Phillip Morris has bought control of the Czech cigarette manufacturing company Tabak for $413 million. PM beat a rival offer of RJ Reynolds.

Coca-Cola has invested $89 million in the Czech soft drink company, Praszke.

K Mart has invested heavily in the Prior and Maj Department Store (clothing).

Dow Chemical has invested $250 million in the Chemicke Zavody Sokolov company (chemicals).

NCR Company of Dayton, Ohio, has sold computer infrastructure to Slovak savings bank, among others.

Rockwell International Corp. has formed a joint venture in Czechoslovakia to manufacture automotive parts and sell them to Czech auto makers. Rockwell is also buying a factory complex in Liberec northeast of Prague. The plant will produce window regulators and seat slides.

Crimson Capital Corp., formed by a 15-member group of American bankers and financiers, is now a major dealmaker in Czechoslovakia. Its goal is to find buyers of the thousands of companies the country is selling as it hurries toward capitalism. The corporation has negotiated many deals on behalf of the Czechs: the Phillip Morris takeover of Tabak; American Standard and a Czech toilet maker; the K Mart acquisition of the Prior and Maj department store chain. Other American companies for which Capital Corp. has negotiated deals are Ford, Atlantic West, General Motors, Sara Lee, Searle, Otis, and TRW.

Although Eastern Europe's economies have shrunk by almost 25 percent, the number of private companies in Hungary has shot up to 57,000 from 5,000. There is now optimism that Hungary can achieve sustainable economic growth. About $1.5 billion in foreign investment poured into Hungary in 1991 — well over half the Eastern Europe total. Among the major investors are **General Electric** (in Budapest — Tungsram plant), **General Motors, Suzuki**, and the French pharmaceutical group **Sanofi**.

Bell West, the regional Bell operating company in Denver, is in a 50-50 joint venture with the Hungarian telephone company Matav.

The **United Technologies Company**, specifically its Otis Elevator Company, has formed a joint venture with Poland's state-owned elevator company PRDiE.

International Paper has bought its first manufacturing unit in Eastern Europe: Poland's largest white paper maker Zaklady Celulozowa Papierniecze, northeast of Warsaw.

CPC International purchased an 80 percent stake in a Polish food company Amino S.A. It makes dehydrated soups, desserts, and pasta. CPC in turn will introduce some of its products, including Hellman's mayonnaise, Skippy peanut butter, and Mazola corn oil, to the Polish market.

Company Assistance Ltd., founded by two Harvard Business School grads, is a Polish-registered joint venture to help build world-class Polish enterprises. Working with both the Polish government and individual companies, CAL hopes to facilitate rapid privatization. CAL is also a consultant to a newly privatized company, Prochnik, a manufacturer of men's raincoats and jackets, 60 percent of which are exported to the West.

From 1990 to 1991, Poland's imports, mostly from the West, rose from $6 billion to $15.6 billion. Much of the increase was in consumer goods by companies such as Heinz and Ford. In a year and a half, **Procter and Gamble's** office in Warsaw increased its work force from one person to 100 employees.

General Motors in Warsaw plans a vehicle assembly venture with the Polish state-owned FSO car. In the first year, it is hoped, up to 10,000 cars will be produced.

Boeing has received an initial order of $450 million for seven 737-300 jets from Romania. Additional orders are expected. Boeing has also received orders from other Eastern Europe countries; namely Bulgaria, Poland, and Hungary.

Up to now, U.S. investment in Baltic countries has been moving ahead slowly, partly because so few enterprises have been privatized and partly because 90 percent of Baltic trade continues to be with Russia and the former Soviet republics. The continued presence of 120,000 to 130,000 Russian troops is also an inhibiting factor to potential foreign investors. As a beginning, however, the U.S. and other countries are now looking at programs to rebuild the Baltics' tattered telecommunications system.

Following is a list of other companies to try:

U.S. COMPANIES WITH SPECIAL INTEREST IN RUSSIAN AND EAST EUROPEAN TRADE

American Express Company
World Financial Center
New York, NY 10285

Armco Commercial
440 Sylvan Ave.
Englewood Cliffs, NJ 07632

Bank of America
P.O. Box 3700
Bank of America Center
San Francisco, CA 94137

Caterpillar Tractor Company
100 NE Adams St.
Peoria, IL 61602

Chase Manhattan Bank
One Chase Manhattan Plaza
New York, NY 10005

Citibank
399 Park Ave.
New York, NY 10022

Continental Grain
277 Park Ave.
New York, NY 10017

Cooper Industries
First City Tower, Suite 4000
Houston, TX 77210

Dow Chemical Company
2030 Willard Dow Center
Midland, MI 48674

E. I. DuPont deNemours & Company
DuPont Building
Wilmington, DE 19898

General Electric Company
3135 Eastern Turnpike
Fairfield, CT 06431

General Motors
3044 West Grand Blvd.
Detroit, MI 48202

Hewlett-Packard Company
3000 Hanover St.
Palo Alto, CA 94304

Honeywell, Inc.
2701 Fourth Ave. South
Minneapolis, MN 55408

IBM World Trade
Armonk, NY 10504

Ingersoll-Rand Company
200 Chestnut Ridge Rd.
Woodcliff Lake, NJ 07675

International Harvester Company
401 N. Michigan Ave.
Chicago, IL 60611

Occidental Petroleum Corporation
10889 Wilshire Blvd.
Los Angeles, CA 90024

Pepsico, Inc.
Anderson Hill Road
Purchase, NY 10577

Pullman Corporation
200 S. Michigan Ave.
Chicago, IL 60604

Satra Corporation
645 Madison Ave.
New York, NY 10022

U.S.-USSR Trade & Economic
  Council
805 Third Ave.
New York, NY 10022

WESTERN EUROPE

As of now, the United States is the largest trading partner of Finland after
Sweden. The Finnish government has sent its Ambassador to the heart of
New Jersey's high technology strip to drum up investment from New
Jersey businesses. Similar contacts are expected to be made in Manhattan

and other parts of the United States. Of some help toward future American investment is a thick binder listing Finnish companies looking for American money and technical skills.

Kraft General Foods, a unit of Phillip Morris, has bought Freia Marabou A.S., a Scandinavian candy company.

General Electric and **Volvo** plan a joint venture to provide financial services to Volvo customers and dealers in the United States and Canada.

Waste Management's Swedish subsidiary has acquired the Finnish business of Servi Systems Oy, a waste management company in southern Finland.

The **Digital Equipment Corporation** has acquired Basys Automation Systems of Britain as part of an "aggressive growth strategy" for the media industry.

Among the American companies making significant investments in Germany are **American Express, Burger King, Coca-Cola, Digital Equipment, General Motors, Hewlett-Packard, IBM, NCR Corp., RJ Reynolds International, Procter and Gamble**, and **Woolworth Company**.

Germany's Treuhand privatization agency has sold an eastern German pharmaceutical company to **American Home Products**.

20th Century Fox has formed a joint venture with Bertelsmann Music Group in Germany to form a new record label, Fox Records.

Borden Inc. has acquired Kamps, a retail bakery chain in Dusseldorf, Germany.

Kraft Foods, a unit of Phillip Morris, has agreed to sell its refrigerated dough business in Germany to Grand Metropolitan, a London food retailing concern.

Two big German appliance manufacturers, **Maytag Corp.** and **Bosch-Siemens**, have formed an alliance for joint marketing, distribution, and research. The companies will explore opportunities in the United States, Europe, and elsewhere.

IBM has reached an agreement with Siemens of Germany (and Toshiba of Japan) to develop memory chips that are likely to be a mainstay of computers used in the next century. The two companies are currently manufacturing small memory chips in a factory in France and developing larger chips. According to a Harvard economist, "The global economy respects no borders and these companies are becoming extensions of one another. It's truly the arrival of the global economic web."*

On the other hand, there is increasing German investment in things American. Western German manufacturers find that the rising costs of doing business in Germany are forcing them to set up new production plants abroad. The location of choice seems to be the United States. According to the Mayor of New York City, who made a business trip to Germany in 1992, New York is perceived in Germany as the premier place in the United States to invest, especially in the financial services, and the entertainment and fashion industries.

New York Times, July 13, 1992.

General Motors is talking with Spanish government officials about building a vehicle manufacturing plant in northern Spain's Basque region.

Bristol-Myers Squibb is working with an Italian company, Inverni della Beffa, to develop a semi-synthetic alternative for a new anti-cancer drug now found only in the rare Pacific Northwest yew tree.

ASIA

Pepsi-Cola International and **A and W Brands** have agreed to increase distribution of A and W's bottled products in Asia. Both companies expect to sell $500 million of A and W soft drinks in Asia in the next ten years. Pepsi-Cola already distributes A and W root beer in Guam and Indonesia.

Eastman Kodak and **Canon** of Japan have an informal alliance in which Canon makes copiers for Kodak. The two companies will also jointly develop and make office products.

Johnson & Johnson has formed an alliance with Olympus Optical Company of Tokyo. The companies will focus on the development of new products and procedures, as well as training surgeons.

The **Bechtel Group** in San Francisco is part of a consortium of companies that has been awarded a contract to construct a $245 million office building in Tokyo for the Nippon Telegraph and Telephone Co.

General Electric and Hitachi, Tokyo, extended for ten years their joint venture to market high-voltage breakers in the United States, to develop GE exports to Japan, and to share technology.

Ford Motor Co. will increase its equity and overall involvement in a joint venture with Mazda Motor Co. of Japan. Ford currently owns 34 percent and Mazda 39 percent of the venture, Autoama, which distributes Ford products in Japan.

American Telephone and Telegraph Co., won a contract worth about $110 million from the Nippon Telegraph and Telephone Corp. of Japan for a traffic management and administration system.

IBM has formed an alliance with Toshiba to work toward the development of sophisticated color computer screens.

Toyota, the largest auto maker in Japan, has been making station wagons in Kentucky and sending them back to Japan at the rate of 700 wagons a month. Now it seems likely that Ford will manufacture and sell Toyota parts for these wagons.

Hughes Aircraft Co. and the Victor company of Japan have formed a joint venture to make video projectors for the coming market for advanced television systems.

McDonnell-Douglas will supply China with 40 mid-range jets in a deal worth more than $1 billion. The planes will be assembled in China with components from the United States and Canada.

China already has McDonald's and Kentucky Fried Chicken. Now it is getting
its first **7-Eleven** stores. Hong Kong Convenience Stores, which controls
7-Eleven operations in Hong Kong, will work with the Shenzhen Luohu
Economic Development Corp. of China to operate 15 stores in China, the
first one located in Shenzhen.

Motorola is constructing a $125 million factory complex in the northern
Chinese city of Tianjin. The plant will initially make semiconductors and
pagers, and later cellular phones and auto ignitions.

Gillette Co., Boston has formed a joint-venture blade and razor manufacturing company with the Shanghai Razor Blade Factory.

LATIN AMERICA

Four South American countries (Brazil, Argentina, Paraguay, and Colombia)
have agreed to a time table for creating a free-trade zone.

Benton Oil and Gas Company, Royal Dutch Shell, one Japanese company,
and two Venezuelan concerns will put $720 million into reviving most of
the country's 55 inactive oil fields in the next decade. It is the first time
Venezuela has opened its government-controlled oil reserves to private investment since the industry was nationalized in 1976.

Many U.S. companies are starting to take advantage of a little-heralded amend-
ment of 1975 to the American embargo that allows them to trade nonstra-
tegic goods with Cuba.

In the void left by trade with the former Soviet Union, Cuba is trying
to replace subsidized supplies of everything from industrial spare parts
and oil to flour for making bread. To implement this change of policy,
Cuba has set up attractive new investment regulations that permit repatria-
tion profits, majority foreign ownership in some instances, and control
over management decisions such as hiring and firing.

Petroleos Mexicanos has signed a joint venture with the Shell Oil Company
to process Mexican oil into unleaded gasoline at a refinery near Houston.

MIDDLE EAST

McDonnell Douglas has awarded contracts worth $520 million to two Israeli
companies (Israel Aircraft Industries and Elbit Ltd. of Haifa) to overhaul a
fleet of 26 DC-9 commercial jets that McDonnell Douglas bought from
Delta and will be leased back to Delta after being refurbished.

CPC International, a consumer food concern based in Englewood Cliffs, New
Jersey, has acquired a 51 percent interest in Israel Edible Products, also
known as Tami.

Paramax Systems Corp., a subsidiary of Unisys Corp., was awarded a $27
million contract for mine-hunting systems for three ships being built for
the Egyptian Navy by Swiftships Inc. in Louisiana.

Iran will allow foreigners to own 100 percent of businesses in Iran, a policy change to attract hard currency. There are also guarantees of free return of capital and payments of damages if properties are nationalized or confiscated.

Gillette is now serving the Turkish market with blades and razors under the Gillette and Permasharp labels. Gillette's agreement is with Permasharp, the leading blade manufacturer in Turkey.

OTHER COUNTRIES

Phillips Petroleum, based in Oklahoma, signed an agreement with Sonatrach, a state-owned Algerian company, to explore for oil and gas on about 1.5 million acres. Phillips is to invest $67 million in seven pilot wells.

H.J. Heinz Co. bought the largest food company in New Zealand, Wattie's Ltd., to expand its business in Australia and Asia.

Digital Equipment Corp. has contracted with Optus Communications, an Australian telecommunications carrier, to provide all information technology and services and some minicomputers for the Optus Operational Support System, a digital telecommunications network.

Procter and Gamble joined with Link-Up investments of Nigeria to sell health care products. The Nigerian venture brought to 54 the number of countries which have P&G facilities.

6

THE FEDERAL GOVERNMENT

Most of you considering an international career with the federal government focus promptly on the Foreign Service of the Department of State. The Department, as it is popularly known, is the focal point of foreign policy and primary source of jobs for those with international training, but other government agencies also offer opportunities for an international career. Many of these agencies are in the executive branch; some are in the legislative.

EXECUTIVE BRANCH: FOREIGN-ORIENTED AGENCIES

The main foreign-oriented agencies of this branch of interest to those with an international background are the Department of State, the U.S. Information Agency, the Agency for International Development, the National Security Agency, the Central Intelligence Agency, the Defense Intelligence Agency, the Arms Control and Disarmament Agency, the Peace Corps, the Office of the U.S. Trade Representative, the Overseas Private Investment Corporation, the Export-Import Bank, the U.S. International Trade Commission, and the Inter-American Foundation. For each one, we will look at the type of jobs available, procedures for applying, and optimum academic preparation.

Agency for International Development (AID)

> International Development Intern Program
> Recruitment Staff, FSP/RSS
> Agency for International Development
> Washington, DC 20523-0114

AID operates U.S. economic assistance programs in approximately 80 developing countries in Africa, Asia, Eastern Europe, Latin America, the Caribbean, and the Near East. The Administrator of AID currently serves as the Acting Director of the International Development Cooperation Agency (see above).

AID uses both loans and grants in its development assistance program. It focuses on critical problem areas in developing countries, such as rural and private enterprise, development, nutrition, health (particularly infant and child mortality), population planning, illiteracy, lack of educational opportunity, the environment, energy, and science and technology. Specific programs include Foreign Disaster Assistance, Food for Peace, and Economic Support.

During the 1990s, AID is focusing on four initiatives: support for democracy, business and development partnership, mobilizing the family's resources in development, and the environment.

AID recruits new personnel annually through the *International Development Intern Program* (IDI), a two-year training program in Washington and in field offices that leads to positions of responsibility in AID. Each year perhaps 30 new interns are accepted.

Background Desired

AID positions are quite varied and, therefore, need different curriculum training. The following is a list of some target jobs:

Program officers advise the Mission Director on policy, planning, and evaluation of AID programs. This is the main generalist job in AID on an entering professional level and the one most applicable to students with an international affairs background. International relations, economics, political science, or area studies in Third World countries are appropriate background studies.

Agricultural economists analyze production, distribution, and consumption of food products; identify problem areas; and study methods of increasing and conserving food. A background in agricultural economics is essential to obtain this job.

Program economists study economic conditions in countries applying for U.S. assistance. A graduate degree in economics is a basic requirement.

Education/human resources development officers analyze, advise, and assist with the development of host country educational systems and human resources. Courses in economics, education, and sociology are needed.

Food for Peace officers work on food-aid programs.

Rural development officers work on soil reclamation and conservation, agricultural economics, community development, rural roads, and irrigation. Courses in international economics and development are desirable.

Health and population officers assist in managing family planning, nutrition, and health projects. World resources, population, or health studies would facilitate obtaining this kind of work.

Foreign language proficiency is required for work in the field. Language training, if needed, is provided in Washington before departing on a foreign assignment. The preferred languages are French and Spanish, although this depends on the country of assignment.

Requirements

There is no written examination for the IDI Program of AID. To start the selection process, applicants should send a résumé to the IDI address on page 72.

If you wish to work in a specific country or region, include your preference in the letter that accompanies your résumé. Overseas AID offices determine their own needs for short-term employees.

Candidates are screened to assure that they meet the qualifications for one of the occupational specialities. All applicants for each specialty are rank-ordered. Those ranked highest come to Washington for interviews.

As with the Foreign Service exam of the Department of State (see page 77), there is a long wait between application and eventual appointment. Similar to the Foreign Service, you will spend a major part of your career overseas. Interns are appointed to one of the classes in the salary schedule of the Foreign Service of the Department of State, depending on their qualifications and experience (see page 84).

Arms Control and Disarmament Agency (ACDA)

> 320 21st St., NW
> Washington, DC 20451

ACDA formulates and implements arms control and disarmament policies that will promote the national security of the U.S. and its relations with other countries. At present, to effectively carry out its responsibilities, it prepares and participates in discussions and negotiations with the countries of the former Soviet Union and others on such issues as strategic arms limitations, mutual force reductions in Central Europe, preventing the spread of nuclear weapons to countries that do not now possess them, a prohibition on chemical weapons, and monitoring the flow of arms throughout the world.

It is a semiautonomous agency operating under general policy guidance of the Department of State.

Background Desired

The ACDA uses specialists knowledgeable in foreign policy, international organizations, weapons technology, military strategy, and economics. Academic courses on national security, disarmament, military technology, and Russian studies will be very helpful as well. Personnel working in the international relations field are often Foreign Service officers on loan from the Department of State. Military personnel are also borrowed from the Department of Defense.

There are three ways of getting into the ACDA:

1. Become a Foreign Service officer through the normal channel, and, if accepted, request an assignment with ACDA.
2. Obtain a Civil Service rating (types of ratings and application procedures are discussed in the section on domestic-oriented agencies of the government).
3. Try for a direct appointment — but this really works only for those with considerable experience in the disarmament or related fields.

For those of you without much experience in this specialized field, your best chance of getting into the organization is through the Foreign Service channel. Most ACDA jobs are in Washington.

Central Intelligence Agency (CIA)

> Director of Personnel
> Central Intelligence Agency
> Washington, DC 20505

The CIA is perhaps the most important government agency providing intelligence information in the formulation of foreign policy. Although the cloak-and-dagger operations of the Agency, as it is known in Washington, appeal to the movie-going public because of their melodramatic content, the bulk of CIA work has to do with intelligence-gathering and analysis. The gathering is done primarily in the field; the analysis, at headquarters in Langley, Virginia.

Background Desired

Each year the size and emphasis of the CIA recruitment program vary. Mainly, however, the Agency is interested in graduate students specializing in the following regions of the world: Russia, East Central Europe, East Asia (particularly Japan and China), the Middle East, Africa, and Latin America. Ability to translate original material from the language of these areas, rather than conversational ability, is stressed.

Another basic skill of value to the Agency is international economics, used in the collection, research, and measurement of data relating to the economic performance of foreign countries. Additional disciplines used by the CIA are abstract mathematics, business administration, computer science, engineering, international relations, physics, and chemistry.

A Ph.D. with the above background may have an edge over an M.A. in international affairs because of the Agency's stress on analytical ability and research capabilities. There are more Ph.D.s employed by the CIA than by most other government agencies. At the same time, appropriately qualified students at the masters level have been accepted by the Agency.

The CIA/Career Training Program has been established for those wishing to pursue a career in intelligence. The program is intense and advanced, lasting from several months to over two years. It consists of formal study and on-the-job training.

Defense Intelligence Agency (DIA)

The Pentagon
Washington, DC 20340-0001

Still another intelligence agency is the DIA, which is the intelligence arm of the Department of Defense. The DIA is oriented toward military intelligence and points to its past role in disclosing missiles in Cuba and the North Vietnamese infiltration of South Vietnam as examples of its achievements. Less glamorous aspects of its work include analysis of military capabilities of various countries, transportation intelligence, photo interpretations, and economic analysis of foreign military production and expenditures. To perform these functions, skilled personnel are needed, and each year a few graduate students are hired.

Most DIA jobs are in the United States, although occassional travel abroad may be involved.

Background Desired

Political science, international relations, area studies, and economics are the optimum courses to take for generalist research jobs. For technical or scientific jobs, a background in engineering, computer science, math, communications, physics, or statistics is valued.

Defense Security Assistance Agency

The Pentagon
Washington, DC 20301-2800

The purpose of this agency is to direct, administer, and supervise foreign sales of military items as well as provide military assistance to other countries.

Background Desired

Knowledge of weapons, technology, economics, business administration, and/or accounting is valuable.

Export-Import Bank of the U.S. (Eximbank)

> 811 Vermont Ave., NW
> Washington, DC 20571

The Export-Import Bank helps to finance and facilitate exports of U.S. goods and services. Although about 85 percent of the U.S. manufactured exports go forward without the bank's support, many exports cannot be financed by the private sector alone. Eximbank, accordingly, plays a limited but critical role in the U.S. export effort. Specifically, it assumes commercial and political risks that private financial institutions cannot undertake and assists U.S. exporters to meet the competition of officially supported foreign export credit.

Background Desired

The personnel of Eximbank have degrees in economics, finance, banking, business, and accounting. These skills — preferably a minimum of two or three — are required for the few jobs available.

Foreign Service of the Department of State

> Recruitment Division
> Department of State
> P.O. Box 9317
> Rosslyn Station
> Arlington, VA 22219

It is a good time to enter the Foreign Service. Hundreds of years ago the Republic of Venice threatened with death any Venetians who had relations with foreign diplomats. More recently, in the early 1950s, ambassadors who predicted bad news, such as a communist victory in China, were thrown out of the Service, similar to the old custom of beheading messengers bearing bad tidings. Also, until recently, Foreign Service officers (FSOs) had to have a private income to survive financially. None of this is now true. FSOs are encouraged to have contacts with foreign diplomats; they are not beheaded for accurately reporting developments of potential damage to the United States; and they now receive entertainment allowances — and sometimes hardship and cost-of-living allowances as well — in addition to a very fair salary, so that their economic survival is no longer at stake.

Candidates for the Foreign Service must be at least 20 and no more than 59. Of the officers recently appointed, 54 percent had master's degrees, 11 percent had law degrees, and 6 percent had Ph.D.s. Many had some years of professional work experience as well. Some 45 percent were skilled in at least one foreign language; 7 percent qualified in two or more foreign languages. The principal areas of study of these officers included international relations, political science, history, economics, foreign languages, English/American literature, and law.

Foreign Service jobs exist both in the Department of State in Washington and in U.S. embassies and consulates abroad. Some 4,200 FSOs serve the Department in more than 265 embassies and consulates in over 140 nations. What do they do?

Political officers cover political developments in their country of assignment, analyzing their significance to the United States. They convey U.S. government views on political issues to foreign governments, negotiate agreements, and maintain contact with foreign officials, political and economic leaders, diplomats of other countries, and other influential foreign nationals.

In Washington, political officers analyze reports from overseas, prepare guidance for embassies, and brief senior State Department officials. They also work closely with other U.S. government agencies and with foreign embassies in Washington.

Economic/commercial officers in U.S. embassies and consulates analyze and report on economic trends and events that affect U.S. interests. They gather and interpret economic data, present U.S. economic positions to foreign officials, and negotiate agreements. They also promote U.S. exports and aid American investors abroad. They work closely with the Department of Commerce and American businesses. They often alert U.S. companies to trade and investment opportunities.

In Washington, economic-commercial officers analyze reports from the field and help set U.S. economic policy in trade, monetary, energy, economic development, aviation, transportation, and maritime matters.

Administrative officers abroad manage the support operations of U.S. embassies and consulates. They are responsible for budget and fiscal planning, maintenance of vehicles and other property, procurement of supplies, negotiating leases for housing, general financial functions, travel arrangements for officers and their dependents, personnel matters, and physical security of embassies and consulates.

In Washington, the administrative officer is involved in a variety of functions: coordination of presidential and vice-presidential overseas trips, escorting and making arrangements for congressional travel, developing computer techniques for information and communications systems, preparing budget submissions to Congress, preparing emergency evacuation plans, and setting policy for administrative offices overseas.

Consular officers abroad have more contact with foreign citizens than do other embassy officers. They grant visas to foreigners visiting or emigrating to the United States; issue passports and handle questions concerning U.S. citizenship; help Americans abroad who have been in serious accidents or have other emergencies; try to ensure that Americans in foreign jails are fairly treated; issue birth certificates to Americans born abroad; register absentee voters; and take testimony for U.S. courts.

Background Desired

Every scrap of knowledge may be helpful in passing the written exam (see following section, "How to Apply"). Accordingly there can be no specific guidance on the curriculum you should take, since almost any course at a school of international affairs will be useful. Certainly you should know basic economic theory and its application to current economic woes; U.S. foreign policy, history, and geography; and cultural and international affairs.

Answer the sample exam questions in the Department of State booklet *Application for the Foreign Service Officer Program*. The results, which you can score yourself, will show you your areas of weakness and strength. Gaps in your knowledge can be filled by taking the appropriate courses or by working on your own. If, for example, you are weak on cultural matters, you should read the art, book, and theater sections of any of the weekly news magazines or the Sunday *New York Times*. At a minimum, you should be able to identify major American names and their contributions in each cultural field. If you are weak in economics or U.S. history, read a basic text in these subjects. If you know little of the functions of U.S. embassies and can't describe what a consular officer does, glance through some of the reference books listed in the exam booklet.

How to Apply for the Exam

The Foreign Service written exam is given annually in November, and applications for it must be submitted by October. The exam varies slightly from year to year, but is usually a multiple-choice test with questions covering English expression, international relations, current events, economics, U.S. history, and geography, to U.S. art, literature, and culture, as well as the historical antecedents of international affairs, foreign political systems, basic principles of economics, commercial issues, the U.S. Constitution and political process, and the U.S. educational system. Over the past few years, the Foreign Service Exam has concentrated on economics and eased up on basic management questions. All facets of U.S. foreign policy, customs, and culture are stressed, since FSOs need a solid background in Americana to be effective U.S. representatives abroad.

A booklet describing the exam format and listing sample exam questions is available generally in August of each year. It can usually be picked up in college placement offices. Otherwise, write to the Recruitment Division of the Department of State (see address on page 77) and ask for *Application for the Foreign Service Officer Program,* and also *Foreign Service Careers.*

Written Exam Questions

Test your skills on these sample questions:*

1. Two key precepts of the Constitution that were not present in the Articles of Confederation were to
   a. Buffer the government from the immediate impact of popular impulse and to extend the vote to all
   b. Promote the power of individual states over that of the federal government and to keep the branches of the federal government separate but linked
   c. Keep the President closely tied to the will of the majority and to promote the power of individual states over that of the federal government.
   d. Buffer the government from the immediate impact of popular impulse and to keep the branches of the federal government separate but linked
2. Which of the following columnists is known for the conservative tone of his or her work?
   a. Russell Baker
   b. Carl Rowan
   c. Meg Greenfield
   d. George Will
3. All of the following were objectives of the common, or public school, movement of 1840–60, except
   a. Primary school education for all white Americans regardless of sex
   b. A professionally trained teaching force
   c. Establishment of a uniform national curriculum
   d. Introduction of new pedagogy based on the idea that children were capable of infinite improvement

*Answers: 1, d; 2, d; 3, c; 4, b; 5, c.

4. All of the following statements concerning dumping in international trade are correct except
   a. It is defined as selling at less than fair value
   b. It forms the basis for a claim in the World Court
   c. It constitutes an unfair trade practice under GATT
   d. It is subject to U.S. law
5. A major difference between U.S. political parties and political parties in European parliamentary systems is that
   a. European parties are less ideologically rigid
   b. U.S. parties have stronger local organizations
   c. European parties exercise more discipline over their elected representatives in the legislature
   d. U.S. parties better represent special interests

Each year about 10,000 eager applicants take the Foreign Service written exam and answer questions such as those above. About 2,000 pass and are eligible to take the "oral assessment" exam. Eventually some 250 may be given probationary appointments for a period of five years.

Oral Assessment and Other Tests

Candidates who pass the Written Examination will be eligible for an all-day Oral Assessment that includes a variety of simulation techniques and other appraisals:

1. An oral exam with two examiners
2. A written essay on an assigned topic
3. A written exercise designed to test the ability to summarize provided materials
4. A two-part group exercise. The first part consists of a short oral presentation of a proposal to a group by each candidate based on material provided; the second part is a leaderless group to discuss and seek agreement on the disposition of the various proposals
5. A written "In-Basket" test in which the candidate deals with a series of problems and situations presented in writing

If you are successful in the Oral Assessment, you will then be investigated to determine eligibility for a security clearance. You are also required to take a medical exam, submit a 1,000-word autobiography, and obtain transcripts from each institution of higher learning that you attended.

A Final Review Panel weighs a candidate's qualifications against those of others. The names of those who pass the entire examination and selection process will be placed on rank-order registers in the functional fields for which they have been judged qualified: administrative, commercial, consular economic, information/cultural, and political. Candidates from the information/cultural register will become FSO Career Candidates for the USIA. Candidates from the commercial register will become Career Candidates for the Department of Commerce. All other candidates will become Career Candidates with the Department of State.

If you get a low, though passing, grade, your name will be near the bottom of the list and you may never be called. If you have not been given an offer within a year and a half, your chances will grow progressively slimmer as new applicants with higher scores from the following year's exam are placed above your name on the register.

Timing

The length of time between applying to the Foreign Service and — if you're lucky — getting a job offer is at least nine or ten months, and frequently longer. The timing may seem inordinately long, but is more readily understood in light of the detailed steps required. Applications are due in October, the written exam is held in November and papers are graded and results sent to applicants by the end of January or the beginning of February.

If you pass the subsequent Oral Assessment, a security check takes from four to six months and sometimes longer if you have lived abroad. Then comes your medical exam.

The length of the whole process means that many students who apply may graduate before the final verdict is in. Therefore, even if a job with the Foreign Service is your primary career objective, keep your lines open to other careers. You may well find you have to take a temporary job in an unrelated field while waiting for the hoped-for bid from the Department of State.

Must You Take the Exam?

Practically all the professional jobs in the Department of State and in U.S. embassies are staffed with FSOs who have successfully passed the written and personal assessment exams, as well as the security check and a medical exam. Exceptions are:

TECHNICAL JOBS. Lawyers, trained economists, and others with desired technical skills may be brought in from the outside. Also, those with media experience may be considered for jobs in the Office of Media Services.

RESEARCHERS. Very occasionally the Bureau of Intelligence and Research may be unable to obtain an FSO with particular skills to staff a research vacancy. In this case, it may be authorized to recruit from outside.

INTERPRETERS AND TRANSLATORS.   People with these skills may be hired for full- or part-time work.

VISA PERSONNEL, CLERKS, AND SECRETARIES.   These are low-level jobs with limited career potential.

FOREIGN SERVICE SPECIALISTS.   The Department of State offers additional career opportunities in specialized functions, appointment to which does not require taking the written exam. Some of these specialized functions are communications electronics officer, security engineering officer, systems manager, building and maintenance specialist, construction engineer, financial management officer, general services officer, personnel officer, and security officer. If interested, write to the Recruitment Division of the Department of State (see address on page 77).

SPECIAL RECRUITMENT PROGRAMS.   As equal opportunity employers, the Departments of State and Commerce and the USIA have certain programs for the appointment of FSO career candidates. A limited number of such appointments may be made annually.

There is an affirmative action program for minority entry-level FSO Career Candidates with at least a bachelor's degree from a college or university, and there is an affirmative action program for minority Mid-Level FSO Career Candidates with a bachelor's degree and at least five additional years of education and work experience.

All applicants are required to take the annual written examination. When the results are known, the Board of Examiners will determine which candidates are qualified for further consideration. Write to the Recruitment Division of the Department of State (see address on page 77).

Languages

Contrary to popular belief, knowledge of a foreign language is not essential to get into the Foreign Service. If you don't have a second language under your belt, however, you will be appointed as a language probationer and not granted tenure until language competency is acquired. If necessary, an officer will attend classes at the Foreign Service Institute, which offers training in more than forty languages.

The Departments of State and Commerce and the USIA particularly seek people with knowledge of Arabic, Chinese, Japanese, or Russian.

There is a reverse twist to the language question. If you have language competence in Arabic, for example, you may assume you'll spend all or most of

The Foreign Service Salary Schedule for 1992 was:

Foreign Service Class	Approximate Civil Service General Schedule* Equivalent	Salary Range
FS-1	15	$64,233–$77,079
FS-2	13/14	$46,210–$65,527
FS-3	12/13	$42,174–$55,450
FS-4	11/12	$34,174–$46,631
FS-5	9/10	$27,691–$35,415
FS-6	8/9	$24,755–$32,156
FS-7	7/8	$22,130–$29,116
FS-8	6/7	$19,784–$26,286
FS-9	5	$17,686–$21,226

*The Civil Service's General Schedule of service grades 1 through 15. See discussion on page 101.

Newly appointed/junior officers are generally hired at the level of GS grade 6 or 5, depending on education and experience. These figures may change, so check before you apply.

your career in the Middle East. Not so. The Department will try to use your language skills but it will not guarantee that all your assignments will be in a specific country or area. In fact, you may on occasion be assigned to a non-Arabic-speaking area solely to expand your knowlege of the world and the variety of its foreign policy problems.

First Assignment

If you are lucky, your first assignment may be a rotational one at an embassy. You will then spend six months in each of the four sections of the embassy: *Political, Economic, Administrative,* and *Consular.* At the end of your two-year tour of duty you will have learned a great deal about the operations and functions of all parts of an embassy.

Another first assignment might place you for your full tour of duty in a specific section of an embassy or consulate general — or perhaps in Washington, assisting a country desk officer. During your career you will bounce many times between Washington and abroad. In general, you should expect about half of your career to be spent overseas.

Inter-American Foundation (IAF)

901 N. Stuart St.
Arlington, VA 22203

The IAF is an independent government corporation that supports social and economic development in Latin America and the Caribbean. It makes grants primarily to private indigenous organizations that carry out self-help projects benefiting the poor. It has also arranged with the Inter-American Development Bank to channel some of its resources to foundation projects, such as workers' self-managed enterprises, credit and production cooperatives, self-help housing, agricultural extension services, legal aid clinics, a bank run by and for workers, peasant associations, and informal education.

Background Desired

The variety of activities of the IAF define the background needed by this agency: economics, economic development, Latin American studies, finance, agriculture, labor, cooperatives, banking, housing, law, industrial management, statistics, labor relations, and a fluency in Spanish and Portuguese. Obviously, no one applicant is going to have that complete a background. The more of these skills you have to offer, however, the better your chances. A Civil Service rating is required.

International Development Cooperation Agency (IDCA)

> 320 21st St., NW
> Washington, DC 20523

IDCA's function is policy planning and coordination on the international economic issues affecting developing countries. Its mission is two-fold: (1) to ensure that developmental goals are taken into account in all executive decisions on trade, financing, monetary affairs, technology, and other economic policy issues affecting the less developed nations; and (2) to provide strong direction for U.S. economic policies toward the developing world. The Director of IDCA serves as the principal international development adviser to the President and Secretary of State.

Background Desired

Of primary value is a background (academic and/or experience) in economics, trade, developmental assistance, and developing areas and languages. If you wish a job in a specific part of IDCA, it may be advisable to take time to do a little research and identify the division or section handling that particular kind of job. (The *U.S. Government Manual*, available in most reference libraries, will give you this information).

National Security Agency (NSA)

> College Recruitment Program
> National Security Agency
> Fort Meade, MD 20755-6000
> Attn: Office of Employment (M 322)

NSA is charged with three of the most important and sensitive activities in the U.S. intelligence community:

1. Interception, collection, and analysis of foreign electromagnetic signals of all types, many of them protected by codes, ciphers, and complete electronic countermeasures, to produce intelligence information for the U.S. government
2. Responsibility for communications security for the U.S. government
3. Responsibility for establishing computer security standards for use throughout the government

Background Desired

NSA puts a premium on people with a technical background that can be applied to electronics, computer, and cryptographic work. Majors in engineering, computer science, and mathematics are particularly desired. NSA is also interested in people with proficiency in certain exotic languages, particularly Slavic languages, Chinese, Japanese, and Arabic. An ability to translate from original sources, rather than conversational ability, is required. Sometimes individuals with exceptional capabilities in an exotic language will be hired without taking the test discussed below.

Requirements

Applicants usually must take an aptitude test, called a Professional Qualification Test, which measures the aptitudes and abilities needed by NSA. This test is usually given in November of each year.

The first step in applying for an NSA job is to obtain a Professional Qualification Test booklet early in the fall. If it is not available locally, write to the College Recruitment Program of the NSA (address above). The test is administered at a number of test centers located on college campuses. If you pass the exam, an interview will subsequently be arranged with an NSA recruiter or panel. Again, there is a premium on time because of the span between application and possible appointment, so apply early.

Most NSA jobs are in the United States, although occasional travel abroad may be required.

Office of the United States Trade Representative

> 600 17th St., NW
> Washington, DC 20506

The U.S. Trade Representative is responsible for setting and administering U.S. trade policy as well as the direction of all trade negotiations. Negotiators, analysts, and support staff all work in the office on policy making and negotiations. Staffs are maintained in Washington and Geneva.

Background Desired

A high degree of skill in economics, with an emphasis on trade and negotiations, is required of applicants for the occasional job opening that develops in this office. A Ph.D. in economics or trade is preferred.

Overseas Private Investment Corporation (OPIC)

> 1615 M. St., NW
> Washington, DC 20527

OPIC is an executive agency that fosters economic development and progress in the developing countries of Latin America, Asia, Africa, and Europe. It does this by providing U.S. investors with political risk insurance and financial assistance to support their investments in these countries. OPIC finances investment projects through direct loans and guarantees and provides the investor with various services, such as counseling and country investment kits. The investors may be large or small, corporate or individual.

All projects supported by OPIC must assist in the economic or social development of the country and also be consistent with the economic and foreign policy interests of the United States.

OPIC insurance is of particular importance in protecting investments against: (1) the ability to convert into U.S. dollars any local currency received by investors as profit; (2) the loss of investments from nationalization or confiscation of facilities; (3) war, revolution, or insurrection.

Background Desired

Since many OPIC functions revolve around insurance and finance, a background in either or both fields is essential. Economics, economic development, Third World area studies, banking, and statistics are also helpful. A Civil Service rating is required (see the section on domestic-oriented agencies, page 92, for more on this).

Panama Canal Commission

> 2000 L St., NW
> Washington, DC 20036

The Panama Canal Commission operates the Panama Canal and coordinates the operations of the waterway with the Republic of Panama. After 1999, the Republic of Panama will assume full responsibility for the Canal.

Background Desired

Most employees of the commission work in Panama, with only a handful located in Washington and New Orleans. In light of the projected turnover of operations of the Panama Canal to Panama in 1999, opportunities for U.S. citizens are extremely limited. Applicants with a business, maritime, or engineering background will be most likely to receive a serious hearing.

Peace Corps

> 1990 K St., NW
> Washington, DC 20526

The Peace Corps, formerly part of ACTION, is now an independent agency with a specialized task of training people of developing nations. Positions are available in many fields throughout Latin America, Africa, the Near East, Asia, the Pacific, and now Europe. Ever since the organization was established in 1961, thousands of Americans have been Peace Corps volunteers in more than 70 countries. Volunteers work in six program areas: education, agriculture, health, small business development, urban development, and the environment.

Background Desired

Three to five years of work experience and/or a college degree are required. Specifically, generalists (with a B.A.) as well as graduate students in business, economics, agriculture, education, engineering, fisheries, the health professions, and many other areas are encouraged to apply for field positions.

A living allowance in the local currency is given to cover housing, food, and essential expenses. When service is completed, volunteers receive a $200 readjustment allowance for every month served.

Occasional positions may also be available in Washington headquarters, where policy is set up, personnel are processed, and work in the field is supervised. Those with administrative interests, a finance background, or economics qualifications are needed.

Selection involves completing an application form, then entering a training program lasting from 8 to 14 weeks preparatory to a two-year assignment in a developing country.

Special Note: Returning Peace Corps volunteers who are looking for another international job have recourse to the *Bulletin of Career, Educational, and Re-entry Information and Opportunities for Returned Peace Corps Volunteers*, a bi-monthly publication of the Peace Corps that includes current openings in the private and public sectors of the U.S. as well as openings abroad. Also, a booklet titled *International Careers — Career Information for Returned Peace Corps Volunteers*, 1991 ed., may be helpful. Both of these publications are available through the Washington, DC Peace Corps office.

United States Information Agency (USIA)

The U.S. Information Agency, formerly the U.S. International Communication Agency, has its headquarters in Washington, DC. Overseas, USIA is known as the USIS (U.S. Information Service). It has 204 posts in 127 countries.

In conjunction with the State Department, USIA defines policy for disseminating the American image abroad. Primary aims are to increase foreign understanding of U.S. policies and to counter attempts to distort the objectives and policies of the United States.

Washington headquarters has four associate directorates, each performing certain functions:

1. *Broadcasting* (Voice of America, or VOA) produces and broadcasts radio programs in English and 44 foreign languages for overseas audiences.

   Radio broadcasts to Cuba on the VOA's Cuban Service, or Radio Marti Program, began in 1985. Named for Cuban patriot José Martí, this program provides, "news, commentary, and other information about events in Cuba and elsewhere to promote the cause of freedom in Cuba."

   USIA uses the latest satellite technology to beam important programs live to foreign audiences through local TV stations. It also acquires and produces videotape programs and films for distribution through its overseas posts.

2. *Management* handles administrative, personnel, and comptroller services.

3. *Programs* uses press and publications to project an accurate image of the United States and its foreign policy abroad. Foreign media reaction to U.S. policies is reviewed, speakers are recruited, and exhibits are displayed overseas. Programs publishes 14 magazines in 20 languages and distributes pamphlets in more than 100 countries. One of its best-known publications is *America Illustrated*, a monthly magazine in Russian for distribution in the former USSR.

4. *Educational and Cultural Exchange*, as its name suggests, operates the U.S. government's programs of educational and cultural exchange, formerly administered by the Department of State.

    The best known of its exchanges is the Fullbright or academic exchange program, which operates in 120 countries. Each year the USIA also invites approximately 5,000 foreign leaders in all fields to the United States, and administers a program for the exchange of young people from 15 to 30 years of age.

    Cultural presentations for overseas audiences, logistical support for libraries, English-teaching programs abroad, and programs for visitors from overseas all come within the purview of this associate directorship.

Each USIA office abroad usually has at least a press officer, a cultural affairs officer, and a librarian. No matter which of these positions you may fill, you will spend a major part of your career overseas.

If you are a *press officer*, you will be responsible for objective reporting of events in the United States in the press of the country of assignment, a particularly thankless job in an unfriendly country. Further, you may write the ambassador's speeches, issue press releases, and arrange press conferences for the ambassador or for visiting U.S. officials.

The *cultural affairs officer* in a typical week may arrange for the visit of an American orchestra or dance group, organize lectures and seminars on American topics, and perhaps plan for student exchanges.

The *librarian* is in charge of the American library, generally located in the center of the city and usually more visible than other U.S. establishments, which explains why it is sometimes the focus of anti-American demonstrations.

Whether you are a press officer, a cultural affairs officer, or a librarian, you will spend a major part of your career overseas.

Background Desired

Journalism and cultural studies in particular are desired. Area studies, languages, foreign policy, international relations, and adminstration are also helpful. The desirable background for a VOA intern includes academic work or experience in broadcasting and/or journalism and international affairs.

Requirements

For most non-VOA jobs in Washington and for overseas jobs, the timing and procedure are the same as for the Foreign Service. You will be required to take the Foreign Service Officer exam. Get the FSO exam booklet in August or September so that you can submit your application before the October deadline.

This booklet should be available at college placement offices. If not, write to the Recruitment Division of the Department of State (see address on page 77).

As with the Foreign Service, the length of time between applying and getting an offer is unbearably long. The advice remains the same: Explore other career opportunities and keep your options open in case you don't pull through.

Procedures are different for VOA. Each year VOA offers a limited number of two-year paid broadcast internships that can lead to careers in radio journalism with VOA. Successful candidates receive on-the-job training, developing their skills in voicing, directing, producing, and writing. During this time they rotate among the most important divisions of the News and English Broadcast Complex. For VOA work, write to:

> Officer of Personnel, Room 1543
> Voice of America
> United States Information Agency
> 301 Fourth St., SW
> Washington, DC 20547

USIA also has positions for guides who accompany exhibits to the former USSR and Eastern Europe for one to seven months. Fluency in the language is required, as is a better-than-average knowledge of the American scene — political, economic, social, and cultural. As a guide at an exhibit in Russia, you are expected to have the answers for any question on America that may be posed by Russian visitors. Write to:

> Special Recruitment Staff
> Office of Personnel
> U.S. Information Agency
> Room 518
> 301 Fourth St., SW
> Washington, DC 20547

Since the USIA is a comparatively small agency, fewer positions are available each year than in the Foreign Service. If you are motivated to work for USIA, however, don't be deterred. Any job that is worthwhile will be highly competitive.

U.S. International Trade Commission

> Director of Personnel
> 500 E St., SW
> Washington, DC 20436

This organization is concerned with international trade and tariff matters. Specifically, it analyzes the effects of imported products on U.S. industries.

The commission has a trade monitoring system that checks imports into the United States from countries without a market economy and, in particular, investigates whether increased imports of articles produced in other countries are causing market disruptions in the United States.

Background Desired

The commission states that it is primarily interested in applicants with the following specializations: international economics, international trade, marketing, and international law. A Civil Service rating is required.

Requirements

Applicants should send a completed Standard Form 171 (Personal Qualification Statement).

EXECUTIVE BRANCH: DOMESTIC-ORIENTED AGENCIES

Most students specializing in international affairs and looking for a federal government job think only of the foreign-oriented U.S. agencies mentioned in the previous section. Don't forget the so-called domestic agencies, however. They also have positions of potential interest to you.

All the large government agencies, such as the Department of Labor, Department of Agriculture, Department of Commerce, and the Department of Energy, have international divisions with jobs for those with an international background, even though the bulk of their work concerns domestic matters.

Unlike the foreign-oriented agencies with their own procedures for recruiting personnel, domestic-oriented agencies use a standardized system for evaluating the qualifications of applicants. This system was devised by the Office of Personnel Management (OPM) which, when it started operations in 1978, took over many of the functions of the former U.S. Civil Service Commission.

OPM is responsible for nationwide recruiting and for examining applicants for positions in the Federal Civil Service at General Schedule (GS) grades 1 through 15. Within each grade there are ten steps, each corresponding to a certain salary. Although you are usually hired at the beginning salary of each grade, an unusually strong background may get you started at a higher step and salary. There are several ways of landing a federal job.

1. *Public Announcements*   About once or twice a month, OPM issues announcements of job openings in the federal government, and posts them at the Job Information Centers (JICs) it maintains in nearly every state. Jobs may range

from a low-level janitor to a senior economist or engineer. Look at the notices in the nearest JIC, and determine which jobs you are interested in and qualified for, and apply according to the instructions given.

If you want to relocate, contact the office that is nearest the location where you would like to work for information on the job opportunities in that area and the forms needed to apply.

Office of Personnel Management Federal Job Information Centers

Alabama	Southerland Building 806 Governors Drive, NW Huntsville, AL 35801 (205) 453-5070
Alaska	Federal Building 701 C St., Box 22 Anchorage, AK 99513 (907) 271-5821
Arizona	U.S. Postal Service Building Room 120 522 N. Central Ave. Phoenix, AZ 85004 (602) 261-4736
Arkansas	Federal Building Room 1319 700 W. Capital Ave. Little Rock, AR 72201 (501) 378-5842
California	Linder Building, 3rd Floor 845 S. Figueroa Los Angeles, CA 90017 (213) 894-3360
	Federal Building 650 Capital Mall Sacramento, CA 95814 (916) 440-3441
	Federal Building, Room 4-S-9 880 Front St. San Diego, CA 92188 (619) 557-6165
	Federal Building Room 1001 450 Golden Ave. San Francisco, CA 94102
Colorado	1845 Sherman St. Denver, CO 80203 (303) 837-3506
Connecticut	Federal Building, Room 613 450 Main St. Hartford, CT 06103 (203) 244-3096

Delaware	Federal Building 844 King St. Wilmington, DE 19801 (302) 571-6288
District of Columbia	1900 E St., NW, Room 1416 Washington, DC 20415 (202) 737-9616
Florida	80 North Hughey Ave. Orlando, FL 32801 (305) 420-6148
	330 Biscayne Blvd. Suite 410 Miami, FL 33131 (305) 350-4725
Georgia	Richard B. Russell Federal Building Room 960 75 Spring St., SW Atlanta, GA 30303 (404) 331-4315
Guam	238 O'Hara Street Room 308 Agana, GU 96910 (671) 344-5252
Hawaii	Federal Building, Room 5316 300 Ala Moana Blvd. Honolulu, HI 96850 (808) 541-2791
Idaho	See Washington listing
Illinois	Dirkson Building Room 1322 219 S. Dearborn St. Chicago, IL 60604 (312) 353-5136
Indiana	46 East Ohio St. Room 123 Indianapolis, IN 46204 (317) 269-7161
Iowa	210 Walnut St. Room 191 Des Moines, IA 50309 (515) 284-4546
Kansas	One-Twenty Building, Room 101 120 S. Market St. Wichita, KS 67202 (316) 269-6794
	In Johnson, Leavenworth, and Wyandotte counties, dial (816) 426-5702
Kentucky	Federal Building 600 Federal Plaza Louisville, KY 40202 (502) 582-5130

Louisiana	1515 Poydras St., Suite 608 New Orleans, LA 70112 (504) 589-2764
Maine	Federal Building Room 611 Sewall St. & Western Ave. Augusta, ME 04330 (207) 622-6171, ext. 269
Maryland	Garmatz Federal Building 101 W. Lombard St. Baltimore, MD 21201 (301) 962-3822
Massachusetts	Thos. P. O'Neill Federal Building 3 Center Plaza Boston, MA 02108 (617) 565-5900
Michigan	477 Michigan Ave., Room 565 Detroit, MI 48226 (313) 226-6950
Minnesota	Federal Building Ft. Snelling Twin Cities, MN 55111 (612) 725-3355
Mississippi	100 West Capitol St. Suite 335 Jackson, MS 39201
Missouri	Federal Building, Room 134 601 E. 12th St. Kansas City, MO 64106 (816) 374-5702
	Federal Building Room 129 1520 Market St. St. Louis, MO 63103 (314) 425-4285
Montana	Federal Building & Courthouse 301 S. Park, Room 153 Helena, MT 59601 (406) 449-5388
Nebraska	U.S. Courthouse & Post Office Building Room 1014 215 N. 17th St. Omaha, NE 68102 (402) 221-3815
Nevada	Mill & S. Virginia Streets P.O. Box 3296 Reno, NV 89505 (702) 754-5535
New Hampshire	Thomas J. McIntyre Federal Building Room 104 80 Daniel St. Portsmouth, NH 03801-3875 (603) 436-7720, ext. 762

New Jersey	Peter W. Rodino, Jr., Federal Building 970 Broad St. Newark, NJ 07102 (201) 645-3673 In Camden, dial (215) 597-7440
New Mexico	Federal Building 421 Gold Ave., SW Albuquerque, NM 87102 (505) 766-2557 In Dona Ana, Otero, and El Paso counties, dial (505) 766-1893
New York	Jacob K. Javits Federal Building 26 Federal Plaza New York, NY 10278 (212) 264-0422
	James M. Hanley Federal Building 100 S. Clinton St. Syracuse, NY 13260 (315) 423-5660
	590 Grand Concourse Bronx, NY 10451 (212) 292-4666
	111 West Huron St. Room 35 Buffalo, NY 14202 (716) 846-4001
	90-04 161st St. Room 200 Jamaica, NY 11432 (212) 526-6192
North Carolina	Federal Building 310 New Bern Ave. P.O. Box 25069 Raleigh, NC 27611 (701) 237-5771
North Dakota	See Minnesota listing
Ohio	Federal Building 1240 East 9th St. Cleveland, OH 44199 (216) 522-4232
Oklahoma	200 NW Fifth St., 2nd Floor Oklahoma City, OK 73102 (405) 231-4948 (Mail or phone only)
Oregon	Federal Building, Room 376 1220 SW Third Ave. Portland, OR 97204 (503) 221-3141
Pennsylvania	Federal Building, Room 168 P.O. Box 761 Harrisburg, PA 17108 (717) 782-4494

Wm. J. Green Jr., Federal Building
600 Arch St., Room 1416
Philadelphia, PA 19106
   (215) 597-7440

Federal Building
1000 Liberty Ave., Room 119
Pittsburgh, PA 15222
   (412) 644-2755

Puerto Rico

Frederico Dagetau Federal Building
Carlos E. Chardon St.
Hato Rey, PR 00918
   (809) 766-5242

Rhode Island

John O. Pastore Federal Building
Room 310, Kennedy Plaza
Providence, RI 02903
   (401) 528-5251

South Carolina

Federal Building
334 Meeting St.
Charleston, SC 29403
   (803) 724-4328

South Dakota

Federal Building
Room 202
U.S. Court House
515 9th St.
Rapid City, SD 57701
   (901) 521-3956

Tennessee

Federal Building
167 N. Main St.
Memphis, TN 38103
   (901) 521-3956

Texas

1100 Commerce St.
Dallas, TX 75242
   (214) 767-8035
   (Mail or phone only)

Property Trust Building
Suite N302
2211 East Missouri Ave.
El Paso, TX 79903
   (915) 543-7425

702 San Jacinto St.
Houston, TX 77002
   (713) 226-5501

643 E. Durango Blvd.
San Antonio, TX 78206
   (512) 229-6600
   (Mail or phone only)

Utah

1234 South Main St.
2nd Floor
Salt Lake City, UT 84101
   (801) 524-5744

Vermont

Federal Building
Room 614
P.O. Box 489
Elmwood Ave. & Pearl St.
Burlington, VT 05402
   (802) 862-6712

Virginia	Federal Building, Room 220 Granby St. Norfolk, VA 23510-1886 (804) 441-3355
Washington	Federal Building 915 Second Ave. Seattle, WA 98174 (206) 442-4365
West Virginia	See Ohio listing
Wisconsin	Residents in Grant, Iowa, Lafayette, Dane, Green, Rock, Jefferson, Walworth, Waukesha, Racine, Kenosha, and Milwaukee counties should dial (312) 353-6189 All other Wisconsin residents should refer to the Minnesota listing
Wyoming	See Colorado listing (303) 236-4166
Overseas	See Hawaii listing (808) 541-2784

2. *Presidential Management Intern Program (PMIP)*   PMIP is a government-wide program to attract into the federal service outstanding graduate students with a potential to become top-level career executives.

You are allowed to apply for PMIP *only* during the fall of your last year of graduate school. The application process includes an initial written application which is screened by an independent agency. If your written application is accepted, you go through a rigorous PMIP interview process and then an interview for specific job openings within the government.

Each year up to 400 exceptionally talented individuals receive two-year appointments in the government agency of their choice. They may be assigned to staff units in administrative and managerial services or to operating program offices. In any case, they will be exposed to a wide variety of jobs within the organization. At the beginning of their internship they start at GS9.

At the end of their two-year internship, depending on the quality of their performance, they may be granted Civil Service status without further competition.

Application materials are usually available at graduate schools in the early fall of each year. Application packets include an institutional nomination form to be filled out by the school, an application form for the student, and independent evaluation forms for each applicant.

If not available at school, applications can be obtained by contacting:

Presidential Management Intern Program
Executive Office of the President
Office of Management and Budget
New Executive Building
725 17th St., NW
Washington, DC 20503

3. *Entry-level jobs* Entry-level positions are generally for those with a B.A. or B.S. On this level, usually GS5-GS7 (e.g., program analyst, personnel specialist), OPM provides two ways in which candidates can enter the federal service. The usual way is to take a written test, which includes questions that test not only the applicant's knowledge but also, for the first time, personal characteristics indicative of successful performance. Most jobs at the entry level are in low-level administration and usually involve little international content.

To learn more about the exam, contact:

Office of Personnel Management
Washington Examining Services
1900 E Street, NW
Washington, DC 20415

There is an easier way of entering the federal service if you are a college grad with a high (over 3.50) grade-point average. In that case, no written exam is needed and you will be judged exclusively on your background and general qualifications. For applications and information, contact the nearest Job Information Center.

4. *Mid-level jobs* Mid-level positions are generally for those with graduate degrees. For mid-level grades GS9-12, individuals should apply directly to the agency that they are interested in or feel the most qualified for.

In the mid-level openings that may appeal to you, such as economist, researcher, or financial analyst, you may find that the precious international background you have accumulated over the years is of slight relevance. Don't necessarily let that deter you from applying. If you should be offered a job in the noninternational operations of a government agency, you may wish to consider it with the thought that once on the inside you may be given priority for possible job openings in the international division of that agency.

If you do land an international job in any of these domestic-oriented agencies of the government, you will work in Washington with perhaps an occasional trip overseas.

Special Tips for Those Applying at the Mid-Level

The above procedures may imply that you should wait by the phone to be summoned for a job interview once your papers are submitted to the Office of Personnel Management, but don't. You increase your chances immeasurably by taking certain actions.

While your papers are being processed in OPM, consult the *U.S. Government Manual.** This manual, in addition to describing the mission and functions of each government agency, provides information on the chain of command in these offices, including names and titles of top-level people. It also discusses agencies in the legislative and judicial branches.

This volume should enable you to identify the sections within each agency that particularly interest you. The manual will also give you the names of the individuals in charge of those sections. College placement offices can be helpful as well in providing you with contacts in some government agencies.

Since most government agencies do not recruit on campus, students will have to conduct a mail campaign to lay the groundwork for face-to-face meetings in Washington. Your communication with an agency should consist of a cover letter and a résumé or filled-out Standard Form 171, available at all JICs. Keep the letter brief. Send it to the director of the international division or other office to which you are applying. You can send letters to several offices within the same agency.

An effective time for starting your mail campaign will be several weeks before a planned visit to Washington. Mention the approximate date of your trip and indicate that you will phone the office director or other recipient of the letter for an appointment before or on arrival.

Phone for an appointment at the time indicated. You may find to your annoyance that the person to whom you have written does not remember hearing from you or may even have misplaced your letter. Often enough, however, you will find the recipient of your letter aware of your application and willing to meet with you. If you do get an appointment, find out if any vacancies exist or are anticipated. If you impress the employer, he or she may ask OPM to submit your name for consideration when vacancies arise. If you are lucky, you may even have the job description rephrased to include specifics of your background and qualifications, thus giving you an edge over your competition.

Check the various addresses of the offices you will be visiting on a map of downtown Washington before making appointments. Knowledge of agency locations and careful planning can double the number of people you can see in a day.

---

*Available at most libraries, it can also be ordered from the U.S. Government Printing Office, Washington, DC 20402 for $23.00.

**Selected Federal White-Collar Pay Schedules
Effective January 1992***

General Schedule (4.2%)		Grade		
Step	1	2	3	4	5
1	$11,478	$11,861	$12,242	$12,623	$13,006
2	12,905	13,212	13,640	14,003	14,157
3	14,082	14,551	15,020	15,489	15,958
4	15,808	16,335	16,862	17,389	17,916
5	17,686	18,276	18,866	19,456	20,046
6	19,713	20,370	21,027	21,684	22,341
7	21,906	22,636	23,366	24,096	24,826
8	24,262	25,071	25,880	26,689	27,498
9	26,798	27,691	28,584	29,477	30,370
10	29,511	30,495	31,479	32,463	33,447
11	32,423	33,504	34,585	35,666	36,747
12	38,861	40,156	41,451	42,746	44,041
13	46,210	47,750	49,290	50,830	52,370
14	54,607	56,427	58,247	60,067	61,887
15	64,233	66,374	68,515	70,656	72,797

General Schedule (4.2%)		Grade		
Step	6	7	8	9	10
1	$13,230	$13,606	$13,986	$14,003	$14,356
2	14,573	14,989	15,405	15,821	16,237
3	16,427	16,896	17,365	17,834	18,303
4	18,443	18,970	19,497	20,024	20,551
5	20,636	21,226	21,816	22,406	22,996
6	22,998	23,655	24,312	24,969	25,626
7	25,556	26,286	27,016	27,746	28,476
8	28,307	29,116	29,925	30,734	31,543
9	31,263	32,156	33,049	33,942	34,835
10	34,431	35,415	36,399	37,383	38,367
11	37,828	38,909	39,990	41,071	42,152
12	45,336	46,631	47,926	49,221	50,516
13	53,910	55,450	56,990	58,530	60,070
14	63,707	65,527	67,327	69,167	70,987
15	74,938	77,079	79,220	81,361	83,502

*Salaries may well be higher by the time you read this.

Avoid scheduling your trip to Washington during major holiday periods. It is preferable to go during the middle of the week. This increases the likelihood of the top management people being there.

Caution: One of the first questions you are likely to be asked is "Have you sent in your application to OPM?" If you reply in the negative, you will probably be asked to return when you have started the whole process. Therefore, do not descend on Washington unless you are well on the way toward getting a GS rating from the OPM.

Types of Jobs

A degree in international affairs will probably qualify you for one or more of the following jobs in the federal domestic-oriented agencies:

ECONOMIST OR INTERNATIONAL ECONOMIST.   Research into economic problems, analysis and interpretation of economic data, and preparation of reports on economic facts, activities, and trends.

Requirements: Twenty-one semester hours in economics plus three semester hours in statistics, accounting, or calculus. Both undergraduate and graduate courses are accepted. Almost any course with the words "economic" or "economy" in the title is apt to be acceptable. If in doubt, list the course and add a few lines to explain its economic content. Courses to be considered for this rating are negotiable with OPM.

FOREIGN AFFAIRS ANALYST.   Research on subjects related to foreign affairs. (This rating is not used by the Department of State or any of the foreign-oriented agencies, but the Treasury Department and Department of Commerce, for example, might use it for some jobs relating to their international activities.)

Requirements: Twenty-four semester hours in one of the social sciences, including international relations, political science, economics, and international law.

INTERNATIONAL RELATIONS OFFICER.   Work on the formulation and implementation of U.S. foreign policy in the conduct of its relations with other governments.

Requirements: Same as for foreign affairs analyst.

INTELLIGENCE RESEARCH SPECIALIST.   Research in military science, international relations, and related fields. Interpretation of relevant facts to help in the formulation and implementation of U.S. foreign policy.

Requirements: A blend of academic work and professional experience depending on the grade for which applied. Academic work should focus on subjects concerning foreign policy, military technology, and general international relations.

There are hundreds of federal government agencies, some small, some large. Only the largest ones — those with jobs of interest to people specializing in international affairs — will be covered in this section.

Department of Agriculture

> Director, Personnel Division
> Foreign Agriculture Service
> U.S. Department of Agriculture
> Washington, DC 20250

The *Foreign Agriculture Service (FAS)* of the Department of Agriculture is the export promotion agency for U.S. agriculture. It improves access to foreign markets for U.S. farm products through representations to foreign governments and through participation in trade negotiations. The FAS also appraises overseas marketing opportunities and makes this information available to the U.S. agricultural trade.

Of particular interest to students of international affairs is the global operation of FAS. It maintains an overseas network of *agricultural attachés* who report and analyze world agicultural production, trade, and policies affecting U.S. agriculture. These attachés are stationed at approximately 60 key posts, usually embassies, covering more than 110 countries.

Background Desired

As might be expected, a Civil Service rating is almost always a prerequisite for these jobs. If interested, take courses in international economics or agricultural economics.

Requirements

Qualified applicants should submit a Standard Form 171, a notice of eligibility from OPM, and college transcripts.

Department of Commerce

> International Trade Administration
> Travel Services, U.S.
> Department of Commerce
> 14th St. and Constitution Ave., NW
> Washington, DC 20230

This department, with its wide variety of programs, offers unusual opportunities for those with an international background and business interests. Of particular importance is the International Trade Administration (ITA), which aims to promote world trade and strengthen the international trade and investment position of the United States.

In ITA there are several offices that may be of interest to you. The Office of *International Economic Policy (IEP)* analyzes, formulates, and implements international economic policies of a bilateral or multilateral nature. IEP represents the United States on trade matters in international organizations. It is broken down geographically into four areas: Europe; the Western Hemisphere; East Asia and the Pacific; and Africa, the Near East, and South Asia. Each of these offices has responsibility for trade and investment issues with countries in its area.

The Office of *Trade Development* advises domestic business on international trade matters and carries out programs to promote world trade and strengthen the international trade and investment position of the United States.

The Office of *Trade Administration* is responsible for developing and implementing policies and programs dealing with exports and imports.

Of further interest to you may be the *Foreign Commercial Service (FCS)* of ITA. The FCS is a part of the Foreign Service system (see pages 77–84 on the Foreign Service of the Department of State), and aims to assist U.S. business in its international activities. The FCS supervises the work of the Foreign Commercial Service Officers attached to U.S. embassies and consulates abroad in 124 posts located in 64 countries.

Also under the Department of Commerce is *Travel Services, U.S.* Its aims are to maximize the contribution of tourism to economic prosperity and full employment, to minimize any restrictions on U.S. tourism throughout the world, and to assist in the collection and distribution of tourism data. It has regional offices in London, Paris, Frankfurt, Amsterdam, Milan, Sydney, Tokyo, Toronto, and Mexico City.

Background Desired

Academic studies that will get you a hearing for ITA jobs are international economics, trade and tariff courses, area studies, languages, and business administration. A combination of two or three of the above will be particularly helpful.

Those of you who are not employees of the Department of Commerce and who wish to work as Foreign Commercial Service Officers overseas should take the Foreign Service Exam (see pages 77–80). Sometimes businessmen are also recruited from the outside for these jobs.

Courses in international economics, tourism, and a knowledge of French, Spanish, Japanese, or German will help you in a job bid with Travel Services, U.S.

Department of Defense (DOD)

> Office of Assistant Secretary of Defense
> International Security Affairs
> Department of Defense, Pentagon
> Washington, DC 20301-1155

You should pay particular attention to the *International Security Affairs Division*. ISA develops defense positions in political-military and foreign economic affairs, including arms control and disarmament. Among its functions are negotiating and monitoring agreements with foreign governments concerning military facilities and the status of armed forces. Policy guidance is provided to military personnel stationed in U.S. embassies and to U.S. representatives at international organizations and conferences.

Background Desired

Academic studies of optimum use are national security, military technology, international economics, U.S. foreign policy, Russian studies, Chinese studies, and East Central European studies and languages.

Department of Energy (DOE)

> Assistant Secretary, International Affairs
> Department of Energy
> 1000 Independence Ave., SW
> Washington, DC 20585

DOE was established in 1977 to bring together the many fragmented energy programs and offices created over the years in the federal government. Its purpose is to ensure that the supply of energy available to the United States is sufficient to meet our needs.

This department has an *Assistant Secretary for International Affairs and Energy Emergencies*, whose office develops and implements U.S. international energy policies and deals with energy emergencies. It provides the energy perspective on all international negotiations between the United States and other nations. The office also develops policy options on energy relationships between producer and consumer nations, analyzing the options' impact on these relationships and on U.S. energy objectives. Another function is to recommend U.S. policy toward the international oil industry and assess world price and supply trends. Of particular importance is the office's role in evaluating the future adequacy of world energy resources.

Background Desired

All these analytical and technical functions are met by personnel qualified in engineering, economics, and energy matters. Here, as elsewhere, a heavy dose of economics at school may get you the appropriate rating.

Department of Health and Human Services (HHS)

> Office of International Health
> Department of Health and Human Services
> 200 Independence Ave., SW
> Washington, DC 20201
>
> or
>
> Social Security Administration
> 6401 Security Blvd.
> Baltimore, MD 21235

This department includes the *Public Health Service* and the *Social Security Administration*, both of which have international activities.

The *Office of International Health* of the Public Health Service administers a program of sharing U.S. health-care expertise and institutional capabilities with other countries. Cooperative activities take the form of scientific exchange of information, training opportunities for scientists, and research and consultations.

The public health program for China, for example, provides opportunities for joint research and exchange of information on causes of cancer and factors that contribute to cardiovascular disease. With India, the program has involved the transfer of new technologies to India for advancing laboratory research in reproductive physiology.

International activities of the Social Security Administration include research on various social security systems throughout the world, as well as the administration of programs for those in the system who are living abroad.

Background Desired

Courses on health, nutrition, medicine, chemistry, physics, and physiology are helpful for HHS's international health activities; and social sciences, statistics, and business administration for those interested in international social security matters.

Department of Housing and Urban Development (HUD)

> Assistant to the Secretary for International Affairs
> U.S. Department of Housing and Urban Development
> 451 7th St., SW
> Washington, DC 20410

HUD tries to improve the quality of life in U.S. cities and towns as well as ensure that future community growth is more orderly than it has been. This department gives financial and technical assistance to help states and cities solve urban problems.

In HUD there is an office concerned with international affairs, headed by an *Assistant to the Secretary for International Affairs*. This office coordinates the exchange of research and experience between HUD's programs and those of foreign governments. Housing and urban programs throughout the United States presumably benefit from the information exchanged under these cooperative arrangements. Some foreign programs that are said to have proved applicable to HUD's operations include industrialized building in Japan; consolidation of local governments in Sweden, France, and Great Britain; regional planning in France and Poland; housing management in Great Britain; housing allowances in several European countries; and national and urban growth policy throughout the developed countries.

Background Desired

In its researching of urban and housing programs of other countries, HUD uses economists, program analysts, financial analysts, realty specialists, and loan specialists. A Civil Service rating is, of course, a requirement.

Requirements

Send a Standard Form 171 and a notice of OPM eligibility.

Department of Justice

> Office of International Affairs
> Office of the Attorney General
> Criminal Division
> Department of Justice
> 10th and Pennsylvania Ave., NW
> Washington, DC 20530

or

Board of Immigration Appeals
Immigration and Naturalization Services
425 I Street, NW
Washington, DC 20536

or

Drug Enforcement Administration
600–700 Army-Navy Dr.
Arlington, VA 22202

This department has an *Office of International Affairs,* which supports the Criminal Division in the formulation and execution of transnational criminal justice enforcement policies, including international extradition proceedings, prisoner transfer, and mutual legal assistance.

Within this department, the *Immigration and Naturalization Service (INS)* administers the immigration laws relating to the admission, deportation, and naturalization of citizens. The INS has offices throughout the United States to provide information to those seeking U.S. citizenship. INS also works to eliminate the flow of illegal drugs into the country. The *Board of Immigration Appeals* is the highest tribunal in immigration matters.

Another part of the Department of Justice of interest to those with international backgrounds is the *Drug Enforcement Administration (DEA),* which conducts domestic and international investigations of major drug traffickers, and exchanges information with certain foreign countries.

Background Desired

In these immigration and drug enforcement functions, economists, investigators, lawyers, and statisticians are needed.

Department of Labor

Bureau of International Labor Affairs
Department of Labor
200 Constitution Ave., NW
Washington, DC 20210

The *Bureau of International Labor Affairs (ILA)* carries out the international responsibilities of the Department of Labor. The bureau helps to formulate international economic trade and immigration policies affecting American workers. ILA also represents the United States in trade negotiations and in such international bodies as the General Agreement on Tariffs and Trade (GATT), the International Labor Organization (ILO), and the Organization for Economic Cooperation and Development (OECD). The bureau also provides direction to the U.S. labor attachés at embassies abroad.

Background Desired

Some temporary jobs dealing with trade matters are exempt from Civil Service rating, but even in these cases your qualifications will be more impressive if you have a mid-level economist rating. Courses in trade and labor relations are other subjects that will be helpful in getting a job in the bureau.

Department of Transportation (DOT)

> Assistant Secretary for Policy and International Affairs
> Department of Transportation
> 400 7th St., SW
> Washington, DC 20590
>
> or
>
> Director, Office of International Activities
> Maritime Administration
> Department of Transportation
> 400 7th St., SW
> Washington, DC 20590
>
> or
>
> Director of International Aviation
> 800 Independence Ave., SW
> Washington, DC 20591

This departments aims to enroll the cooperation of federal, state, and local governments, carriers, labor, and other interested parties in achieving a more effective transportation network throughout the United States.

DOT has an *Assistant Secretary for Policy and International Affairs* who is responsible for carrying out the department's international programs. Among these are conducting research on transportation problems in other countries and providing policy and guidance to U.S. representatives attending international conferences involving transportation matters.

Under the DOT is the *Maritime Administration*. It administers programs to aid in the development and promotion of the U.S. merchant marine. It also operates the subsidy program under which the United States pays the difference between certain costs of building and operating ships under the U.S. flag versus similar costs under foreign flags.

Also under DOT is the *Federal Aviation Administration*, which promotes civil administration abroad by exchanging aeronautical information with foreign aviation authorities, negotiating international agreements to facilitate the import and export of aircraft, and providing technical representation at international conferences, including participation in the International Civil Aviation Organization.

Background Desired

For this specialized work, economics will be a help. Even more pertinent for the necessary Civil Service rating, however, are courses in transportation, trade, technology, and maritime and aviation problems.

Environmental Protection Agency (EPA)

> Associate Administrator of International Activities
> Environmental Protection Agency
> 401 M St., SW
> Washington, DC 20460

The purpose of the EPA is to protect and improve our environment. It aims to check and/or eliminate pollution of all types, from excess garbage to noise to radiation. A director is in charge of the international aspects of these functions. Some research is undertaken on environmental standards and problems faced by other countries. The office is also involved in providing guidance to U.S. representatives at international conferences dealing with environmental matters.

Background Desired

In-depth academic studies in economics, environment, energy, population, and related courses are of major importance in getting the mid-level rating of interest to this organization.

Requirements

Submit a Standard Form 171 and a college transcript.

Executive Office of the President

> Administration Office
> Office of Management and Budget
> Executive Office Building
> Washington, DC 20503

The major function of the *Office of Management and Budget (OMB)* is to make government service more efficient and economical. OMB has two units of potential interest to you, *National Security* and *International Affairs*. In these units are concentrated the international aspects of the following OMB functions: assisting the President in evaluating budgets for the foreign-oriented agencies (Department of State, USIA, NSA, CIA, and the Department of Defense); and keeping the President informed of the work proposed, initiated, and completed by these agencies.

Background Desired

A mid-level rating with a background in economics, international economics, business administration, foreign affairs, and international relations will be helpful.

Requirements

Applicants should forward copies of their résumé and completed Standard Forms 171. Applicants should also establish eligibility for employment simultaneously with the Office of Personnel Management (see pages 99–101).

Federal Maritime Commission (FMC)

> 1100 L St., NW
> Washington DC 20573-0001

The FMC regulates the waterborne foreign and domestic commerce of the United States, assures that U.S. international trade is open to all nations on equitable terms, and guards against monopoly situations in U.S. waterborne commerce.

Background Desired

To obtain the necessary Civil Service rating for FMC jobs, take courses in trade, economics, finance, and maritime shipping.

Federal Reserve System

> International Finance Division
> Board of Governors of the Federal Reserve System
> 20th St. and Constitution Ave., NW
> Washington, DC 20551

The system is composed of twelve Federal Reserve Banks located throughout the country and a Board of Governors in Washington, DC. The Board's primary function is to formulate monetary policy. To assist the Board, there is a staff of more than 1,000 employees assigned to various divisions, among which is the *International Finance Division*. This division analyzes international policies and operations of the Federal Reserve, major financial and economic developments abroad that affect the U.S. economy, and problems related to the international monetary system. Staff members of the division serve on U.S. delegations to international financial conferences and maintain liaison with central banks of foreign countries.

Background Desired

As you might surmise, the most pertinent elements in the curriculum to prepare for jobs in the International Finance Division are international economics, international finance, money and banking, accounting, and statistics. This is one of those rare government agencies for which a Civil Service rating is not required. A Ph.D. in one of these fields is usually preferred, but exceptionally talented people with an M.A. are given consideration.

Foreign Claims Settlement Commission of the U.S.

> Room 400
> 1111 20th St., NW
> Washington, DC 20579

This organization, which is under the Department of Justice, determines claims of U.S. citizens against foreign governments for loss or injury. Special claims programs have been undertaken against the governments of Yugoslavia, Panama, Poland, Bulgaria, Hungary, Romania, Italy, the former Soviet Union, Cuba, Czechoslovakia, the People's Republic of China, Vietnam, Egypt, and Ethiopia. The commission also administers claims of ex-prisoners of war from Vietnam and civilians who were interned during the Vietnam conflict.

Background Desired

This agency has only a small staff, and vacancies do not often occur. Still, if you have special interest in claims work and if you have an academic background in finance, law, or specialized knowledge of the countries listed above, you should give it a try.

General Services Administration (GSA)

> General Services Building
> 18th and F St., NW
> Washington, DC 20405

The GSA is concerned with the management of U.S. property and records, including the construction and operation of buildings, procurement and distribution of supplies, use and disposal of property, and stockpiling of strategic materials.

Since much U.S. property is located abroad, there is an international aspect to GSA work. The government-wide supply system means that purchases ranging from automobiles to paper clips are made for federal agencies in the United States and abroad. GSA also determines the amounts of travel and relocation allowances for personnel of the nonforeign affairs agencies of the government.

Background Desired

Courses in business administration, finance, and economics constitute an optimum academic background to get a Civil Service rating for these jobs.

National Aeronautics and Space Administration (NASA)

> Director, International Relations Division
> NASA
> 600 Independence Ave., SW
> Washington, DC 20546

This organization conducts research for the solution of problems of flight within and outside the earth's atmosphere. NASA also arranges for the most effective use of U.S. scientific resources with other nations engaged in space activities.

Background Desired

A science, engineering, and aeronautical background is clearly indicated for the technical jobs in this organization. At the same time, there are some administrative jobs for which a background in accounting, personnel work, or administrative practices will be helpful.

National Science Foundation (NSF)

> Division of International Programs
> National Science Foundation
> 1800 G St., NW
> Washington, DC 20550

The NSF supports many programs for scientific research. Its *Division of International Programs* encourages American participation in international science programs and activities. The division also fosters the exchange of information between scientists in the United States and in foreign countries. Other international programs include the exchange of American and foreign scientists and engineers, as well as travel to international conferences.

Background Desired

Few jobs are available, but if you are interested in a career with this organization, a scientific background in addition to economics or area studies will be helpful.

Nuclear Regulatory Commission (NRC)

> Director, Office of International Programs
> Nuclear Regulatory Commission
> 1717 H St., NW
> Washington, DC 20555

The NRC licenses and regulates the uses of nuclear energy to protect public health and safety and the environment. Its *Office of International Programs* analyzes and processes applications for the export of nuclear material abroad. It also concerns itself with international safeguards.

Background Desired

Credentials in law, political science, economics, trade, and science will be helpful in your bid for the occasional NRC job available.

LEGISLATIVE BRANCH

The search for government jobs does not end with the obvious executive agencies. The legislative branch offers a variety of positions with international content.

Unlike jobs in the executive branch, however, in the legislative branch there is little reliance on the Office of Personnel Management or Civil Service ratings. Leave your résumé in the placement offices of the House and Senate, but spend more time in cultivating contacts with staff assistants and their friends in congressional offices. This network is usually the key to available jobs in the legislative branch.

Congressional Budget Office (CBO)

> Second and D St., SW
> Washington, DC 20515

The CBO was established in 1974 to provide Congress with an overview of the federal budget and to enable it to make decisions on spending and taxing levels.

CBO is the mechanism through which Congress weighs priorities for the allocation of national resources. It prepares budget studies relating to U.S. defense and international economic programs. The CBO also examines the impact on the economy and the federal budget of foreign programs, such as commodity agreements, aid, tariff and subsidy programs, and international monetary agreements.

Background Desired

Courses in economics, finance, national security, accounting, trade, and tariffs would certainly be a plus if you are eyeing positions in the CBO.

General Accounting Office (GAO)

National Security and International Affairs Division
General Accounting Office
441 G St., NW
Washington, DC 20548

The GAO is in the legislative branch of government and reports directly to Congress. It analyzes the efficiency and effectiveness of the operations of federal government agencies in the executive branch. Its recommendations ostensibly lead to improved management practices in these agencies. Even though the GAO is in the legislative branch, it uses Civil Service ratings for entry positions.

Overseas offices of the GAO are located in Frankfurt and Honolulu. Its *National Security and International Affairs Division* administers these offices and supervises GAO reports to Congress on various foreign policy problems. Typical of these reports are *Foreign Assistance and Combatting HIV/AIDS in Developing Countries; Foreign Investment Issues Raised by Taiwan; Proposed Investment in McDonnell Douglas;* and *Foreign Technology: Federal Process for Collective Dissemination.*

Background Desired

Far from being an accountant's paradise, the GAO is more often in search of the international relations expert, the student specializing in area studies or international economics, and the business administration graduate.

Library of Congress

Congressional Research Service
Library of Congress
101 Independence Ave., SE
Washington, DC 20540

The title of this organization is deceptive and does not hint at the scope of its functions. True, the library has an extensive collection of books on every subject and in a multitude of languages, and it administers the copyright laws. But it also engages in a variety of research tasks of an international nature.

The *Congressional Research Service (CRS)* is an important source of jobs for the international relations scholar. The CRS works exclusively as the research arm of members of Congress and their staffs. Two CRS units will be of particular interest to you: (1) the *Foreign Affairs and National Defense Division*, which has three sections — *Global Issues* (international organizations, international economics, and global strategy), *Regional Issues* (Latin America, Europe, and Africa/Asia), and *Policy Management* (budget and management); and (2) the *Environment and Natural Resources Policy Division*.

In addition, the CRS has an internship program lasting for three-month periods in which successful applicants receive a stipend and work on short-term analytical projects.

Typical CRS projects might examine American cults abroad and relations with their host governments or the influence of Castro in the Caribbean.

Background Desired

Area studies, international economics, national security, foreign policy, environmental studies, and/or world resources would be valuable.

Requirements

Send a résumé and Standard Form 171.

Office of Technology Assessment (OTA)

> International Security and Commerce Program Manager
> Office of Technology Assessment
> 600 Pennsylvania Ave., SE
> Washington, DC 20510

This office reports to Congress on the scientific and technical impact of government policies and proposed legislative initiatives.

Background Desired

Although a scientific background is most pertinent for OTA work, this organization has an occasional need for an international generalist or one trained in world trade and international economics.

Senate and House

> House Foreign Affairs Committee
> House Office Building
> New Jersey and Independence Ave., SE
> Washington, DC 20515

> or

> Senate Foreign Relations Committee
> Senate Office Building
> First St. and Constitution Ave., NE
> Washington, DC 20510

The Senate Foreign Relations Committee and the House Foreign Affairs Committee both have small staffs, which research international issues of interest to Congress and participate in drafting those sections of bills with international content.

Depending on its strength and the prestige of its chairman, the Senate Foreign Relations Committee in particular can have an important influence on the formulation of foreign policy by the State Department. Sometimes the influence is an adversarial one, sometimes a cooperative one; but if you are interested in the formulation of foreign policy you would do well to include both congressional committees in your job hunting.

Since Civil Service ratings are usually not needed for the legislative branches, how do you go about your job hunt? If you know a friend of your congressperson — or better yet, a contributor to his or her campaign — you will be welcomed and may perhaps receive an introduction to one or both committees.

You have no congressional contacts? Don't let that discourage you from making a direct approach. Go to the offices of your representative or Senators. You may not get to see any of them, but you will be able to see a staff assistant who may give you suggestions and perhaps help on the job hunt.

Another tip: If you aren't able to get a paying job and can support yourself for a while, by all means offer your services on a voluntary basis. Once you are in the office, you will be on the inside track the next time there is a job vacancy.

Background Desired

An academic background in area studies, national security, international economics, economic development, and foreign policy is helpful in getting consideration for the few job openings on the House and Senate committees.

PUBLICATIONS

The following publications will give you additional information on each government agency, its functions, organization, and top personnel:

U.S. Government Manual

> U.S. Government Printing Office
> North Capital and H St., NW
> Washington, DC 20402

This manual is published annually by the Office of the Federal Register, the National Archives and Records Service. It costs $23.

Washington Information Directory

> Congressional Quarterly, Inc.
> 1414 22nd St., NW
> Washington, DC 20037

This is also an annual directory.

Federal Yellow Book Directory, Congressional Yellow Book Directory

> Washington Monitor, Inc.
> 1301 Pennsylvania Ave., NW
> Washington, DC 20045

The former lists the top-level employees of the federal agencies; the latter lists members of Congress as well as their committees and key aides. Both books can be found in large reference libraries.

7

THE UNITED NATIONS AND RELATED INTERNATIONAL ORGANIZATIONS

Many of you with backgrounds in international affairs naturally think of the United Nations and its specialized agencies as the best sources of jobs after graduation. Some years ago that was true. Today, however, there are few U.N. positions open, even for the most talented.

In addition to the dearth of jobs, a personnel quota system adds to the difficulty in getting work in some U.N. organizations. These quotas, whether rigidly enforced or used only as informal guidelines, are tied to the funds contributed by each member country. If you are an American and the organization to which you are applying receives 25 percent of its funds from the United States, the target figure for all American employees would presumably be one quarter of the total personnel. In many organizations, however, you will find Americans overrepresented.

Even without definite quotas, the United Nations — with some justification — tries to unearth qualified talent from developing nations that are currently underrepresented. For these reasons, if you are a qualified national of Upper Volta or Chad, for example, you probably have a better chance for a U.N. job than if you are a qualified American. However, at higher levels — and in specialized fields such as law and economics — Americans with the appropriate graduate degrees and a few years of experience have a somewhat better chance.

Staffing, as you can see, is not entirely dependent on the skills and background you offer. Contacts, energy, and initiative in locating job opportunities are all-important.

Should I Take Courses on the United Nations to Get a U.N. Job?

Courses on the United Nations may be interesting and informative, but don't expect them to lead to a U.N. job. The United Nations values, in particular, M.A.s and Ph.D.s in economics, economic development, and area studies, with fluency in French and Spanish in addition to English. An academic specialization in the U.N. system is nice to have, but it's not what you get hired for.

Can Pressure Help?

The higher the position for which you are applying, the more you will have to cope with political considerations. In addition to the difficulties presented by the quota or guideline system mentioned above, your application is liable to languish unless you get support from your government. The Russian states, the United States, and several other countries as well vie for the top jobs, and indeed often stake out a claim to positions considered politically sensitive and therefore especially desirable. The decision on whether you or someone of a different nationality gets a position is often made far from the personnel office.

Strong and consistent pressure on your behalf, if obtainable from your government, is of utmost importance. The United Nations has been known to resist light pressures from member governments, but often buckles under more determined efforts. In other words, get all the political support you can — from your Mission to the United Nations, from your Foreign Ministry or Department of State, from influential friends and relatives. All such support will be crucial in your effort to join the U.N. household.

THE U.N. SECRETARIAT: NEW YORK

The Secretariat services the Secretary General of the United Nations, who is the chief administrative officer of the whole system: the General Assembly, the Security Council, the Economic Social Council, and the Trusteeship Council. Much of the research, public relations, and administrative work in the Secretariat is generated by resolutions of the General Assembly.

The greatest need is for specialists with a concentration in economics, economic development, area studies, administration, agriculture, communications, and social sciences (among others). Languages, particularly French and Spanish in addition to English, are usually required.

In filling professional vacancies, the Secretariat pays more attention to maintaining a fair balance of employees among member countries, several of which have few nationals on the Secretariat staff, than do the specialized agencies. The United States is neither underrepresented nor overrepresented on the Secretariat. It is said to be "within range but above the midpoint." In other words, even though there may be a few too many Americans on the payroll, the doors are not closed to you if you have strong credentials and, it is hoped, some political pull.

Types of Jobs

Lower-level research jobs are the ones for which many of you may be best qualified, but for which only a few of you will be given serious consideration. Administrative vacancies are also few and usually filled by the reassignment of existing staff.

The following positions, some of which are equally difficult to get, should still be looked at by those who have appropriate qualifications and strong motivation for U.N. work. Generally an M.A. or Ph.D. is required, plus several years of experience.

PUBLIC INFORMATION OFFICER. This type of position is found primarily in the *UN Department of Public Information (UNDPI)*. One unit of UNDPI, called the *Center for Economic and Social Information (CESI)*, coordinates, plans, and, where necessary, helps finance information programs to stimulate international development. CESI tries to involve developed and developing countries in cooperative programs aimed at accelerating economic and social progress in developing countries.

Requirements: Professional posts in this office call for substantial experience in journalism, publications, radio, films, and visual media. Even junior posts ordinarily require considerable experience, not merely a degree in journalism or international communications.

LEGAL OFFICERS. The *Office of Legal Affairs* has a very small staff.

Requirements: Only those with a specialization in public international law are considered.

TRANSLATORS. Recruitment for these positions is by competitive exam and interview, usually held annually.

Requirements: A candidate will have to translate written material from at least two official languages into his or her mother tongue, which must be one of the six official U.N. languages (Arabic, Chinese, English, French, Russian, and Spanish).

INTERPRETERS. Here, too, recruitment is by individual examination.

Requirements: Applicants mut be able to interpret into their mother tongue (again, one of the six official languages) and must have full auditory comprehension of at least two other official languages.

DEMOGRAPHERS AND POPULATION PERSONNEL. A need for trained staff in this field sometimes exists.

Requirements: A doctorate in the social sciences with a major in demography is usually required. A world resources specialization in academic work is helpful.

CLERICAL AND SECRETARIAL POSTS. Most vacancies in this category are for secretaries and typists. Occasionally there is a need for high-speed conference typists to serve on a shift basis in large typing pools. A knowledge of word processors and computers is valuable.

Requirements: Applicants should be bilingual (English plus French or Spanish).

U.N. GUIDES. Guides are recruited locally, usually once a year, and begin their training in March. Personal interviews at headquarters may be arranged, usually for the fall, by writing to:

> U.N. Central Employment Section
> United Nations
> New York, NY 10017

Requirements: Candidates generally should be 20 to 30 years old and have a college degree. Fluency in English and one other official U.N. language is a requirement.

Internship Programs

> Recruitment Programmes Section
> Office of Personnel Services
> United Nations
> One U.N. Plaza
> New York, NY 10017

Enclose a U.N. Personal History Form P-11, together with a transcript of your undergraduate and graduate grades, a sample of your research work, and a description of the type of project desired. The U.N. Personal History Form P-11 can usually be obtained from college placement offices. Otherwise, write to the U.N. recruitment office above.

All of this documentation should be accompanied by at least one letter of recommendation — from your employer, your university, or your permanent mission to the United Nations. On receipt of this material, the Office of Personnel Services will try to arrange a suitable assignment in one of the deparments.

A summer internship program is conducted annually by UNDPI for college students and those doing graduate work in economics, law, international relations, sociology communications, and related subjects. Each year about 50 candidates are selected for the New York program and about 80 for a similar program in Geneva. Again, no stipend is paid to interns on either assignment. Obtain special application forms from your college placement office. If not available, write to:

> UNDPI
> U.N. Secretariat
> United Nations
> One U.N. Plaza
> New York, NY 10017

The United Nations seldom recruits paid staff for the summer months only. The main exception is the addition of a few extra guides to the Visitors' Service, to handle the seasonal influx of vacationers.

The *UN Development Programme (UNDP)* also has a summer internship lasting eight to ten weeks. It is aimed at on-the-job training for a limited number of students taking graduate studies in development work or disciplines related to UNDP's work. Candidates should be enrolled in a graduate program and ideally have full working knowledge of two of the United Nations official languages. About 60 interns are accepted each summer. Internships are awarded through the office in New York. Occasionally, interns will be hired during the year. Those interested and qualified should contact:

> UNDP Summer Intership Program
> One U.N. Plaza
> New York, NY 10017

The *U.N. Institute for Training and Research (UNITAR)* accepts a few interns for work in research training, or administration for periods between two months and a year. Write to:

> Executive Director
> UNITAR
> 801 U.N. Plaza
> New York, NY 10017

Some of the specialized agencies of the U.N. located outside New York also conduct internship programs. Interested students should write to them directly. Some of their addresses are included in this chapter.

U.S. Government Involvement

Although each U.N. organization makes the final decision on hiring personnel, various parts of the U.S. government are sometimes drawn into the recruitment process. The Department of State is officially charged with recommending, and sometimes even recruiting, U.S. citizens for U.N. positions; for technical positions, the department generally delegates this responsibility to other federal agencies.

INTERNATIONAL ORGANIZATION	RESPONSIBLE U.S. AGENCY
UNESCO (teachers)	U.S. Department of Education
World Health Organization (medical personnel)	International Division, Public Health Service
FAO (nutrition/agriculture)	Office of International Organization Affairs, Department of Agriculture
International Atomic Energy (nuclear physics)	Office of International Affairs, U.S. Atomic Energy Commission
ILO (labor, vocational education)	International Division Department of Labor

If you are interested in any of these U.N. technical jobs, send the responsible federal agency an appropriate résumé. If you feel qualified for a professional post of a more general nature that is not covered by the technical posts mentioned above, send a U.S. Standard Form 171 to:

> Recruitment Division
> Bureau of International Organization Affairs
> Department of State
> P.O. Box 9317
> Rosslyn Station
> Arlington, VA 22209

Also send a U.N. Personal History Form P-11 to:

> Recruitment Programmes Section
> Office of Personnel Services
> United Nations
> One U.N. Plaza
> New York, NY 10017

Net salaries for professional workers (after a staff assessment has been conducted by the U.N.) are modest. P-1, the lowest grade, ranges from $22,030 to $30,020; P-5, the highest, ranges from $46,400 to $61,450, depending on the professional "step" and your marital status. These are March 1992 salaries and will probably be higher when you read this. Note also that the salaries quoted are not subject to U.S. income tax.

THE U.N. SECRETARIAT: OUTSIDE NEW YORK

Geneva Office and Regional Economic Commissions

> Recruitment Programmes Section
> Office of Personnel Services
> United Nations
> One U.N. Plaza
> New York, NY 10017

The U.N. office in Geneva is the only regional office of the U.N. Secretariat. In addition, there are five regional commissions aimed at economic and social development of the area in which they are located:

1. Economic Commission for Europe (ECE), Geneva, Switzerland
2. Economic and Social Commission for Asia and the Pacific (ES-CAP), Bangkok, Thailand
3. Economic Commission for Latin America (ECLA), Santiago, Chile
4. Economic Commission for Africa (ECA), Addis Ababa, Ethiopia
5. Economic Commission for Western Asia (ECWA), Amman, Jordan

Aside from administrative personnel, who are usually provided through the reassignment of existing staff from headquarters or from one of the other offices, U.N. regional offices are staffed primarily with specialists experienced in economics, statistics, sociology, and various aspects of industry.

U.N. Department of Public Information (UNDPI)

> United Nations Secretariat
> Room 1060A
> New York, NY 10017

UNDPI also has about 66 centers overseas, which service more than 130 member countries. These offices are involved in all areas of press, publications, radio, television, films, graphics, exhibitions, and public liaison. They cover the whole spectrum of U.N. activities in political, economic, social, and humanitarian matters. Information center directors contact government officials, educational authorities, and media personnel in order to increase awareness in that country of U.N. aims and activities.

Following is a list of all U.N. Information Centers (UNIC) with their addresses. Write them directly for information on their specific functions and available jobs. Send all employment applications to the address above.

United Nations Information Centers

Accra (Ghana and Sierra Leone)	United Nations Information Center Roman Ridge Ambassadorial Estate Extension Area, Plot N78 Gambel Abdul Nassar Liberia Roads Accra, Ghana
Addis Abada (Ethiopia)	United Nations Information Service Economic Commission for Africa P.O. Box 3001 Addis Ababa, Ethiopia
Algiers (Algeria)	Centre d'information des Nations Unies B.P. 823 Algiers, Algeria
Ankara (Turkey)	United Nations Information Centre P.K. 407 Ankara, Turkey
Antananarivo (Madagascar)	Centre d'information des Nations Unies B.P. 1348 Tananarive, Madagascar
Asunción (Paraguay)	Centro de Información de las Naciones Unidas Casilla de Correo 1107 Asunción, Paraguay
Athens (Cyprus, Greece, Israel)	United Nations Information Centre 36 Amalia Avenue GR-105, 58 Athens, Greece
Baghdad (Iraq)	United Nations Information Service Economic and Social Commission for Western Asia (ESCWA) P.O. Box 27 Baghdad, Iraq
Bangkok (Democratic Kampuchea, Hong Kong, Lao People's Democratic Republic, Malaysia, Singapore, Thailand, Vietnam)	United Nations Information Service Economic and Social Commission for Asia and the Pacific United Nations Building Rajdamnern Avenue Bangkok 10200, Thailand
Beirut (Jordan, Kuwait, Lebanon, Syrian Arab Republic	United Nations Information Centre P.O. Box 4656 Beirut, Lebanon
Belgrade* (Albania, Yugoslavia)	United Nations Information Centre P.O. Box 157 Belgrade Yugoslavia YU-11001
Bogotá (Colombia, Ecuador, Venezuela)	Centro de Información de las Naciones Unidas Apartado Aéreo 058964 Bogotá 2, Colombia
Brazzaville (Congo)	Centre d'information des Nations Unies B.P. Box 13210 Brazzaville, Congo

*Check to see whether this office still exists before you apply.

Brussels
(Belgium, Luxembourg,
Netherlands)

Centre d'information des Nations Unies
Avenue de Broqueville 40
1200 Brussels, Belgium

Bucharest
(Romania)

United Nations Information Centre
P.O. Box 1-701
Bucharest, Romania

Buenos Aires
(Argentina, Uruguay)

Centro de Información de las Naciones
Unidas
Junín 1940, piso 1
1113 Buenos Aires, Argentina

Bujumbura
(Burundi)

Centre d'information des Nations Unies
B.P. 2160
Bujumbura, Burundi

Cairo
(Egypt, Saudi Arabia, Yemen)

United Nations Information Centre
P.O. Box 262
Cairo, Egypt

Colombo
(Sri Lanka)

United Nations Information Centre
P.O. Box 1505
Colombo, Sri Lanka

Copenhagen
(Denmark, Finland, Iceland,
Norway, Sweden)

United Nations Information Centre
37 H.C. Andersen Boulevard
DK-1553 Copenhagen V, Denmark

Dakar
(Cape Verde, Gambia,
Guinea, Guina-Bissau,
Ivory Coast, Mauritania,
Senegal)

Centre d'information des Nations Unies
B.P. 154
Dakar, Senegal

Dar es Salaam
(United Republic of
Tanzania)

United Nations Information Centre
P.O. Box 9224
Dar es Salaam
United Republic of Tanzania

Dhaka
(Bangladesh)

United Nations Information Centre
G.P.O. Box 3658
Dhaka 1205, Bangladesh

Geneva
(Bulgaria, Poland,
Switzerland)

United Nations Information Service
United Nations Office at Geneva
Palais des Nations
1211 Geneva 10, Switzerland

Harare
(Zimbabwe)

United Nations Information Centre
P.O. Box 4408
Harare, Zimbabwe

Islamabad
(Pakistan)

United Nations Information Centre
P.O. Box 1107
Islamabad, Pakistan

Jakarta
(Indonesia)

United Nations Information Centre
Gedung Dewan Pers, Fifth Floor
32-34 Jalan Kebon Sirih
Jakarta, Indonesia

Kabul
(Afghanistan)

United Nations Information Centre
P.O. Box 5
Kabul, Afghanistan

Kathmandu (Nepal)	United Nations Information Centre P.O. Box 107 Pulchowk Kathmandu, Nepal
Khartoum (Somalia, Sudan)	United Nations Information Centre P.O. Box 1992 Khartoum, Sudan
Kinshasa (Zaire)	Centre d'information des Nations Unies B.P. 7248 Kinshasa, Zaire
Lagos (Nigeria)	United Nations Information Centre P.O. Box 1068 Lagos, Nigeria
La Paz (Bolivia)	Centro de Información de las Naciones Unidas Apartodo Postal 9072 La Paz, Bolivia
Lima (Peru)	Centro de Información de las Naciones Unidas Apartado Postal 14-0199 Lima, Perú
Lisbon (Portugal)	Centro de Informaçao das Nações Unidas Rua Latino Coelho No. 1 Edifício Aviz, Blaco, A-1 10 1000 Lisbon, Portugal
Lomé (Benin, Togo)	Centre d'information des Nations Unies B.P. 911 Lomé, Togo
London (Ireland, United Kingdom)	United Nations Information Centre Ship House 20 Buckingham Gate London SW1E 6LB, England
Lusaka (Botswana, Malawi, Swaziland, Zambia)	United Nations Information Centre P.O. Box 32905 Lusaka, Zambia
Madrid (Spain)	Centro de Información de las Naciones Unidas Apartado Postal 3400 28080 Madrid, España
Managua (Nicaragua)	Centro de Información de las Naciones Unidas Apartado Postal 3260 Managua, Nicaragua
Manama (Bahrain, Qatar, United Arab Emirates)	United Nations Information Centre P.O. Box 26004 Manama, Bahrain
Manila (Papua New Guinea, Philippines, Solomon Islands)	United Nations Information Centre P.O. Box 7285 (DAPO) MIA Road Pasay City, Philippines

Maseru
(Lesotho)

United Nations Information Centre
P.O. Box 301
Maseru 100, Lesotho

Mexico City
(Cuba, Dominican Republic,
Mexico)

Centro de Información de las Naciones
Unidas
Presidente Masaryk
29-7° Piso
11570 México D.F., México

Monrovia
(Liberia)

United Nations Information Centre
P.O. Box 274
Monrovia, Liberia

Moscow
(Byelorussian SSR,
Ukrainian SSR)

United Nations Information Centre
4/16 Ulitsa
Lunacharskogo
Moscow 121002, USSR

Nairobi
(Kenya, Seychelles,
Uganda)

United Nations Information Centre
P.O. Box 34135
Nairobi, Kenya

New Delhi
(Bhutan, India)

United Nations Information Centre
55 Lodi Estate
New Delhi 110003, India

Ouagadougou
(Burkina Faso, Chad, Mali,
Niger)

Centre d'information des Nations Unies
B.P. 135
Ouagadougou, Burkina Faso

Panama City
(Panama)

Centro de Información de las Naciones
Unidas
Apartado Postal 6-9083 El Dorado
Urbanizacion Obarrio
Callo 54 y Avenida
Terceru Sur
Casa No. 17
Panama

Paris
(France)

Centre d'information des Nations Unies
1 rue Miolles
75732 Paris Cedes 15, France

Port of Spain
(Antigua and Barbuda,
Bahamas, Barbados, Belize,
Dominica, Grenada, Guyana,
Jamaica, Netherlands,
Antilles, Saint Kitts and
Nevis, Saint Lucia, Suriname,
Trinidad and Tobago,
St. Vincent, Grenadines)

United Nations Information Centre
P.O. Box 130
Port-of-Spain, Trinidad

Prague
(Czechoslovakia)

United Nations Information Centre
Panska 5
11000 Prague 1, Czechoslovakia

Rabat
(Morocco)

Centre d'information des Nations Unies
B.P. 601
Rabat, Morocco

Rio de Janeiro
(Brazil)

Centro de Informaçao das Nações
Unidas
Palacio Intamaraty
Avenida Marechal
Floriano 196
20080 Rio de Janeiro, Brazil

Rome
(Holy See, Italy, Malta

United Nations Information Centre
Palazzetto Venezia
Piazza San Marco 50
Rome, Italy

San Salvador
(El Salvador)

Centro de Información de las Naciones
      Unidas
Apartado Postal 2157
San Salvador, El Salvador

Santiago
(Chile)

Jefa del Servicio de Información de las
      Naciones Unidas
Avendia Dag
Hammarskjold s/n
Casilla 179-D
Santiago, Chile

Sydney
(Australia, Fiji, Kiribati,
Nauru, New Zealand,
Samoa, Tonga, Tuvalu,
Vanuatu)

United Nations Information Centre
P.O. Box 4045
Syndey, N.S.W. 2001 Australia

Teheran
(Islamic Republic of Iran)

United Nations Information Centre
P.O. Box 15875-4557
Teheran, 620891

Tokyo
(Japan, Trust Territory
of the Pacific Islands)

United Nations Information Centre
Shin Aoyama Building
Nishikan
22nd Floor
1-1 Minami Aoyama
1-chome
Minato-ku
Tokyo 107, Japan

Tripoli
(Libyan Arab Jamahiriya)

United Nations Information Centre
P.O. Box 286
Tripoli, Libyan Arab
Jamahiriya

Tunis
(Tunsia)

Centre d'information des Nations Unies
B.P. 863
Tunis, Tunisia

Vienna
(Austria, Germany)

United Nations Information Service
United Nations Office at Vienna
P.O. Box 500
A-1220 Vienna, Austria

Windhoek
(Namibia)

United Nations Information Centre
Sanlan Centre, 154
Independence St.
Windhoek, Namibia

Yangon
(Myanmar — formerly Burma)

United Nations Information Centre
P.O. Box 230
Yangon, Myanmar

Yaounde
(Central African Republic,
Cameroon, Gabon)

Centre d'information des Nations Unies
B.P. 836
Yaoundé, Cameroon

The United Nations also sponsors programs of technical cooperation, administered by the *U.N. Conference of Trade and Development (UNCTAD)*, the *U.N. Industrial Development Organization (UNIDO)*, and nine of the specialized agencies supervised by the U.N. Development Programme. Requests from countries for technical assistance are distributed to participating organizations on the basis of field of specialization. The requests are usually for senior expert advisers. Candidates who are relatively junior, without much experience in their fields, are seldom nominated. More on these organizations on pages 137–138 and 155.

U.N. SPECIALIZED AND RELATED AGENCIES

Consultative Group on International Agricultural Research (CGIAR)

c/o World Bank
1818 H St., NW
Washington, DC 20433

This group was organized by the FAO, the World Bank, and the UNDP. Its purpose is to stimulate agricultural progress in the tropics and subtropics, where most of the less-developed countries lie. It tries to achieve this aim through research programs and the training of scientists and specialists in the developing world.

CGIAR supports 17 centers engaged in the investigation of the problems of tropical agriculture. Among those are:

1. International Rice Institute (Philippines)
2. International Maize and Wheat Improvement Center (Mexico)
3. International Center for Tropical Agriculture (Colombia)
4. International Institute of Tropical Agriculture (Nigeria)
5. International Potato Center (Peru)
6. International Crops Research Institute for the Semi-Arid Tropics (India)
7. International Laboratory for Research on Animal Diseases (Kenya)
8. International Livestock Center for Africa (Ethiopia)
9. West Africa Rice Development Association (Liberia)
10. International Board for Plant Genetic Resources (Italy)
11. International Center for Agricultural Research in the Dry Areas (Lebanon)

Background Desired

Agricultural sciences, economics, and Third World area studies.

Food and Agriculture Organization (FAO)

Via delle Terme di Caracalla
00100 Rome, Italy

or

Liaison Office for North America
1001 22nd St., NW
Washington, DC 20437

The purpose of the FAO is to raise levels of nutrition as well as improve the efficiency of production and distribution of food and agricultural products. It has regional offices in Ghana, Ethiopia, Thailand, Chile, Egypt, and Washington, DC.

The *World Food Programme* is an agency set up by the FAO to provide food aid to all developing countries. The program is supported by voluntary pledges from participating countries in the form of commodities, cash, or services such as shipping. Food aid has been given by the program for a diversity of projects, recipients, and reasons: resettlement of Bedouin tribes, dairy and livestock improvement, community development, land improvement schemes, victims of natural disasters, and refugees and displaced persons.

Background Desired

Economics (particularly agricultural economics), economic development, world resources, and nutritional subjects.

General Agreements on Tariffs and Trade (GATT)

Palais des Nations
154 Rue de Lausanne
CH-1121 Geneva 21, Switzerland

GATT, an autonomous organization within the U.N. system, is the focus for intergovernmental efforts to remove trade barriers. It also aims to expand international trade and economic development.

Background Desired

Economics, economic development, and trade and tariff studies.

Intergovernmental Committee for Migration (ICM)

P.O. Box 71
CH-1211 Geneva 19
Switzerland

or

New York Office, ICM
1123 Broadway
New York, NY 10010

or

Washington Office, ICM
440 National Press Building
529 14th St., NW
Washington, DC 20045

ICM, formerly the Intergovernmental Committee for European Migration, has three major objectives: the processing and movement of refugees to countries offering them permanent resettlement; the promotion of orderly migration to meet the specific needs, (e.g., employment) of emigration and immigration countries; and the transfer of technology through migration to promote the economic, educational, and social advancement of developing countries.

ICM has a membership of 29 countries. Operational offices are located in 34 countries.

Background Desired

Economics, law, sociology, international relations, area studies, and languages.

International Atomic Energy Agency (IAEA)

Vienna International Center
Wagramerstrasse
P.O. Box 100
A-1400 Vienna, Austria

This agency seeks to enlarge the contribution of atomic energy to national welfare. Through an international safeguards system, it also tries to ensure that its assistance to any country is not used for military purposes. Technical assistance to developing countries is provided by the IAEA in the form of fellowships, training courses, and study tours.

Background Desired

Although a scientific background is of major interest to the IAEA, there is some place for those trained in economics, administration, public relations, and general international relations.

International Bank for Reconstruction and Development (IBRD)

> Young Professionals Program
> World Bank
> 1818 H St., NW
> Washington, DC 20433

The IBRD assists in the reconstruction and development of member countries by making loans out of its own funds when private capital is not available on reasonable terms. It also promotes private foreign investment by offering guarantees on loans and investments made by private investors.

The World Bank (the unofficial name for the IBRD) system encompasses four institutions:

1. *World Bank*   This is the oldest and largest international organization providing development finance. In addition to loans, the Bank helps developing countries evaluate projects and draw up national programs.
2. *International Development Association*   The IDA lends on exceptionally easy terms to very poor countries that cannot afford conventional borrowing to meet their needs for development capital.
3. *International Finance Corporation*   The IFC invests in private or "mixed" (i.e., joint ventures between private enterprise and government) ventures. Unlike the Bank and the IDA, the IFC neither seeks nor accepts government guarantees. It is one of the few international development organizations that makes both equity investments and loans.
4. *International Center for Settlement of Investment Disputes*   The ICSID provides a mechanism for solving disputes between governments and investors.

Entry into the World Bank structure is formalized through a *Young Professionals Program (YPP)*, a mechanism for hiring talented individuals for junior professional posts. Upon entry, you are given two or three rotational assignments of four to eight months. In each assignment, you are treated as a full-fledged member of the department to which you are assigned and are expected, through on-the-job training, to make a significant contribution.

For example, one assignment might be as *loan officer* in one of the Bank's country program departments; another assignment might be to work as a *project economist* or *financial analyst* in a regional projects department, or as an *economist* or *investment officer* in the IFC. Upon satisfactory completion of the rotational assignments, you join one of the departments of the Bank on a regular basis.

Participants in the program are selected on a highly competitive basis. Applications are sought from all member countries. Qualifications are screened and interviews arranged for the most promising applicants. Final selection is made by a panel of senior staff members "on the basis of professional merit." Offers of appointment are made annually, usually in March, and candidates then have up to six months to join the program.

Background Desired

Have knowledge of as many of the following as possible: banking and finance, economics, economic development, business administration, and Third World studies. In addition, professional experience in one of the above areas is highly desirable. The average age of a program entrant is about 28. If you have an M.A. or Ph.D. degree without practical experience, you will probably be encouraged by the Bank first to get a job elsewhere in the banking or economic development field and then apply to the Young Professionals Program. A Ph.D. does have an edge over an M.A., however.

International Civil Aviation Organization (ICAO)

> P.O. Box 400
> Succursale Place de L'Aviation International
> 100 Sherbrooke St. West
> Montreal H 3A 2R2, Canada

ICAO was established as a specialized agency of the United Nations to achieve international cooperation in the air. One of ICAO's chief activities has been the establishment of international standards in all aspects of aviation: licensing of personnel, rules of the air, aeronautical charts, operation of aircraft, registration marks, airworthiness of planes, accident inquiries, and aircraft noise. This organization has six regional offices, located throughout the world, for planning navigation facilities and ground services for aircraft. A particular aim of ICAO is to promote civil aviation in developing countries. To this effect, a program of technical assistance is carried out through the U.N. Development Programme.

Background Desired

Aeronautics, meteorology, economics, and business administration.

International Fund for Agricultural Development (IFAD)

> 107 Via del Serafico
> 00142 Rome, Italy

or

Room S 2955
United Nations
New York, NY 10017

IFAD is a relatively new and important specialized agency within the U.N. system. With initial resources of a billon dollars, its primary purpose is to help increase agricultural production in developing countries. To this effect, it disburses loans on easy terms to these countries.

Background Desired

Economics (primarily agricultural economics), economic development, finance, sociology, world resources with an emphasis on food, and Third World area studies.

International Labor Organization (ILO)

Personnel Department
International Labor Oganization
4 Route des Morillons
CH-1211 Geneva 22, Switzerland

or

Washington Branch
International Labor Organization
1750 New York Ave., NW
Washington, DC 20006

The ILO's main purpose is to improve labor conditions, raise living standards, and promote economic stability throughout the world. It is distinct from all other international organizations in that a tripartite body representing government, workers, and employers from each member country shapes ILO policies. The standards developed by the annual conference, while not obligatory, are guides for countries to follow and form an international labor code covering employment, hours of work, protection of women and young workers, worker's compensation, trade unionism, and related matters.

Note: U.S. relations with the ILO have wavered from wholehearted support to resignation because of political differences with ILO policies. Accordingly, the prospects for employment will depend, among other factors, on whether the U.S. is a full dues-paying member at the time you apply.

Background Desired

The type of work undertaken by this organization points to the following optimum background for employment: economics, particularly labor economics;

industrial relations; statistics; area studies; languages; and some experience in trade unions or the Department of Labor.

International Monetary Fund (IMF)

> Economists Program
> Recruiting and Training Division
> International Monetary Fund
> 700 19th St., NW
> Washington, DC 20431

The IMF is the foremost international organization involved in global monetary issues. It keeps informed of member countries' economic problems, and often provides financial assistance to help them overcome balance-of-payments difficulties. The IMF has also established a system of special drawing rights to supplement existing reserve assets of its member countries.

There are 14 departments in the IMF. Five are area departments concerned with analyzing economic developments and financial policies in specific countries. Other departments are concerned with exchange rates, restrictions on international payments, and international liquidity.

The IMF has a *Young Professionals Program (YPP)* primarily to recruit economists. The fund's program for young professionals starts twice a year, in spring and fall. Work assignments are interspersed with courses and seminars. Over a two-year period, successful applicants will normally have assignments in one area department and one functional department in Washington headquarters, and will also take part in a mission overseas. The assignment given a candidate after this two-year stint depends on his or her background and interests.

Background Desired

Because of the specialized technical nature of IMF work, Ph.D.s in economics, finance, and statistics are normally needed. There are occasions, however, when M.A.s in these fields may be considered if candidates also have impressive practical experience in the economic and financial fields. Area studies, business administration, and languages are additional useful qualifications.

U.N. Conference on Trade and Development (UNCTAD)

> United Nations Office
> Palais des Nations
> 1211 Geneva 10
> Switzerland

UNCTAD is a permanent organ of the U.N. General Assembly. Its major thrust is to raise the standard of living in all countries. It views international trade as an important instrument for economic development and makes comprehensive reviews of problems of trade, particularly those problems which affect developing countries.

Background Desired

A knowledge of developing countries and areas as well as a background in economics, economic development, and trade are highly desired.

United Nations Children's Fund (UNICEF)

> 3 U.N. Plaza
> New York, NY 10017

As its title indicates, UNICEF is involved with the needs of children on a global scale. About 70 percent of UNICEF's long-term aid goes to equipping health centers, schools, and day-care and community centers throughout the world. About 30 percent goes to training needed staff: nurses, health and nutrition workers, teachers, and child welfare workers. UNICEF's resources are also used for relief and rehabilitation of children suffering from natural disasters and civil disturbances.

Background Desired

Social work, welfare, health, nutrition, teaching, education, economics, area studies, and languages.

United Nations Development Programme (UNDP)

> Recruitment Section
> Division of Personnel
> United Nations Development Programme
> One U.N. Plaza
> New York, NY 10017

UNDP is the central funding, planning, and coordinating body for technical cooperation in the U.N. system. Its activities are directed toward helping developing countries throughout Asia, Africa, Latin America, the Middle East, and part of Europe in their efforts to make effective use of available natural resources and manpower. UNDP helps developing countries provide their people with adequate nutrition, housing, human development, employment, education, health care, and public services. It also conducts projects related to sustainable economic growth in the areas of agriculture, forestry and fisheries, industry, natural resource management and development, transportation, communications, and science and technology. As a result of the United Nations Earth Summit held in the spring of 1992 in Brazil, UNDP has focused on the environment and has programs in more than 150 countries related to environmental concerns.

Toward these ends, UNDP evaluates requests from developing countries for technical assistance. As in previous years, UNDP has dedicated the largest regional share of spending to Africa, followed by Asia and the Pacific, the Arab States and Europe, and Latin America and the Caribbean. A total of 1,002 new projects were approved, and $1,430.7 million was spent on development projects in 1991. These projects are most closely linked with overall national development plans. Most recently, there has been a 4-percent increase in funding provided to UNDP by donors.

UNDP has 115 field offices and headquarters for 31 executing agencies. Because of its global representation, other U.N. organizations doing business in foreign countries are sometimes housed in UNDP offices. See the list of UNDP overseas offices on page 140.

Each year, UNDP recruits a small group of outstanding young graduates for its professional staff, placing these people at the entry level, P-1 or P-2. Successful candidates serve at any of the UNDP field offices throughout the world and usually spend the greater part of their careers overseas. A four-year tour of duty in each assignment is normal.

UNDP has six associated programmes, each funded separately through voluntary contributions, which provide specific services through the UNDP network. They are: *United Nations Capital Development (UNCDF), United Nations Sudao-Sahelian Office (UNSO), United Nations Development Fund for Women (UNIFEM), United Nations Fund for Science and Technology for Development (UNFSTD), United Nations Revolving Fund for Natural Resources Exploration (UNRFNRE),* and the *United Nations Volunteers (UNV).*

UNDP also has a *Junior Professional Officer Program (JPOP),* which trains young officers sponsored by their governments. These young professionals join for one- or two-year assignments, generally at a field office after which they are expected to return to their countries. From the sponsoring country's point of view, the program provides a fine opportunity to build up a core of personnel trained in development work. Some industrialized countries have signed agreements with UNDP to sponsor JPOs from developing countries that are not able to afford the expense of subsidizing their own nationals.

More than 100 JPOs are in the field at any one time. Graduates of this program sometimes become full-fledged UNDP employees, although candidates are warned from the beginning that the "JPOP is emphatically not a backdoor to a UNDP career."

Background Desired

The emphasis on development work immediately points to the major qualification demanded of most applicants: a thorough grounding in economic development and economics. Graduate academic work in these fields is expected. Courses in sociology and public administration are helpful, and experience in developing countries is desirable. As with most U.N. organizations, fluency in French and Spanish is usually required.

Requirements

For ordinary employment, as well as for the JPOP, send a Personal History Form P-11 and a one-page statement of your motivation for UNDP work. For specific functions of UNPD and job availability, contact each office directly.

Following is a list of U.N. Development Programme County Offices.

United Nations Development Programme Country Offices

Afghanistan	David Lockwood Resident Representative, a.i. United Nations Development Programme P.O. Box 5 Kabul, Afghanistan
Albania	Mr. John-Nicole Marchal Resident Representative United Nations Development Programme Desh Mort E4 Shkurtit St. Villa 35 Tirana, Albania
Algeria	Mr. Finn Tore Rose Resident Representative, a.i. United Nations Development Programme Boîte postale 823 Algiers 16000, Algeria
Angola	Mr. Miguel Da Graca Resident Representative United Nations Development Programme Caixa Postal 910 Luanda, People's Republic of Angola
Argentina	Ms. B. Katica Cekalovic Resident Representative United Nations Development Programme Casilla de Correo 2257 1000 Capital Federal Buenos Aires, Argentina

Bahrain	Mr. Ahmed Dhakkar Officer-in-Charge United Nations Development Programme P.O. Box 26814 Manama, Bahrain
Bangladesh	Mr. Charles Larsimont Resident Representative United Nations Development Programme G.P.O. Box 224 Dhaka 1000, Bangladesh
Barbados	Mr. Jan Wahlberg Resident Representative United Nations Development Programme P.O. Box 625 C Bridgetown, Barbados
Benin	Mr. Paolo Coppini Resident Representative United Nations Development Programme Boîte postale 506 Cotonou, People's Republic of Benin
Bhutan	Paul Matthews Resident Representative United Nations Development Programme G.P.O. Box 162 Thimphu, Bhutan
Bolivia	Mr. Gonsalo Perez del Castillo Resident Representative United Nations Development Programme Casilla 686 La Paz, Bolivia
Botswana	Ms. Elizabeth Fong Deputy Resident Representative United Nations Development Programme P.O. Box 54 Gaborone, Botswana
Brazil	Eduardo Gutierrez Resident Representative United Nations Development Programme Caixa Postal 07-2085 70000 Brasilia, Brazil
Burkino Faso	Ms. Agnes Guimba-Ouedraogo Resident Representative United Nations Development Programme Boîte postale 575 Ouagadougou, 01 Burkina Faso
Burundi	Ms. Jocelline Bazile-Finley Resident Representative United Nations Development Programme Boîte postale 1490 Bujumbura, Burundi
Cameroon	Mr. Herbert M'Cleod Resident Representative United Nations Development Programme Boîte postale 836 Yaounde, Cameroon

Cabo Verde	Mr. Pierre Ly Resident Representative United Nations Development Programme Caixa Postale 62 Praia, Cabo Verde
Cambodia	Mr. Edouard Wattez Liaison Officer c/o UNPD P.O. Box 877 Phom Penh, State of Cambodia
Central African Republic	Mr. Roger Maconick Resident Representative United Nations Development Programme Boîte postale 872 Gangui, Central African Republic
Chad	Mr. Emmanuel Dierckx de Casterie Resident Representative United Nations Development Programme Boîte postale 906 N'Djhamena, Chad
Chile	Mr. Luis Thais Resident Representative United Nations Development Programme Casilla 197-D Santiago, Chile
China	Mr. Roy Morey Resident Representative United Nations Development Programme 2 Dongqijie Sanlitun Beijing, China
Colombia	Mr. Arthuro Hein-Caceres Resident Representative United Nations Development Programme Apartado Aero, No. 091369 Bogotá, Colombia
Comoros	Mr. Jean-Marie Lorge Resident Representative United Nations Development Programme Boîte postale 648 Moroni, Comoros Federal Islamic Republic of Comoros
Congo	Mr. Ragnar Gudmundsson Resident Representative United Nations Development Programme Boîte postale 465 Brazzaville, People's Republic of Congo
Costa Rica	Mr. Bruno Guandalini Resident Representative United Nations Development Programme Apartado Postal 4540 San Jose, Costa Rica
Cuba	Mr. Joachim von Braunmuhl Resident Representative United Nations Development Programme Apartado Postal 4138 La Habana, Cuba

Cyprus	Mr. Johannes Swietering Resident Representative United Nations Development Programme P.O. Box 5605 Nicosia, Cyprus
Djibouti	Ms. Halinka Akrouf Resident Representative United Nations Development Programme Boîte postale 2001 Djibouti, Djibouti
Dominican Republic	Mr. Cesar Miguel Resident Representative United Nations Development Programme Apartado 1424 Santa Domingo, Dominican Republic
Ecuador	Mr. Mario Salzmann Resident Representative United Nations Development Programme P.O. Box 4731 Quito, Ecuador
Egypt	Mr. Pedro Mercader Resident Representative United Nations Development Programme P.O. Box 982 Postal Code No. 11511 Cairo, Egypt
El Salvador	Mr. Walter Franco Resident Representative United Nations Development Programme P.O. Box 1114 San Salvador, El Salvador
Equatorial Guinea	Mr. Markku Visapaa Resident Representative United Nations Development Programme Grand Central Station New York, NY 10163-1608
Eritrea	Mr. Sean Finn Liaison Officer UNDP Liaison Office Nyala Hotel, Room 208 Nation Way Asmara, Eritrea
Ethiopia	Mr. Timothy Painter Resident Representative United Nations Development Programme P.O. Box 5580 Addis Ababa, Ethiopia
Fiji	Mr. Somsey Norindr Resident Representative United Nations Development Programme Private Mail Bag Suva, Fiji

Gabon	Mr. Jean-Pierre Gernay Resident Representative United Nations Development Programme Boîte postale 2183 Libreville, Gabon
Gambia	Mr. Jose Da Silva Angelo Resident Representative United Nations Development Programme P.O. Box 553 Banjul, Gambia
Ghana	Mr. Joseph Byll-Cataria Resident Representative United Nations Development Programme P.O. Box 1423 Accra, Ghana
Guatemala	Mr. Ricardo Tichauer Resident Representative United Nations Development Programme Apartado Postal 23 "A" 01909 Guatemala City, C.A. Guatemala
Guinea	Mr. Ernest Nzekio Resident Representative United Nations Development Programme Boîte postale 222 Conakry, Republic of Guinea
Guinea Bissau	Mr. Cyr Samake Resident Representative United Nations Development Programme C.P. 179 P.O. Box 1011 Bissau Codex Republic of Guinea — Bissau
Guyana	Mr. Juan Luis Larrabure Resident Representative United Nations Development Programme P.O. Box 10960 Georgetown, Guyana
Haiti	Ms. Carroll Long Resident Representative United Nations Development Programme Boîte postale 557 Port-au-Prince, Haiti
Honduras	Mr. Paolo Oberti Resident Representative United Nations Development Programme Apartado Postal 976 Tegucigalpa D.C., Honduras
India	Mr. Erling Dessau Resident Representative United Nations Development Programme P.O. Box 3059 New Delhi 110003, India

Indonesia	Mr. Casper Kamp Resident Representative United Nations Development Programme P.O. Box 2338 Jakarta 10001, Indonesia
Iran	Mr. Michael Schulenburg Resident Representative, a.i. United Nations Development Programme P.O. Box 15875-4557 Tehran, Iran
Iraq	Mr. Salah Bourjini Resident Representative United Nations Development Programme P.O. Box 2048 (Alwiyah) Baghdad, Iraq
Ivory Coast	Mr. Normand Lauzon Resident Representative United Nations Development Programme 01 Boîte postale 1747 Abidjan 01, Republique de Cote d'Ivoire
Jamaica	Mr. Denis Benn Resident Representative, a.i. United Nations Development Programme P.O. Box 280 Kingston, Jamaica
Jordan	Mr. Osman Hashim Resident Representative United Nations Development Programme P.O. Box 35286 Amman, Jordan
Kenya	Mr. David Whaley Resident Representative, a.i. United Nations Development Programme P.O. Box 30218 Nairobi, Kenya
Korea (North)	Mr. Henning Karcher Resident Representative United Nations Development Programme P.O. Box 27 Pyongyang, Democratic People's Republic of Korea
Korea (South)	Mr. Jacob Guijt Resident Representative United Nations Development Programme Central Post Office Box 143 Area Code 100-601 Seoul, Republic of Korea
Kuwait	Mr. Khaled Philby Officer-in-Charge United Nations Development Programme P.O. Box 2993 SAFAT 13030 Safat, Kuwait

Lebanon	Mr. Hendrik van der Kloet Resident Representative United Nations Development Programme P.O. Box 11-3216 Beirut, Lebanon
Lesotho	Mr. Qais Noaman Resident Representative United Nations Development Programme P.O. Box 301 Maseru 100, Lesotho
Liberia	Mr. Ross Mountain Resident Representative United Nations Development Programme P.O. Box 10-0274 1000 Monrovia 10, Liberia
Libya	Mr. Awni Al-Ani Resident Representative United Nations Development Programme P.O. Box 358 Tripoli, Great Socialist People's Libyan Arab Jamahiriya
Madagascar	Mr. Christopher Metcalf Resident Representative United Nations Development Programme P.O. Box 1348 Antananarivo 101, Madagascar
Malawi	Mr. Michael Heyn Resident Representative United Nations Development Programme P.O. Box 30135 Lilongwe, 3 Malawi
Malaysia	Mr. Carl-Erik Wiberg Regional Representative United Nations Development Programme P.O. Box 12544 50782 Kuala Lampur, Malaysia
Maldives	Mr. Mohammed Farashuddin Resident Representative United Nations Development Programme P.O. Box 2058 Male, Republic of Maldives
Mali	Mr. Kya Kaysire Gitera Resident Representative United Nations Development Programme Boîte postale 120 Bamako, Mali
Mauritania	Mr. Hean-Jacques Edeline Resident Representative United Nations Development Programme Boîte postale 620 Nouakchott, Mauritania
Mauritius	Mr. Olubanke King-Akerele Resident Representative United Nations Development Programme P.O. Box 253 Port Louis, Mauritius

Mexico	Mr. Frederick Lyons Resident Representative United Nations Development Programme Apartado Postale 105-39 11581 Mexico, D.F. Mexico
Mongolia	Mr. Erick De Mul Resident Representative United Nations Development Programme P.O. Box 49/207 Ulaanbaater, Mongolia
Morocco	Mr. Luc Jacque Franzoni Resident Representative United Nations Development Programme CASIER ONU, Rabat-Chellah Rabat, Morocco
Mozambique	Mr. Peter Simkin Resident Representative United Nations Development Programme P.O. Box 4595 Maputo, Mozambique
Myanmar	Mr. Gerd Merrem Resident Representative United Nations Development Programme P.O. Box 650 Yangon, Myanmar
Namibia	Mr. Fidele Dionou Resident Representative United Nations Development Programme Private Bag 13329 Windhoek 9000, Namibia
Nepal	Mr. Jerrold Berke Resident Representative United Nations Development Programme P.O. Box 107 Kathmandu, Nepal
Nicaragua	Mr. Francesco Vincenti Officer-in-Charge United Nations Development Programme Apartado Postal 3260 Managua, Nicaragua
Niger	Mr. Aliou Diallo Resident Representative United Nations Development Programme Boîte postale 11207 Niamey, Niger
Nigeria	Mr. Assefa Fre-Hiwet Resident Representative United Nations Development Programme P.O. Box 2075 Lagos, Nigeria
Oman	Mr. Saleem Kassum Resident Representative United Nations Development Programme P.O. Box 5287 Ruwi, Muscat, Sultanate of Oman

Pakistan	Mr. Hans Von Sponeck
	Resident Representative
	United Nations Development Programme
	P.O. Box 1051
	Islamabad, Pakistan

Panama	Mr. Eduardo Niño-Moreno
	Resident Representative
	United Nations Development Programme
	Apartado 6314
	Panama 5, Panama

Papua New Guinea	Mr. Siba Kumar Das
	Resident Representative
	United Nations Development Programme
	P.O. Box 1041
	Port Moresby, Papua New Guinea

Paraguay	Mr. Hans D. Kurz
	Resident Representative, a.i.
	United Nations Development Programme
	Casilla de Correo 1107
	Asunción, Paraguay

Peru	Mr. Pierre den Baas
	Resident Representative
	United Nations Development Programme
	Apartado 4480
	Naciones Unidas
	Lima, Peru

Philippines	Mr. Keven McGrath
	Resident Representative
	United Nations Development Programme
	P.O. Box 1864
	Manila 2801, Philippines

Poland	Mr. Gary Gabriel
	Resident Representative For UNDP
	United Nations Centre
	P.O. Box 1
	Warsaw 12, Poland

Qatar	Mr. Fuad Mohammed
	Resident Representative
	United Nations Development Programme
	Box 3233
	Doha, Qatar

Romania	Mr. Ottorino Jannone
	Resident Representative
	United Nations Development Programme
	Strada AurelVlaicu nr. 16
	Sectorul 2, P.O. Box 1-701
	79362 Bucharest, Romania

Rwanda	Mr. Amadou Abdoul Ly
	Resident Representative
	United Nations Development Programme
	Boîte postale 445
	Kigali, Rwanda

Samoa	Mr. Matthew Kahane Resident Representative United Nations Development Programme Private Mail Bag Apia, Samoa
Sao Tome	Ms. Aissatou Kone-Diabi Resident Representative United Nations Development Programme Caixa Postal 109 São Tomé, Sao Tome and Principe
Saudi Arabia	Mr. Hassan Issa S.H. Issa Resident Representative, a.i. United Nations Development Programme P.O. Box 558 Riyadh 11421, Saudi Arabia
Senegal	Mr. Dramane Ouattara Resident Representative United Nations Development Programme Boîte postale 154 Dakar, Senegal
Sierra Leone	Mr. Joseph Kotta Resident Representative United Nations Development Programme P.O. Box 1011 Freetown, Sierra Leone
Somalia	Mr. Peter Schumann Resident Representative United Nations Development Programme P.O. Box 24 Mogadiscio, Somalia
Sri Lanka	Mr. Robert England Resident Representative United Nations Development Programme P.O. Box 1505 Colombo, Sri Lanka
Sudan	Mr. Per Janvid Resident Representative United Nations Development Programme P.O. Box 913 Khartoum, Republic of the Sudan
Swaziland	Mr. Solomon Akpata Resident Representative United Nations Development Programme Private Bag Mbabane, Swaziland
Switzerland	Mr. Jean Fabre Chief, Information Section United Nations Development Programme Palais de Nations Ch-1211 Geneva 10 Switzerland
Syria	Mr. Kyaw Lwin Hia Resident Representative United Nations Development Programme P.O. Box 2317 Damascus, Syria Arab Republic

Thailand	Mr. Alan Doss Resident Representative United Nations Development Programme c/o UNDP GPO Box 618 Bangkok, 10501 Thailand
Togo	Mr. Bernard Ntegeye Resident Representative United Nations Development Programme Boîte postale 911 Lomé, Togo
Trinidad and Tobago	Mr. Charles Perry Resident Representative United Nations Development Programme P.O. Box 812 Port-of-Spain, Trinidad and Tobago
Tunisia	Mr. Fawaz Fokeladeh Resident Representative United Nations Development Programme Boîte postale 863 1035 Tunis, Tunisia
Turkey	Mr. Edmund Cain Resident Representative United Nations Development Programme P.K. 407 06043 Ulus Ankara, Turkey
Uganda	Mr. Tedia Teshome Resident Representative United Nations Development Programme P.O. Box 7184 Kampala, Republic of Uganda
United Arab Emirates	Mr. Abdel Rahman Abdalla Resident Representative United Nations Development Programme P.O. Box 3490 Abu Dhabi, the United Arab Emirates
Tanzania	Mr. Wally N'Dow Resident Representative United Nations Development Programme P.O. Box 9182 Dar-es-Salaam, Tanzania
Uruguay	Mr. Paul van Hanswijck de Jonge Resident Representative United Nations Development Programme Casilla de Correo 1207 Montevideo, Uruguay
Venezuela	Ms. Seyril Siegel Resident Representative United Nations Development Programme Apratado 69005 Caracas 1062-A, Venezuela

Vietnam	Mr. David Smith Resident Representative United Nations Development Programme c/o UNDP GPO Box 618 Bangkok, Thailand
Yemen	Mr. Michael Hyland Resident Representative United Nations Development Programme P.O. Box 551 Sana'a, Yemen Arab Republic
Yugoslavia	Mr. Constante Muzio Resident Representative United Nations Development Programme P.O. Box 644 11001 Belgrade, Yugoslavia
Zaire	Mr. Joseph Cavalli Resident Representative United Nations Development Programme Boîte postale 7248 Kinshasa, Republic of Zaire
Zambia	Mr. Onder Yucer Resident Representative United Nations Development Programme P.O. Box 31966 Lusaka, Zambia
Zimbabwe	Mr. Dusan Dragic Resident Representative United Nations Development Programme P.O. Box 4775 Harare, Zimbabwe

Liaison Offices

Italy	Director U.N. Information Center Palazzeto Venezia Piazza San Marco 50 Rome, Italy
Japan	Mr. Makoto Hinei Liaison Officer United Nations Development Programme Shin Aoyama Building, Room 2254 1-1, Minami-Aoyama 1-Chome Minato-Ku Tokyo 107 Japan
United States	Mr. David Scotton Liaison Officer United Nations Development Programme 1889 F St., NW Washington, DC 20006

United Nations Educational, Scientific, and Cultural Organization (UNESCO)

> 7 Place de Fontenoy
> 75700 Paris, France
>
> or
>
> UNESCO Liaison Office
> United Nations
> U.N. Plaza
> New York, NY 10017

UNESCO, a specialized agency of the United Nations, functions in the fields of education, science, mass communications, and cultural matters.

EDUCATION. One of UNESCO's priorities is the problem of illiteracy. In addition, UNESCO recognizes the need for educational innovation and works with countries individually and in regional groupings to improve the quality of education offered. Much of this organization's educational business is doné through large-scale conferences.

SCIENCE. UNESCO seeks to advance the cause of science globally and also helps countries build up their scientific capabilities. It has set up special funds for research, established an international exchange of information on the application of science and technology to development, and organized regional conferences of ministers of science and technology.

COMMUNICATIONS. UNESCO is charged by its constitution to promote "the free flow of ideas by word and image." To this end, it aims to increase each country's access to information. It has worked to help launch national and regional news agencies in order to promote rural newspapers and help create training centers for journalists. It pays increasing attention to television and helps train personnel to bring TV to villages throughout the developing world.

CULTURE. UNESCO's best-known effort in this arena has been its international campaigns to save the great monuments of the world. Artistic, engineering, and archeological skills have been mobilized globally to launch cultural rescue operations, such as for the Egyptian temples that were almost submerged by the waters of the Aswan Dam. Long-term study projects are also under way to preserve and disseminate traditional and contemporary cultures of all regions of the world.

Background Desired

Because of the variety of UNESCO activities, you should determine in advance which parts or functions interest you, since qualifications will differ according to section and division. If you are educationally inclined, teaching experience and a background in academe are desirable. If you are interested in UNESCO's cultural activities, you should have some background in the arts, cultural studies, archaeology, or engineering. If communications is your field, you should be qualified in journalism, broadcasting, publishing, and communication skills.

If interested in applying, first check with UNESCO on current employment possibilities for Americans.

United Nations Environment Programme (UNEP)

P.O. Box 30552
Nairobi, Kenya

or

2 U.N. Plaza
New York, NY 10017

The U.N. General Assembly, in establishing UNEP, recognized that environmental problems of the international level required a special approach. Since environment is the logical concern of many U.N. organizations, it was considered unwise to make environmental problems the province of one agency. Thus, in contrast to the concept that shaped other U.N. organizations, UNEP was created as a small coordinating body to give leadership and direction to international initiatives — not to do the work itself, but to see that it gets done.

Background Desired

Economics, economic development, world resources, population studies, energy studies, and environmental studies.

United Nations Fund for Population Activities (UNFPA)

Chief, Personnel Section
UN Fund for Population Activities
220 East 42nd St.
New York, NY 10017

The Population Fund, as it is popularly called, was set up in 1967 to help developing countries with high population rates and low national incomes solve their population problems. This U.N. organization is recognized as the focal point for the promotion and coordination of international population programs. The fund assists national efforts by: (1) promoting government awareness of the consequences of a high population growth rate; (2) providing assistance to countries seeking relief from their population problems; (3) helping organizations within the U.N. system to be more effective in planning and implementing population projects; and (4) assuming the leading international role in developing global population strategies.

Background Desired

A similar background to that required for UNDP applies to the fund: economics, economic development, and developing area studies. Emphasis is also placed on population, demography, and statistics. Fluency in languages is a great plus.

United Nations High Commissioner for Refugees (UNHCR)

> Case Postale 2500
> CH-1211 Geneva
> 2 Depot
> Switzerland
>
>   or
>
> 1718 Connecticut Ave., NW
> Suite 200
> Washington, DC 20009

This organization is concerned with any individual who lives outside his or her home country and who does not receive its protection for reasons of race, nationality, membership in a particular social group, or political opinion. UNHCR has two main functions: (1) encouraging the practice of asylum and then safeguarding the rights of refugees concerning employment, education, residence, freedom of movement, and security against being returned to a country where their lives may be in danger; and (2) helping governments and private organizations in countries of asylum in their task of enabling refugees to become self-supporting.

In recent years the U.N. Secretary General has designated UNHCR to coordinate several major U.N. programs. One concerned emergency relief for some ten million East Bengali refugees in India; another, the return of thousands of refugees to the South Sudan and their resettlement in that region. UNHCR also has provided aid to hundreds of thousands of uprooted people from Vietnam, Cambodia, Laos, and other countries.

Background Desired

Social work, work with displaced persons or refugees, economics, economic development, and international relations.

United Nations Industrial Development Organization (UNIDO)

> Vienna International Center
> P.O. Box 300
> A-1400 Vienna, Austria

UNIDO was established in 1967 to "promote and accelerate the industrialization of the developing countries." Fifty-three countries are represented on the policy-making *Industrial Development Board*. The technical assistance activities of UNIDO are financed mainly by UNDP. One of UNIDO's aims is to increase the developing nations' share of world industrial production from 7 percent to 25 percent by the year 2000. UNIDO also administers an *Industrial Development Fund* of voluntary contibutions for special operational tasks.

To summarize, UNIDO helps developing countries expand and modernize their industries; acts as liaison between developing and industrialized countries in their joint efforts toward industrialization of the former; assists developing nations to obtain financing for industrial projects; and undertakes the transfer of needed technology and the training of personnel.

Background Desired

Business administration, industrial relations, and a liberal supply of economics courses, economic development, and Third World area studies. Languages are also desirable.

United Nations Institute for Training and Research (UNITAR)

> 801 U.N. Plaza
> New York, NY 10017

UNITAR was established in 1963 as an autonomous institute within the U.N. framework for specialized training and research. The training function involves individuals primarily from the developing nations who need to improve their qualifications for U.N. work or for work in their own countries. Research performed is "related to the functions and objectives of the U.N.," thus allowing wide latitude for the studies undertaken.

Background Desired

A research and/or training ability is clearly indicated for all applicants. Specific courses in support of your application are: economics, economic development, area studies, world resources, international relations, and foreign policy.

Requirements

Send your Personal History P-11 Form.

United Nations International School

24-50 East River Dr.
New York, NY 10010

The U.N. International School is not part of the U.N. structure, but is included here because of its close relationship to the United Nations. The school is for students whose parents are associated with the United Nations and have come to New York from abroad. It is a day school, beginning with the five-year-old level and continuing through preparation for college and university. It has two locations: on the East River south of U.N. headquarters, and in Queens (an elementary branch).

Background Desired

Teaching experience, area studies, languages.

United Nations University

Toho Sheimei Building
15-1 Shibuya 2-Chome, Shibuya-ku
Tokyo 150, Japan

The U.N. University was established for scholars, economists, and political analysts to "improve the conditions of human existence throughout the world." It is not organized on the basis of traditional academic departments; instead, the university's institutes employ multidisciplinary approaches to specific world problems. It is strongly oriented toward the needs of the developing countries. The University Council has chosen world hunger as the first priority. Long-range analysis of food policy, water resources, human rights, international trade, and the uses of oceans are other matters of concern.

Background Desired

Teaching credentials and experience; knowledge of agriculture and world resources; Third World area studies; and, of course, languages, especially Japanese, because the university is headquartered in Tokyo.

United Nations Volunteers (UNV)

> International Secretariat for Volunteer Service
> Palais des Nations
> CH-1211 Geneva 10, Switzerland
>
> or
>
> U.N. Volunteers
> United Nations Plaza
> New York, NY 10017

UNV is somewhat similar to the Peace Corps in that it enrolls the youth of many countries in a collective effort to help developing nations. The help offered ranges from community development to road construction, well digging, health services, education — in other words, much the same territory covered by the UNDP in its technical assistance work. For this reason, volunteers are associated with UNDP-assisted projects and form another wing of that organization. The primary aim of UNV is to make a contribution to the development of the recipient country. Volunteers are paid transportation expenses and a small living stipend.

Background Desired

Economics, business administration, teaching, health services, community development, engineering, and almost any other skills needed by impoverished countries.

Requirements

Applicants must be over 21 and are recruited from both developed and developing countries. UNV does not recruit volunteers directly; applications are channeled through existing volunteer organizations. To this end, UNV cooperates with the *International Secretariat for Volunteer Service* and the *Coordinating Committee for International Voluntary Service,* two international volunteer organizations with a membership of more than 500 affiliated organizations. Applicants should seek sponsorship from local UNDP offices or recognized volunteer organizations in their own country. For a list of these organizations, as well as general information on the U.N. Volunteers, write to the addresses above. U.S. citizens may also apply for the UNV through the Peace Corps.

World Health Organization (WHO)

Palais des Nations
CH-1211 Geneva 27, Switzerland

or

Pan American Sanitary Bureau
Pan American Health Organization
525 23 St., NW
Washington, DC 20037

WHO plans and coordinates health action on a global basis. It assists member countries to carry out health programs, strengthen their health services, and train their health workers. It also promotes medical research and exchange of scientific information, makes health regulations for international travel, keeps communicable diseases under surveillance, collects and distributes data on health matters, and sets standards for the control of drugs and vaccines.

WHO has six regional offices: African region (headquarters, Brazzaville, Congo); the Americas (Washington, DC); Eastern Mediterranean (Alexandria, Egypt); Europe (Copenhagen, Denmark); Southeast Asia (New Delhi, India); and Western Pacific (Manila, Philippines).

Background Desired

The type of work performed by WHO defines the type of personnel needed: medical officers, nurses, sanitary engineers, entomologists, bacteriologists, health educators, and occasionally economists and statisticians. Third World experience is desirable, as is fluency in the languages of the area applied for.

World Intellectual Property Organization (WIPO)

32, Chemin des Colombettes
CH-1211 Geneva 20, Switzerland

or

WIPO Liaison Office
United Nations DC2-0560
New York, NY 10017

WIPO is responsible for the protection of intellectual property throughout the world, and for the administration of various "unions," each founded on a multilateral treaty and dealing with the legal and administrative aspects of intellectual property. Intellectual property consists of: (1) industrial property (chiefly inventions, trademarks, and designs), and (2) copyrights (chiefly of literary, musical, artistic, photographic, and cinematographic work).

Background Desired

Law, business administration, cultural work, library sciences, and transfer of technology.

World Tourism Organization (WTO)

> Calle Capitan Haya 42
> Madrid 28020, Spain

The WTO promotes tourism for the economic, social, and cultural advancement of all countries. It fosters the adoption of measures making travel easier by simplifying frontier formalities and removing barriers to the free movement of tourists. It drafts international agreements on tourism, and in cooperation with other interested organizations, helps their implementation. The WTO is actively involved in trying to solve problems of maintaining an adequate supply of trained personnel for the various branches of tourism.

The WTO has six Regional Commissions: Africa, the Americas, Europe, Middle East, Pacific and East Asia, and South Asia.

Background Desired

Academic and practical background in all phases of tourism, area studies, languages, administration, and cultural studies.

Other Agencies

Four other specialized U.N. agencies, whose names are self-descriptive, follow:

> International Maritime Organization (IMO)
> 4 Albert Embankment
> London SE 1 7SR
> England

> International Telecommunication Union (ITU)
> Palais des Nations
> CH-1211 Geneva 20
> Switzerland

> Universal Postal Union (UPU)
> Case postale
> Welt Post Strasse 4
> CH-3000 Bern 15
> Switzerland

> World Meteorological Organization (WMO)
> 41, avenue Giuseppe Motta
> Geneva 20
> Switzerland

REGIONAL U.N. ORGANIZATIONS

The following organizations, also related to the U.N. system, are listed separately because they have a particular regional emphasis.

Asian Development Bank

> 2330 Roxas Boulevard
> Pasay City, Philippines

The bank's function is to promote economic growth in member countries, most of which are from Asia. The United States became a member in 1966 and provides significant funding for the organization.

Background Desired

Banking and finance, economics, economic development, and Asian studies.

Inter-American Development Bank

> Recruitment Office
> Inter-American Development Bank
> 1300 New York Ave., NW
> Washington, DC 20005

The purpose of the bank is to promote economic development of its member countries from Latin America. The United States and several countries from Europe and Asia have also been admitted as members. The bank finances high-priority economic and social development projects in the private and public sectors; it provides technical cooperation, research, and training in the development field; and it acts as a clearing house for the exchange of information on economic and social questions in Latin American countries. Bank offices are located in most Latin American countries.

Background Desired

Finance and banking, economics, economic development, Latin American studies, and Spanish and Portuguese.

Organization for Economic Cooperation and Development (OECD)

> 2 rue André-Pascal
> F-75018 Paris, France

The OECD is the successor to the Organization for European Economic Cooperation, which administered the Marshall Plan for European recovery after World War II. The organization is composed primarily of European countries, although the United States, Canada, Japan, and several other countries are also members. The OECD tries to achieve the highest sustainable economic growth, employment, and standard of living in member countries while maintaining financial stability. Another purpose of the organization is to expand world trade.

Background Desired

The specialized economic nature of this organization puts a premium on doctorates in economics, industrial relations, manpower studies, economic development, statistics, and finance. Business administration, European studies, and languages are also helpful.

Organization of American States (OAS)

> General Secretariat
> Organization of American States
> Constitution Ave. & 17th St., NW
> Washington, DC 20006

The OAS is one of the world's oldest international organizations. It unites the countries of the western hemisphere "in a community of nations dedicated to the achievement of peace, security, and prosperity for all Americans." The OAS is thought of as a regional agency of the United Nations. In fact, its relation is limited to the maintenance of peace and the peaceful settlement of disputes. In other fields — economic, social, legal — the OAS operates independently. The *Council of the OAS* is the executive body of the organization and it functions with eight permanent committees:

1. General
2. Program and Budget
3. Inter-American Conferences
4. Inter-American Organizations
5. Economic and Social Affairs
6. Juridical-Political Affairs
7. Cultural Affairs
8. Public Information, Regulations, and Procedures

The titles of the committees represent the general scope of overall OAS functions.

The *Pan American Union* is the Secretariat of the OAS. In addition, there are five inter-American specialized organizations with which the OAS Council maintains working agreements:

1. Pan American Health Organization (headquarters in Washington, DC)
2. Inter-American Children's Institute (headquarters in Montevideo)
3. Inter-American Commission of Women (headquarters in the Pan American Union in Washington, DC)
4. Pan American Institute of Geography and History (headquarters in Mexico City)
5. Inter-American Institute of Agricultural Sciences (headquarters in the Pan American Union in Washington, DC)

This prolific network of agencies and organizations, all dedicated to the improvement of the quality of life for North and South Americans, has personnel working in a wide variety of arenas: economics, political, social, health.

Background Desired

Latin American studies, Spanish and Portuguese, economics, economic development, communications, and public relations.

U.N. Relief and Works Agency for Palestine Refugees in the Near East (UNRWA)

> Vienna International Center
> P.O. Box 700
> A1400 Vienna, Austria
>
> or
>
> Liaison Office
> 2 U.N. Plaza
> Room 550
> New York, NY 10017

UNRWA has existed as a temporary U.N. agency since 1950, with its mandate being renewed periodically by the General Assembly. It provides services to Palestinian refugees, specifically those persons (or their descendants) who were residents of Palestine for the last two years before the 1948 Arab-Israel conflict and who then lost their homes and means of livelihood.

UNRWA operates almost 600 schools for refugee children and employs more than 8,000 teachers, mostly Palestinians, to staff these schools. The educational program is run jointly with UNESCO. UNRWA's health program for refugees is also run jointly — in this case with the WHO. Its other major program is a relief program consisting of food distribution, staffed mostly with local personnel. The agency's areas of operation are Lebanon, Syria, East Jordan, and the West Bank.

Background Desired

UNRWA's international staff is limited in number, and the organization requires the following specializations as well as experience: law, accounting, information and public relations, administration, personnel, education, health, nutrition and feeding, and languages.

PUBLICATIONS

Additional information on international agencies and their functions, organization, and personnel can be found in the following publications:

1. *Europa Year Book: A World Survey, Vol. I, Part I, International Organizations* (London: Europa Publications, Ltd.).
2. *Yearbook of the United Nations* (New York: United Nations).

8

INTERNATIONAL BUSINESS AND BANKING

INTERNATIONAL BUSINESS

So far we have looked at the government and the United Nations, both non-profit. Now we turn to quite a different world, sometimes called "the real world." Since profit is the motivating force in business, it is only natural that you, too, may be motivated by "What's in it for me?" The starting salary in many businesses and banks is in the $40,000–$50,000 range, compared to more modest figures in nonprofit organizations.

The two worlds, real and unreal (if they exist at all in such raw terms), are similar in one important respect: Before you are offered a job in any profit or nonprofit organization, you will have been evaluated in terms of the help you are expected to give that organization in carrying out its task. The salient point on which you are judged by the employer really is: How much can this person help me to do my job? Whether the employer's job is to increase some company's international profit, enhance the U.N. image in the eyes of the American public, or increase the effectiveness of American policy in Central America, the criterion of potential usefulness is the same. But with a business, the results of your performance tend to be more measurable.

Unlike in a nonprofit organization, where your performance is often difficult to evaluate — how does an employer measure your success in helping a refugee adapt to America or in making the public aware of a foreign policy issue? — business operations result in hard figures on profit and loss. If profits are lagging, the stockholders are unhappy and may call management to account. The accounting may well entail a good look at personnel and jobs. Reorganization of sections and head rolling are not uncommon as an aftermath.

There are two major kinds of jobs in business that will attract those with an international background (1) political risk analysis (evaluation of the political climate in a country and its effect on the operations of a corporation), and (2) international marketing and finance jobs (either in U.S. headquarters or abroad). We shall look at both of these shortly, but first we should examine the value of your international background to international business.

How Valuable Is Your Background to International Business?

In the past, just because you had an international relations background did not mean that you became a target for eager recruiters from companies looking for personnel to fill slots in their international operations. Likewise, language fluency and a concentration in area studies — say, Russian or Western European — although found valuable by recruiters, did not automatically get you a job with companies doing business in those areas.

For example, some years ago an automotive manufacturer planned to expand in what was then the Soviet Union. Students with a Russian studies background thought they would be needed for the new undertaking. Not so. When asked why not, an official of the organization said that the best marketing experts would be negotiating with the Russians. "But how," one student asked, "can you understand the Russians without having on the negotiating team people steeped in Russian politics, economics, and history?" "No problem at all," came the reply, "We will use interpreters." Too often such a gap existed between corporate operations and the international political analysis.

How, you may well ask, was business not aware of the importance to their operations of international know-how? Don't casually dismiss this attitude as idiocy. After all, if business believed that an international background in itself could increase profits, it would have been foolish not to hire internationally oriented people such as yourselves. The probability is that many of these organizations analyzed the effect on company profits of hiring one or more political experts and concluded that the benefits at that time did not justify the costs.

The record was not all negative, however. In another example, a giant communications conglomerate, bruised from public disclosure of its political dealings abroad, tried to improve its public image and prevent similar errors by starting a small unit of political thinkers headed up by a retired American ambassador.

Another repair job was undertaken by an oil company as a result of adverse publicity received during the oil crisis of the early 1970s. A great deal of research was undertaken, much of it by Ph.D.s in political science and international relations, which has been used to improve the public image of the oil industry.

In the case of the last two organizations, creative use of internationally knowledgeable personnel came into play only as a result of crises. Today much has changed, and international experts in some fields are welcomed into the business world.

Political Risk Analysis

Business is now using political risk analysts, not just to repair an image after a crisis, but to prevent a crisis from happening. Specialists are being hired to interpret political activities in a foreign country and gauge their effect on a company's business. Sometimes the analysis is provided as a guide to a company's manufacturing or marketing functions in a country; sometimes as a guide to a company's investment in native industry.

The movement has gained such momentum in the last few years that an Association of Political Risk Analysts has been organized. The association issues a quarterly newsletter to its several hundred members highlighting political risk in one or more countries as well as general developments in the field. It also publishes a directory of its members and organizes both an annual meeting and regional chapter meetings. The group is located at 13740 Midway Rd., Suite 609, Dallas, TX 75244.

Political risk analysis can take various forms organizationally. The function may be performed for a company by an outside consulting firm, such as Multinational Strategies of New York, or by in-house analysts, as at General Motors. Sometimes a single individual (often a retired high-level Foreign Service officer) performs the functions; sometimes various members of corporate headquarters and division and branch managers provide the company with knowledge of the political environment overseas (Exxon).

Regardless of the form the political analysis function takes, it is a field in which the international affairs specialist can make a contribution. Retired high-level Foreign Service officers are sometimes sought to head up a political risk section or the like. With less experience but with substantial academic background in international affairs, you may qualify for a lower-level position in the same political risk section.

When you are identifying your targets, start off with the *Fortune* 500 list; these are the largest companies and the ones most likely to use political risk people. When making an approach, contact the Chief of the Political Risk Section, if there is such a section; if none, contact a division with a name suggesting political risk, such as international, political planning, political research, public affairs, legal, or economics. Even when there is an International Division, the political risk function may be found elsewhere.

Two useful sources of information in this growing field are Louis Kraar's article, "The Multinationals Get Smarter about Political Risk," which appeared in the March 24, 1980, issue of *Fortune* magazine, and a study, "Assessing the Political Environment: An Emerging Function in International Companies," issued by the Conference Board, 845 Third Ave., New York, NY 10022. Though issued in the early 1980s, this study is still available and pertinent, but must be requested through a member of the board.

For a list of prominent political risk analysis firms, see pages 207–210. For the names of management consultant firms engaging in political risk analysis, see the section of this chapter on management consultants, pages 198–207.

INTERNATIONAL MARKETING AND FINANCE JOBS

Perhaps political risk jobs may seem too specialized and beyond the reach of newly graduated students. At the same time, more companies have larger sales and profits abroad today than in the past. Therefore, you may argue, your international background may give you an edge over competitors who lack your credentials. True and not true.

For one thing, the pool of foreign-born personnel who are getting their training in the business schools of America is expanding. These people are bilingual, have a built-in international content, are technically trained, and are understandably eager to assume responsible positions in their own countries. They may also cost the company less if they are hired abroad. Salaries tend to be lower than in the United States, and there is an additional saving to the company in not having to pay the cost of transportation for the employee and his or her family. This explains why fewer Americans are now being sent abroad for long-term assignments and why an international background for an American is sometimes less valued in the business world than you think it should be.

If you get hired for international work, you will probably do it at the U.S. headquarters of the company, with occasional travel abroad for conferences, negotiations, or consultation. Sometimes, however, assignments to company offices and factories overseas can be arranged for shifts of several years at a time, despite the trend of hiring foreigners for overseas jobs.

In a few cases, language ability may lead directly to a job, regardless of your other qualifications. For example, a Russian-language specialist without business qualifications may be hired by a company trading with Russia, or a Japanese language expert may be hired by an American export firm dealing with Japan, but these are exceptions. The rule still is that you usually don't get hired for your international background alone. You need something more.

What Is This "Something More"?

Simply stated, it is the technical business curriculum: the accounting, marketing, and finance courses that the M.B.A. brings to the job hunt. You don't have to have an M.B.A. to receive serious consideration from some internationally oriented businesses, but you do have to have these technical courses. How many? Perhaps five or six, divided into two basic tracks: accounting-marketing and accounting-finance.

Those of you who hate numbers may be dismayed to see accounting figuring prominently in both tracks. Even though no one wants to turn you into an accountant (unless you want to be one), you do have to know what the work of the accountant is. In the course of a long career in business you will find an understanding of accounting vital for the insight it will give you into overall company policy and prospects.

Marketing is the heart and guts of most businesses. It is often the main highway for fast progress up the promotional ladder. Most companies manufacture a product that has to be sold to other companies or to the consumer. This is what marketing is: sales, advertising, market research, and product management.

In this *accounting-marketing* track the following courses, or their equivalent, are recommended: one course each in basic accounting and basic marketing; two in advanced marketing, such as international and foreign marketing, marketing research, and product management; one in international business; and one or two in finance, especially business finance, money and financial markets, or international investments.

The *accounting-finance* track is a bit more specialized but it has one great advantage. Not only can it be used on the financial side of business, but it will also qualify you for international banking jobs.

Recommended courses for this track are basic accounting and four or five different courses in finance, such as international finance, business finance, money and financial markets, monetary policy, corporate financial reporting, financing international transactions, money markets, or international banking. International business or intermediate accounting is also good.

Don't be sidetracked into other business courses unless you have special reasons for taking them. Courses in statistics, industrial relations, managerial behavior, economics of the firm, and the like, while interesting and beneficial, will not ordinarily help you get a job in international business. Businesses will usually judge you by how many courses you have in accounting, finance, and marketing, and then look at your international courses.

Can I Substitute International Economics for Some of These Courses?

You may think that because business and the economy are dependent on each other, economics is essential to getting a business job. Not really.

Economics is the science — often theoretical — that investigates the laws affecting production, distribution, and consumption. Understanding how the economy works is always useful, employers admit, especially as you rise up the corporate ladder. For a beginning job, however, they usually consider business courses more valuable than an economics background.

However, international economics courses have enormous value in many other fields and will help you get an entry-level job in government, nonprofit organizations, foundations, some banks, and almost every other line of work — except many businesses.

M.B.A. or M.A.?

If you know you want a career in business and you don't much care whether international or domestic, an M.B.A. is better. This degree commands immediate respect from most businesses and may get you further in the long run.

However, if the international aspect is important to you, take your chances on the M.A. track, since your international know-how will be a solid asset when you apply for jobs. But you can maximize your chances by taking the business courses indicated above and by including in your job strategy the following:

1. *Approach with employers*   When interviewing with employers, stress that you offer the best of both worlds: the basic technical business courses that M.B.A.s offer, plus something that most M.B.A.s do not — international know-how.
2. *Define your targets*   It makes no sense to apply to companies that do very little international business. Your targets rightly will be those heavily involved in the international economy. Better yet, consult the annual reports of the major companies and identify those organizations whose profits from international operations are growing faster than domestic profits. Zero in on these companies, since your international training will be offered just when the need for your background may be greatest.

   The largest companies are apt to have the largest amount of international business. It would make sense to start the job hunt with the *Fortune* 500 list unless you have an aversion to large size.

   a. *Special target: export-import companies*   Another way to capitalize on your background is to try export-import companies. There is nothing more international than the work performed by these organizations. These companies usually do not recruit on campus since they are small and have relatively few openings, and M.B.A.s do not usually seek them out.

      Beginning salaries are often less than those offered by the conglomerates, and the initial work may be in the stockroom acquainting yourself with shipping forms, bills of lading, and other documentation you should know about. But promotion comes rapidly for the talented, and long-term career opportunities exist.

For lists of exporters and importers, consult the *American Register of Exporters and Importers*, a directory of some 30,000 manufacturers and export-import buying agencies, broken down by product class. It is published by Thomas International Publishers. For additional information on specific firms, you may want to contact the National Association of Export Companies, P.O. Box 1330, Murray Hill Station, New York, NY 10156 (212) 725-3311. Those with a background in Chinese studies should contact the U.S.–China Business Council, 1818 N St., NW, Washington, DC 20036.

b. *Special target: foreign companies in the United States*   Whether these companies are businesses or banks, you will be better able to compete with the M.B.A. if you have international training plus business-banking courses. For lists of companies, contact the Washington embassies or New York consulates of the following countries: Japan, Germany, England, Israel, Brazil, France, Holland, and Belgium. Also look at the *Directory of Foreign Firms Operating in the United States* published and updated every two or three years by Uniworld Business Publications, 50 East 42nd St., New York, NY 10017, and available at any large reference library. One disadvantage: Your chances for advancement may be limited if the company gives priority for top assignments to its own nationals.

c. *Special target: extractive industries*   More than most other U.S. industries, extractive industries (oils, metals) tend to send American employees overseas.

d. *Special target: computer and high-technology companies*   Since the United States is moving further into an era of high technology, companies in these fields — computer, bio-tech, high-tech — represent the wave of the future. As such, they are likely not only to have more jobs but also more international jobs.

Training Programs

Training programs in business can vary considerably. Sometimes there is no specialized training for a new employee. He or she is ushered into an office, shown the rudiments of a job, and expected to produce.

Where training programs exist they may be small and individually tailored to the successful applicant. Others are elaborate, with each stage of training defined and organized so that a new recruit feels like a product in the process of being packaged. Generally, it can be said that the largest companies have training programs and that recruits entering them are considered to have executive potential.

The length of training may vary from several weeks to several years. In some companies, course work at school is mixed with on-the-job training. Because of the diversity of the training provided, the only typical program is the atypical one.

A rather sophisticated program we have come upon involves one year of on-the-job training in marketing or finance, depending on your specialty. During that year you will be shuttled from one section to another. In each section you may have a specific job or you may act as general assistant to the officers of the section. Occasionally, you may even be made temporary supervisor of a section so that your supervisory talents may be evaluated. At the end of the year you will be assigned a full-time job in the marketing or finance section of the company.

You will notice that no specific assignment to the international division is mentioned. It will probably be included in the training program, but there is no certainty that it will be. Sometimes, even with an international academic background, you may be hired for the domestic operations of the company, with the understanding that when vacancies occur in the international operations you will be given special consideration.

You may decide on a business career when you have insufficient or unrelated academic and professional credentials. In that case, you may find it advisable to take one of the special business programs offered at a number of universities. New York University in particular has an excellent business curriculum for recycling those with Ph.D.s in nonbusiness fields.

An additional suggestion: The American Society for Training and Development offers seminars, institutes, and regional/national/international conferences in training and development. Some of these may be useful to you in broadening your background and in giving you contacts in the business world. For a brochure, write to American Society for Training and Development (ASTD), 1640 King St., Alexandria, VA 22313.

The Job Hunt

When you start your initial job hunt, you will first want to identify the office in charge of the international division of the company, or at least the person responsible for its foreign operations.

Your search begins with a standard reference guide to business: *Moody's Industrial Manual, Dun and Bradstreet's Million Dollar Directory, Standard and Poor's*

Register of Corporations, or *The International Corporate 1,000,* a directory of who runs the world's thousand leading corporations. All are available in large reference libraries. Consult the latest editions of these directories so that you will have up-to-date information on the personnel in this rapidly changing world.

In each of these directories there is a list of officers and managers. Look at the list and try to find someone with the magic word "international" in his or her title, or if not "international," at least "foreign" or "overseas" or "worldwide." If none of these clues can be found, then consult the public relations office of the company and ask who is in charge of the international workings of the organization. That is the person whom you should first contact in your job hunt.

For Non-U.S. Citizens

Intersearch Group, 115 East 87th St., New York, NY 10028, (212) 831-5156, is a recruitment organization providing career opportunities for international students. One of its primary goals is to help foreign students locate employment with multinational corporations either in their home countries or in the United States.

Fees for this service are said to be paid by corporate clients, and no fee is supposed to be charged to the student. But read the fine print before reaching an agreement with this or any other recruiting organization.

For U.S. Citizens

The type of position you will be applying for will probably be in the company's international division at headquarters in the United States. If, however, you are primarily interested in a position abroad, you can try to get a job at U.S. headquarters and work your way into a foreign position after you have proved yourself at home.

Usually, hiring for work in U.S. corporations in other countries is done in those countries. Occasionally, however, representatives from foreign branches of U.S. companies come to the United States for recruiting purposes. Learn when these reps are scheduled to arrive and try to get an interview, either through headquarters or by writing directly to the foreign branch.

The rest of this section deals with a few companies that do substantial international business. The list is obviously incomplete. There are so many businesses with heavy involvement in the international sphere that it would be impossible to list more than a few examples. Refer to Chapter 5 for specifics on job opportunities that have resulted from recent trade pacts and the disintegration of the Soviet Union.

Amerada Hess

> 1185 Avenue of the Americas
> New York, NY 10036
> (212) 997-8500

This is an integrated petroleum company engaged in every phase of the petroleum business, from finding new deposits of crude oil and natural gas to refining and marketing petroleum products.

The corporation's exploration and production activities abroad are conducted in Canada, Abu Dhabi, Libya, and the Norwegian and United Kingdom sectors of the North Sea. Its refineries produce residual fuel oil, heating oil, gasoline, and other petroleum products.

Background Desired

Petroleum engineering, marketing, accounting, finance, business administration, and Middle East studies.

American Cyanimid

> One Cyanimid Plaza
> Wayne, NJ 07470
> (201) 831-2000

This company manufactures pharmaceuticals, vitamin and mineral supplements, hospital supplies, fertilizers, pesticides, animal feed and veterinary products, industrial chemicals, and consumer toiletries and hair preparations. In 1991, foreign sales amounted to 38.6 percent of total sales, and foreign profits 50.5 percent of total profits.

Background Desired

Chemistry, agriculture, environmental studies, marketing, finance, accounting, public relations, and economics.

American Home Products

> 685 Third Ave.
> New York, NY 10017
> (212) 878-5000

American Home Products is an important world supplier of prescription drugs, packaged medicines, household products, housewares, and food and candy products. Over 30 percent of sales are made in Europe, Latin America, Australia and New Zealand, Asia, and Africa. It has the following divisions: *A. H. Robins* (packaged medicines), *Corometrics* (obstetrical monitoring and diagnostic ultrasound products), *Genetics Institute* (biopharmaceuticals), *Sherwood* (medical supplies and hospital products), *Whitehall International* (packaged medicines), and *Wyeth-Ayerst International Ltd.* (prescription drugs). American Home Products is currently joint venturing with Eisia Co. Ltd., one of Japan's first pharmaceutical companies.

Background Desired

Marketing, finance, accounting, chemistry, physics, biology, and business administration.

Amgen

> 1840 Dehavilland Dr.
> Thousand Oaks, CA 91320-1789

Amgen is a global pharmaceutical company that develops, manufactures, and markets human pharmaceuticals based on advanced cellular and molecular biology. Its operating subsidiaries are located in Australia, Belgium, Canada, Germany, France, Italy, Netherlands, Puerto Rico, Spain, Switzerland, and the United Kingdom.

Background Desired

Biology and science for development and manufacturing, marketing, administration, business for marketing Amgen products.

Armco International

> P.O. Box 73688
> Houston, TX 77273

> or

> Armco
> Executive Office
> Parsippany, NJ 07054

Armco has three business units that may be of interest to you:

1. *Armco Worldwide Grinding Systems* develops grinding balls and rods and abrasion-resistant casting liners, among other things. It has overseas offices in Belgium, Italy, Chile, and Peru and joint ventures in three other countries.
2. *Armco Latin America Division* develops carbon and alloy specialty sheet and strip, construction products, and building components.
3. *International Trading Companies* buys and sells steel and manufactured steel products. It has offices primarily in Europe.

Background Desired

Area studies and languages, business administration, economics, marketing, finance, and accounting. Armco offers exceptional opportunities to people with backgrounds in International Affairs, primarily because a specialization in European studies, without marketing, finance, or accounting, is sometimes enough to lead to a job offer.

Baxter International, Inc.

One Baxter Parkway
Deerfield, IL 60015

Baxter is a leading international supplier of health-care products, systems, and services. It offers 120,000 products to health-care providers in more than 100 countries, and owns plants in 23 countries. One of Baxter's largest overseas operations in terms of sales is in Japan, a large market for dialysis products. In Malaysia, home of valuable rubber reserves, Baxter makes medical gloves and catheters. In 1991, international sales rose 11 percent and accounted for about a fourth of total net sales.

Background Desired

Economics, health care, sales, marketing, advertising, administration, area studies, and pharmaceuticals.

Boeing Company

7755 East Marginal Way
Seattle, WA 98108
(206) 655-2121

Boeing is the leading manufacturer of commercial jet aircraft. It also makes missiles, helicopters, hydrofoil boats, and ground transportation systems. Its exports amounted to 20 percent of total sales. Many of Boeing's customers are from Europe and Asia.

Background Desired

Engineering, science, marketing, finance, public relations, and knowledge of aviation and missiles.

Bordens

> 277 Park Ave.
> New York, NY 10172
> (212) 573-4000

Bordens has two operating divisions of the company with international components: *Packaging and Industrial Products International* and *International Consumer Products*. At present, international sales amount to about 31 percent of total sales and international earnings are about 33 percent of total earnings. International operations are found primarily in Europe, Canada, Asia, and Latin America.

Background Desired

Business administration, finance, marketing, and accounting.

Bristol-Myers Squibb

> 345 Park Ave.
> New York, NY 10154-0037

Bristol-Myers Squibb is one of the largest pharmaceutical companies in the world. It has four main segments: *Pharmaceutical Products*; *Medical Devices*; *Nonprescription Health Products*; and *Toiletries, Beauty Aids, and Household Products*. The 50,000 employees of this company are in all parts of the world.

Background Desired

Science, advertising, marketing, finance, and accounting.

Browning-Ferris Industries

> 14701 St. Mary's
> Houston, TX 77079
> (713) 870-8100

Browning Ferris is one of the largest companies engaged in providing waste services. Subsidiaries and affiliates collect, transport, treat, and dispose of commercial, residential, and municipal solid waste and industrial hazardous wastes. More than 27,000 employees operate in the United States, Australia, Hong Kong, Netherlands, Puerto Rico, Spain, the United Kingdom, and Venezuela.

Background Desired

Environmental studies, economic development, economics, engineering, international affairs, finance, accounting, and area knowledge if you wish to work abroad.

Chesebrough-Pond's

> 33 Benedict Place
> Greenwich, CT 06830

This company is a diversified manufacturer and marketer of consumer products, including foods, children's apparel, cosmetics, fragrances, and health-care products. Some of the company's best-known brand names are Vaseline, Pond's, Cutex, Prince Matchabelli, Pertussin, and Q-tips. Overseas sales amount to about 30 percent of total sales.

Background Desired

Business administration, marketing, and accounting.

Church and Dwight

> 469 North Harrison St.
> Princeton, NJ 08543-5297

Church and Dwight Co. is the world's leading producer of sodium bicarbonate, popularly known as baking soda, or bicarb. The company specializes in developing uses for bicarb and related products which are packaged and sold under the Arm & Hammer label. The company is concentrating on laundry detergent as well as new products such as Arm & Hammer Dental Care (the first tooth paste with bicarb). In its marketing efforts, Church and Dwight is emphasizing the European Economic Community, Latin America, and Japan.

Background Desired

Marketing, accounting, finance, and public relations.

Corning Glass International

> General Inquiry
> MP-CH-02
> Corning, NY 14831
> (607) 974-9000

In its worldwide operations, Corning operates 78 plants, has operations or affiliates in more than 21 countries, and exports products to more than 90 nations. Corning produces about 60,000 different products. A large proportion of the business is in glass for electrical and electronic applications. Other substantial market areas are in products used for food preparation, such as Pyrex and Corning Ware, and fiber optics and chemical testing.

In the mid-1960s Corning decided to increase its international operations substantially. To this end, it put increasing emphasis on exports and gained majority ownership in manufacturing facilities in many countries. Most recently it has entered into a joint venture with Vitro SA of Mexico. Corning is now a multinational organization with revenue outside the United States accounting for 15 percent of the corporate total.

Background Desired

Business administration, marketing, finance, accounting, and science.

CPC International

> International Plaza
> Englewood Cliffs, NJ 07632
> (201) 894-4000

CPC is a worldwide family of consumer and industrial food businesses. It has manufacturing plants in more than 51 countries. Sales and earnings from the international market are about 60 percent of total company sales and earnings. Worldwide sales in 1991 were $6.19 billion. Its best-known consumer names are Hellman's, Mazola, Knorr, and Best Foods. For industrial customers, CPC manufactures cornstarch and glucose syrups.

International operations are organized into three divisions: *CPC Europe, CPC Latin America,* and *CPC Asia.*

Background Desired

Business administation, marketing, and accounting.

Digital Equipment Corp.

146 Main St.
Maynard, MA 01754
(508) 897-5111

Digital is a leading supplier of networked computer systems, software, and services. It offers a full range of desktop, client/server, and production and mainframe systems. Applications include research, education, health care, engineering, telecommunications, finance, software development, and industrial control. Clients have included American Express, Union Bank of Switzerland, Philips (a Dutch electronic manufacturer), Hoechst (one of Germany's largest chemical companies), and Scotland Yard. Digital does more than half of its business overseas.

Background Desired

Computer knowledge, economics, engineering and electronics, science, marketing, finance, sales, administration, public relations, and international affairs.

Dow Chemical Company

Midland, MI 48674
(517) 636-1000

Dow is one of the largest chemical companies in the United States. It manufactures primarily chemicals, basic plastics, hydrocarbons, and energy. Its *Specialties Division* produces resins and latex products, and its *Consumer Specialities Division* projects include SaranWrap and Fantastik. Dow operates 181 manufacturing sites in 33 countries.

Background Desired

Chemistry, science, marketing, finance, accounting, public relations, advertising, and international affairs.

Dun and Bradstreet

299 Park Ave.
New York, NY 10171

Dun and Bradstreet is composed of several business segments: *Information Services* (the world's leading supplier of commercial-credit information services, with operations in 27 countries and a worldwide data base covering more than 20 million businesses); *Reuben Donnelley* (compiles, publishes, and sells more than 400 directories representing 15 percent of U.S. yellow pages advertising sales); *Nielsen Marketing Research* (a worldwide leader in marketing research in the United States and 28 countries); and *IMS International* (the leading supplier of marketing-research information and services to the pharmaceutical industry throughout the world).

Background Desired

Statistics, research abilities, marketing, accounting, and finance.

DuPont

> E.I. DuPont deNemours & Company
> Wilmington, DE 19898
> (302) 774-1000

Because this foremost manufacturer of nylon and textiles is heavily engaged in the international market, there are many possibilities for those with an international background. Foreign sales account for about 47 percent of total sales. Perhaps the most available positions are for those with a heavy finance and accounting background in addition to international relations. With this background you should aim for the Treasurer's Department for work in foreign financial affairs.

Foreign financial analysis in DuPont headquarters work closely with the financial officers in DuPont's foreign subsidiaries to help develop and implement financing plans for overseas investments. They establish cash utilization and dividend policies in light of prevailing economic, political, and exchange conditions. They also review foreign financial statements and forecasts. The foreign and banking staffs likewise are involved with devaluation risks of soft currencies and with assisting in financing arrangements for joint ventures.

Background Desired

Accounting and finance for jobs in the Treasurer's Department; otherwise, marketing, chemistry, science, and data systems.

Eastman Kodak

> 343 State St.
> Rochester, NY 14650
> (716) 724-4684

Foreign photographic sales amount to about 45 percent of Kodak's total sales and 38 percent of profit. Primary manufacturing units in this field are located in England, France, Germany, Mexico, Brazil, Argentina, and Australia. The Asian, African, and Australian regions are growing faster than the Latin American region.

Background Desired

Business administration, marketing, finance, accounting, public relations, science, chemistry, and area studies.

Emerson Electric Co.

> 8000 W. Florissant Ave.
> St. Louis, MO 63136

Emerson is one of the foremost electric companies in the country. Its international sales are a major source of growth and, over the past ten years, have grown at an annual rate of 13.3 percent. During 1991, international sales grew 10.1 percent, reaching 40.5 percent of total net sales due to the strong performance of subsidaries in Latin America, the Middle East, and the Asia-Pacific region. As its markets have become increasingly global, Emerson has shifted from an export-led strategy to an investment-led strategy based on committing capital to establish maximum efficiency in Emerson's operations abroad. The company has more than 110 manufacturing locations outside the United States and is positioned to take advantage of the projected relaxation of trade barriers throughout Europe. Nonetheless, its greatest potential markets are in the Far East.

Background Desired

Accounting, finance, marketing, engineering, administration, public relations, depending on the kind of job sought.

Ernst & Young

> 787 Seventh Ave.
> New York, NY 10019

This is an international accounting firm with many multinational clients. It has offices in more than 114 countries.

Background Desired

Accounting (as a CPA in most cases) or administration. Area studies are also useful.

Exxon

225 East John Carpenter Freeway
Irving, TX 75062
(214) 444-1900

Divisions and affiliates of Exxon operate in the United States and 79 other countries. The principal business is energy, involving exploration for and production of crude oil and natural gas, manufacturing petroleum products, and transporting and selling all three. Exploring for, mining, and selling coal and uranium are other concerns of this multinational. Nuclear fuel is also produced. Sixty percent of Exxon's total invested capital is employed in its foreign operations. Foreign earnings account for more than 75 percent of total Exxon earnings. Exxon is currently concentrating its efforts in Europe and the Asia-Pacific area.

Background Desired

Petroleum engineering, business administration, finance, accounting, marketing, and Middle East studies.

Foreign Credit Insurance Association (FCIA)

40 Rector St.
New York, NY 10006
(212) 306-5000

The FCIA was created in 1961 to place American exporters on a par with their foreign competitors. It does this by insuring U.S. exports against commercial and political loss, allowing the exporter to offer credit terms, and facilitating the financing of foreign receivables.

FCIA is an association of some 50 of the leading insurance companies in the United States operating in cooperation with the Export-Import Bank (see page 77). The private insurance industry underwrites the commercial credit risks, and Eximbank covers the political risks.

Background Desired

Accounting, finance, business administration, banking, and insurance.

General Motors

> 3044 West Grand Blvd.
> Detroit, MI 48202
> (313) 556-5000

General Motors is one of the world's largest auto manufacturers. Its foreign sales account for about 33 percent of total sales. GM is targeting Europe and the Asia-Pacific region, although sales in other parts of the world are considerable.

Background Desired

Business administration, finance, marketing, accounting, and personnel.

Gillette Co.

> Prudential Tower Building
> Boston, MA 02199

Gillette is the world's leader in sales of blades and razors. The company holds a major position in North America in sales of toiletries and is among the world's top sellers of writing instruments. Manufacturing operations are conducted at 51 facilities in 26 countries, and products are distributed in more than 200 countries.

Background Desired

Business, accounting, finance, and marketing.

Glaxo Holdings

> Lansdowne House
> Berkeley Square
> London WIX 6BP
> England

Glaxo is a research-based group of companies with the purpose of discovering, developing, manufacturing, and marketing "safe, effective medicines of the highest quality." Glaxo has subsidiaries in 38 countries in Latin America, Europe, Asia, Africa, and North America.

Background Desired

Business, marketing, accounting, finance, and, if interested in the manufacturing and development of products, biology and science.

Hewlett-Packard

> 3000 Hanover St.
> Palo Alto, CA 94304
> (415) 857-1501

H-P, as it is commonly called, is a major designer and manufacturer of precision electronic products and systems for measurement and computation. Major product categories include design, measurement, and manufacturing equipment; computers and computer systems; electronic calculators; and medical electronic equipment and instrumentation. Foreign sales are 55 percent of total sales. H-P has manufacturing facilities in six European countries, seven countries in the Far East, and in Mexico, Brazil, and Australia. It has numerous offices in more than 80 countries throughout the world.

Background Desired

Marketing, electronics, engineering, sales, research, computers, and European and Far East studies.

Imperial Chemical Industries (ICI)

> Imperial Chemical House
> Millbank
> London SW 1P 3JF
> England

ICI aims to be the world's leading chemical company serving customers internationally through application of chemistry and related sciences. It operates in three main economic regions of the world: Europe, North America, and Asia-Pacific.

Background Desired

Science, chemistry, advertising, marketing, and finance.

Ingersoll-Rand

> 200 Chestnut Ridge Rd.
> Woodcliff Lake, NJ 07675
> (201) 573-0123

Operations of this company are organized into three worldwide business segments (1) standard machinery — air compressors, construction equipment, mining machinery; (2) engineered equipment — pumps, gas compressors, turbo machinery; and (3) bearings, locks, and tools. Overall, 40 percent of Ingersoll-Rand's sales are international.

Background Desired

Engineering, construction, mining, marketing, sales, finance, and international affairs.

International Business Machines

Central Employment
IBM
12 Water St.
White Plains, NY 10601

or

IBM Corporate Headquarters
Old Orchard Rd.
Armonk, NY 10504
(914) 765-1900

IBM is one of the largest suppliers of information processing equipment systems in the world. It offers customers solutions that incorporate these systems with software and communications systems to address specific needs. Forty percent of revenue comes from Europe, the Middle East, and Africa; 22 percent from Latin America and the Far East. IBM's subsidiaries overseas are wholly owned.

Background Desired

Business administration, computer technology, engineering, economics, science, area studies, international affairs, marketing, and finance.

International Flavors and Fragrances

521 West 57th St.
New York, NY 10019
(212) 765-5500

IFF is the leading creator and manufacturer of flavors and fragrances used in perfumes, cosmetics, soaps, detergents, foods, beverages, and pharmaceuticals. IFF has manufacturing plants in 23 countries. Foreign operations account for 70 percent of total sales. Sales are particularly strong in the Far East and Latin America. China is one of its fastest growing markets in the 1990s.

Background Desired

Sales, science, public relations, advertising, marketing, finance, accounting, and international relations.

International Specialty Corporation (ISC)

> 1361 Alps Rd.
> Wayne, NJ 07470
> (201) 628-3000

International Specialty Corporation is a major speciality chemical business and a leading manufacturer of building materials (through its subsidiary GAF). As of 1991, ISP's international sales had grown over the past eight years at an annual rate of 20 percent, primarily because of a growth in European sales. Asia-Pacific region sales grew at an average annual rate of 34 percent as well, but accounted for a smaller percentage of the market.

Background Desired

Sales, finance, marketing, chemistry research, area studies, and construction.

Johnson & Johnson

> One Johnson & Johnson Plaza
> New Brunswick, NJ 08933

Johnson & Johnson, with 82,000 employees and $12.45 billion in sales, is the world's largest and most comprehensive manufacturer of health-care products serving the consumer and professional markets. J&J has 166 operating companies in 52 countries around the world, selling products in more than 150 countries.

Background Desired

Marketing, accounting, finance, administration, and international affairs.

Kamsky Associates, Inc. (KAI)

> 780 Third Ave.
> Suite 1600
> New York, NY 10017-2024

Kamsky is a rapidly growing trading company that has forged its reputation in one of the most difficult markets of the world: mainland China. It is one of the relative few foreign firms approved on an official long-term basis by the State Council of China. Kamsky has an office in Beijing where it represents the interests of more than 40 companies in the People's Republic. KAI operates five divisions: projects and joint ventures (helping Western firms establish joint ventures in China); sales of Western technology to the Chinese; a trading division that brokers the exchange of raw materials; a division developing product sources in the People's Republic; and a financing and insurance division. The company is expanding its activities in other countries, including the Philippines and Brazil.

Background Desired

Economics, fluent Mandarin language, Portuguese (if applying for work in the Brazil section), business, and international studies.

McDonnell Douglas

> P.O. Box 516
> St. Louis, MO 63166

McDonnell Douglas manufactures military aircraft, commercial aircraft, missiles, and spacecraft. Its foreign sales amount to about 22 percent of total sales.

Background Desired

Engineering, science, aeronautics, marketing, finance, and public relations.

Merck and Company

> Merck International Division
> 126 East Lincoln Ave.
> Rahway, NJ 07065
> (201) 574-4000

Merck is a worldwide organization engaged primarily in the business of discovering, producing, and marketing medicines and health products. The company's operations outside the United States are conducted primarily through subsidiaries and have grown over the years. Sales outside the United States, including export sales to overseas markets, amount to about 50 percent of total sales.

Background Desired

Marketing, chemistry, finance, science, accounting, and business administration.

Millipore Corp.

> 80 Ashby Rd.
> Bedford, MA 01730
> (617) 275-9200

This company is the world's leading supplier of products used to analyze, purify, and separate the components of fluids. It also supplies biotechnology instruments and intravenous fluid devices. Foreign sales are about 61.4 percent of total sales. Millipore's business in the Pacific Rim grew 26 percent in recent years.

Background Desired

Chemistry, science, economics, marketing, finance, public relations, and accounting.

Mobil Corporation

> 3225 Gallows Rd.
> Fairfax, VA 22037-0001

Mobil is an integrated oil company with global operations. Now 125 years old, it has a strong base in petrochemicals and plastics. With 61 percent of its oil and gas production outside the United States, it processes crude oil into gasoline and sells its lubricants through a worldwide marketing network of more than 20,000 outlets. In exploration, Mobil is putting emphasis on the remote areas of Africa, Latin America, and Indonesia, as well as in the North Sea. It is also building its business in the growing economies of Asia's Pacific Rim.

Background Desired

Engineering, science, geology, marketing, accounting, finance, and international affairs.

New York Life Insurance

> 51 Madison Ave.
> New York, NY 10010
> (212) 576-7000

This company is distinguished because of the way it conducts its business. It is an excellent example of the growth of the global office. The company, though based in New York, processes its insurance claims in Ireland, where wages and operating costs are low and there is an abundant supply of skilled labor; processing costs are about 25 percent lower than those in the United States. The system works as follows: Insurance claims are collected, sent to Kennedy Airport, and put on an Aer Lingus plane each day at six P.M. The claims arrive at Shannon Airport the next morning, are taken by van to New York Life's office in Castle Island, 60 miles away, and processed on IBM terminals within seven days. The claim information is flown back to the United States, and the following day a check or letter is printed and sent to the beneficiary.

Background Desired

Computers, life insurance, accounting, and statistics.

Ogilvy & Mather Worldwide

> 309 West 49th St.
> New York, NY 10019
> (212) 237-4000

Ogilvy & Mather is the world's fifth largest ad agency group. Among its operations engaged in advertising and marketing services are the Marketing Information Sector, which includes Research International, and Retail Marketing Services, which comprise the SGE worldwide consulting and promotion companies. Together the group services more than 3,500 clients in 321 offices in 49 countries. Foreign operations account for about 50 percent of revenues.

Background Desired

Advertising, marketing, finance, research, administration, and international affairs.

Pepsico

> Pepsico World Headquarters
> Purchase, NY 10577
> (914) 253-2000

In addition to soft drinks, Pepsi is now heavily involved in snack foods, transportation, and restaurants. The growth of international profits on soft drinks, at

25 percent, exceeded the domestic growth rate. Pepsi snack food sales have also jumped 16 percent in the international market. Pepsi's international restaurant business has grown by 28 percent. Pepsi has more than 1,000 bottlers around the world, including in the former Soviet Union.

Background Desired

Business administration, economics, accounting, finance, marketing, public relations, and area studies.

Pfizer International

> 235 East 42nd St.
> New York, NY 10017
> (212) 573-2323

Pfizer is a worldwide research-based company with primary interests in health-care products, including pharmaceuticals, medical and dental specialities, and orthopedic devices. Pfizer also has a line of hospital products, specialty chemicals such as caffeine, minerals such as limestone, consumer items such as Wild Musk, animal health products, and seed and poultry gene operations. It has production facilities in more than 60 countries, and 45 percent of its sales come from overseas. Pfizer products are available in virtually every country of the world.

Background Desired

Marketing, business administration, accounting, finance, chemistry, science, and biology.

Phelps Dodge Corp.

> 2600 North Central Ave.
> Phoneix, AZ 85004-3014

Phelps Dodge is a major mining and manufacturing concern, operating mines and plants in 23 countries. It is divided into: *Phelps Dodge Mining Company* (the world's second largest producer of copper, with operations in Chile, Mexico, Peru, and South Africa), and *Phelps Dodge Industries* (its international manufacturing division in the transportation and electrical sectors, with international operations in 15 countries in South America, Europe, Asia, and Africa).

Background Desired

Engineering, marketing, manufacturing, accounting, finance, and geology.

Phillip Morris

> 120 Park Ave.
> New York, NY 10017
>
> or
>
> Phillip Morris International
> 800 Westchester Ave.
> Rye Brook, NY 10573

Phillip Morris is a huge consumer-product business consisting of tobacco (Marlboro), beer (Miller), and foods (Kraft, Oscar Meyer, and many other brands). Its international operations are on the way to achieving the size and profitability of its domestic businesses. It has representatives in most countries of the world.

Background Desired

Marketing, advertising, finance, public relations, and accounting.

Pitney Bowes

> 1 Elmcroft Road
> Stamford, CT 06926-0700
> (203) 356-5000

Pitney Bowes is the world's largest manufacturer of postage meters and mailing equipment. It also markets copiers and facsimile systems and provides financial services. Its *Dictaphone Corp.* sells business supplies and dictating equipment. Foreign Operations, in Europe and Canada primarily, account for 22 percent of total revenues. Its *Monarch Marking* subsidiary sells retail systems and price-marking products.

Background Desired

Computers, electronics, marketing, finance, accounting, public relations, and international affairs.

Texaco

2000 Westchester Ave.
White Plains, NY 10650
(914) 253-4000

Texaco's operations are worldwide, encompassing the production, transport, refining, and marketing of oil and gas products. Its international operations are divided into the following divisions: *Texaco Europe* (exploration or production in 10 countries and manufacturing or marketing operations in 11 countries); *Texaco Latin America/West Africa* (production and/or exploration in Ecuador, Colombia, Brazil, Angola, Mauritania, and Nigeria, as well as a substantial number of retail outlets in these areas); *Texaco Canada*; and *Texaco Middle East/Far East* (including Indonesia, Saudi Arabia, Australia, and the People's Republic of China).

Texaco's operations abroad are staffed largely by nationals of the countries concerned, although some opportunities exist for Americans who wish to work abroad.

Background Desired

Geology, marketing, accounting, engineering, international affairs, and sometimes fluency in European languages.

Toyoda America, Inc.

1 World Trade Center
New York, NY 10048

Toyoda America is a wholly owned American subsidiary of Toyoda Kaisha, Ltd. It imports and exports steel and other metals, textiles, industrial products, bicycles, foodstuffs, and cotton. The company plays such roles as shipping agent, purchasing agent, retailer, distributing agent, marketing research firm, and negotiating agent.

Background Desired

Marketing, trade, finance, accounting, business law, and Japanese studies.

Union Carbide

39 Old Ridgebury Rd.
Danbury, CT 06817
(203) 794-2000

In addition to the manufacture of batteries and antifreeze products, Union Carbide has now diversified into other fields: foamed plastics, electronic materials, biomedical systems, pollution abatement systems, energy, food, and pesticides.

Overseas earnings now represent about one-third of total company earnings. International operations are divided into *Union Carbide Pan America, Union Carbide Europe, Union Carbide Eastern, Union Carbide Africa and Middle East,* and *Union Carbide Canada.*

Background Desired

Business administration, marketing, finance, accounting, science and technology, engineering, and area studies.

Unisys Corp.

> P.O. Box 500
> Blue Bell, PA 19424-0001

Unisys, which acquired Sperry in 1986, manufactures computer-based network systems and software and provides related services to defense and commercial customers such as banks, insurance companies, airlines, and telephone companies. Unisys operates in about 100 countries and foreign business accounts for 50 percent for revenues.

Background Desired

Computers, engineering, science, marketing, finance, accounting, public relations, and international affairs.

Varity Corp.

> 672 Delaware Ave.
> Buffalo, NY 14209

Varity Corp. (formerly Massey Ferguson) is one of the largest manufacturers of farm machinery in the world. It also makes industrial machinery, small diesel engines, truck components, and building products. Its manufacturing facilities and associate companies are located in 15 countries. The majority of its business is in North America (43 percent) and Europe (42 percent). The other 15 percent is distributed in other parts of the world.

Background Desired

Agriculture, marketing, sales, finance, accounting, and area studies.

Waste Management

Oak Brook, IL 60521

Waste Management is one of the world's leaders in providing comprehensive environmental and waste management and related services to industry, government, and consumers. It has facilities in England, France, Italy, the Netherlands, and in South America, the Middle East, and the Asia and Pacific Rim region.

Background Desired

Science, marketing, administration, finance, and accounting, depending on the type of job desired.

WPP Group

466 Lexington Ave.
5th Floor
New York, NY 10017
(212) 210-6900

The WPP Group is a major multinational marketing services company involved in media advertising, public relations, market research, nonmedia advertising, and specialist communications. In total, the WPP Group has 625 offices in 64 countries. WPP has worked with 300 clients in the *Fortune* 500 list and 868 major national or multinational clients. The WPP Group builds and maintains such companies as Oglivy & Mather, Worldwide, J. Walter Thompson, Hill and Knowlton, and Research International. Fifty-five percent of revenues are generated in the United Kingdom or other parts of the world.

Background Desired

Advertising, marketing, research, public relations, international affairs, administration, and area studies.

General Round Up — Special Opportunities
for Those with Language Skills

1. Young and Rubicam of the United States and Dentsu of Japan, both advertising giants, have combined to start agencies in Kuala Lumpur, Malaysia, as well as Japan.
2. General Motors and Toyota cooperate on an auto assembly plant in the United States.

3. Unilever, the big Dutch company, is expanding its American interests.
4. Honda, Toyota, and Volkswagen have built auto plants in the United States.
5. Most countries allow subsidiaries of U.S. companies in its area to employ a small number of Americans. If you are abroad and looking for a job, start with the American companies in that country.

An additional list of companies that ordinarily welcome résumés from those with international training and an accounting-marketing or accounting-finance background follows. A list of companies with special interest in trade with countries of the former Soviet Union and with Eastern European countries can be found in Chapter 5.

Increasing opportunities may be available for Chinese language and area specialists as China–U.S. trade develops. Follow the financial pages of newspapers to find out which companies are doing substantial business with China.

If you wish to pinpoint targets in a specific country, refer to the invaluable *Directory of American Firms Operating in Foreign Countries*, published by Uniworld Business Publications, 50 E. 42 St., New York, NY 10017 (available in many reference libraries). It lists by country all the American firms with subsidiaries and branches in that country. Finally, refer to the Bibliography for directories of businesses and banks.

Other International Businesses

Marketing and/or Finance Organizations

Albany International	Burlington Industries
Allied Stores Marketing Corporation	Caltex Petroleum
American Metal Climax (AMAX)	Cargill, Inc.
American Importers Association	Canada Dry
American Foreign Insurance Association	Celanese Corporation
American International Underwriters Corporation	Chrysler Corporation
	Clairol, Inc.
American Machine & Foundry	Colgate Palmolive
Arabian American Oil Company	Continental Can Company
Elizabeth Arden	Continental Grain
Associated Metals & Minera	Council of the Americas
Avon Products	Crompton & Knowles Corporation
Bache & Company	East-West Trade Council
Bell & Howell	Farrell Lines
Brazilian Government Trade Bureau	Ford Motor Company
Brunswick International	*Fortune* Magazine

General Cable
General Electric
Gibney International
W.R. Grace & Company
Frank B. Hall & Company
Walter E. Heller Overseas Corporation
Hertz, Inc.
International Basic Economy
   Corporation
International Paper Company
Intsel
Intertex
Johnson & Johnson
Journal of Commerce
KLM Royal Dutch Airlines
Koppers, Inc.
Kurt Orban Company
Lehman Brothers
Lever Brothers
Liggett & Myers
Litton Industries
MBA Resources
Merrill Lynch, Pierce, Fenner & Smith
Metropolitan Life
Mitsubishi International

Mobil Oil
North American Phillips
Olin Matheson
Olivetti Corporation
Owens-Illinois
JC Penney Company, Inc.
Phillip Morris International
Phillips Petroleum
Revlon, Inc.
Richardson-Vicks
Schering Plough
J.E. Seagram and Sons, Inc.
Sperry Hutchinson
Sterling Products
E.R. Squibb & Company
Tesoro Petroleum
Trans World Airlines
Uniroyal
U.S. Gypsum
U.S.-Japan Trade Council
Vick International
Webster, Johnson & Stowell (WJS, Inc.)
Westinghouse Electric
Xerox
Young and Rubicam International

Also, as suggested earlier, consult the *Fortune* 500 list of companies.

BUSINESS-SERVICING ORGANIZATIONS

Don't forget to include in your job hunt organizations that service business in one form or another:

1. Institutes that represent a whole industry, such as the *American Petroleum Institute* and the *Aerospace Industries Association*
2. Outfits that provide information and analysis of legislative programs important to business, such as the *Chamber of Commerce of the United States*
3. Organizations that perform research for business with international interests, such as *Business International*
4. Organizations that provide briefings for business people and their families going abroad as well as briefings for U.S. ambassadors, such as the *Business Council for International Understanding*

These organizations are sometimes technically not-for-profit but, with the exception of the Business Council for International Understanding (listed in the chapter on nonprofit organizations), are included here because they are either subsidized by business or at least immediately related to industry.

Aerospace Industries Association of America

1250 I Street, NW
Suite 1100
Washington, DC 20005

This association offers guidance to the exporting segment of the aerospace industry. It also provides for an exchange of views between government and industry in order to increase aerospace exports.

Background Desired

Economics, business administration, public relations, trade, and knowledge of the aerospace industry.

American Management Association (AMA)

135 West 50th St.
New York, NY 10020

The AMA is a membership organization for all types of management development and training. Through conferences, workshops, and publications it provides a forum for members to exchange ideas concerning management education. Its *International Managment Division* is geared to executives responsible for overseas operations and coordination with overseas affiliates. This division has established management centers in Canada, Mexico, Brazil, and Belgium (which serves Western Europe and the Middle East). Programs are given in the local language, mostly by local trainees.

Background Desired

Business administration, economics, management and personnel training, conference and seminar organization, public relations, and work in publishing. Knowledge of foreign languages may be useful.

American Petroleum Institute

1220 L St., NW
Washington, DC 20037

The API fosters foreign and domestic trade in American petroleum products and promotes in general the interests of all branches of the petroleum industry.

Background Desired

Economics, statistics, and petroleum engineering or other petroleum background.

Chamber of Commerce of the United States

> 1411 K St., NW
> Washington, DC 20526

The Chamber of Commerce keeps its members informed of important legislative programs with national and international significance. Among the latter are international economic policy and relations, and international energy and/or environmental decisions.

Background Desired

Business administration, economics, congressional lobbying, and energy and environmental training or experience.

Business International

> 215 Park Ave., South
> New York, NY 10003

BI publishes a wealth of reports based on its own research on problems of interest to internationally oriented business. Among these are compensation surveys; management monographs; short- and medium-term forecasts for every region of the world as well as for individual country markets; and in-depth research reports on Latin America, Europe, and the Asia-Pacific region. Offices are located in New York, Geneva, Hong Kong, Tokyo, and London.

Background Desired

Economics, business administration, research ability, and area and country studies.

MANAGEMENT CONSULTANTS

The field of management consulting is made up of all kinds, shapes, and breeds of consultants. The function common to all consultants, big or small, general or specialized, is to respond to a need for improved performance or for a new strategy or professional advice on the part of an organization or individual.

As the need for advice and help has grown with the increasing complexity of today's world, so have the number, size, and functions of consultants grown. The services of consultants are now used by all occupations: government agencies, nonprofit organizations, banks and businesses, advertisers, accountants, and any other occupation with a problem that needs a professional solution. Nor is the client necessarily a large organization. A doctor may hire a consultant to improve the efficiency of his or her office. A regional theater may hire a consultant to institute a rational bookkeeping system or perhaps to advise how best to publicize a series of plays for a new subscription season.

It has been said that the growth in management consulting has gone "from a stream to a white-water rapid." This illustrates why management consulting can be one of the most highly paid careers in the United States.

The world's largest corporations often act as consultants to improve the performance of other companies not necessarily in the same field. For example, General Electric uses its financial wing, a sizable segment of the huge GE empire, as a consultant on financial services to clients. Some large accounting firms, for example Price Waterhouse, in addition to auditing, offer accounting and administration services to companies with accounting problems. Advertising firms offer public relations advice to companies having a problem with their image. The size of consultant firms ranges from hundreds of employees working in a huge glass-and-steel skyscraper to a single figure in a one-room office or perhaps even the bedroom of a private home.

In general, the motto of all consultants, large or small, specialized or wide-ranging, is "Your problem is my opportunity."

Management consulting may interest you enough to include these companies in your job hunt, although an international affairs background may not be sufficient to get hired.

In the first place, specializations, not necessarily international, may be required. If, for example, a management consultant firm contracts with a foreign government to revise its tax structure, it will form a team of experts to do the job. Experienced economists, taxation specialists, and financial experts will be hired in addition to an international affairs specialist. But in almost all cases these people have to be immediately productive. Because there is no training period, they usually have to arrive on the job with years of experience in their field. Unless needed to support the team, a junior professional without substantial experience is not likely to be considered.

Large engineering firms often have consulting contracts overseas. Even if you are nontechnical by nature, there still may be a place for you in the administrative, financial and general support services of these organizations. Pay is generally higher than in similar jobs at home.

If you are interested in consulting work, one of the best sources of job openings is a knowledge of consulting firms that are given contracts by U.S. government agencies. A listing of consultants awarded such contracts — with types of projects — is carried frequently in the *Federal Register,* a daily publication of the U.S. Government Printing Office. Additional information is provided in *Consultants and Contractors: A Survey of the Government's Purchase of Outside Services,* prepared by the Subcommittee on Reports, Accounting, and Management of the Committee on Governmental Affairs, U.S. Senate. The Agency for International Development also lets out contracts, information on which can be obtained from AID's Office of Contract Management. (For further information on AID, see Chapter 6.)

The following pages include only a representative sampling of consulting organizations. For a listing of directories of consultants, refer to the Bibliography.

Arthur Andersen and Co.

> 69 West Washington St.
> Chicago, IL 60602
> (312) 580-0069

Arthur Andersen specializes in planning, designing, and installing computer-based information systems. It is composed of two business units: (1) audit, business advisory and tax services, and corporate specialty services; and (2) consulting for strategic services, systems integration, systems management, and application of software produced. Its clients are in virtually all industries worldwide. Arthur Andersen has offices in many cities in the United States and in 67 countries.

Background Desired

Accounting, finance, computers, information systems, economics, and an M.B.A.

Association of Management Consulting Firms (ACME)

> 521 Fifth Ave.
> New York, NY 10175
> (212) 697-9693

ACME is a nonprofit organization whose members include domestic and international consulting organizations. Formed in 1929, it serves as a watchdog for the consulting profession, promulgating standards of practice and a code of ethics.

Some 3,400 consulting firms of various sizes currently operate in the United States employing an estimated 60,000 consultants. Some of the largest of these organizations are members of ACME.

Background Desired

Administration, law, research, economics, training skills, and an M.B.A. or Ph.D.

Booz Allen and Hamilton

> 101 Park Ave.
> New York, NY 10178
> (212) 697-1900

Founded in 1914, this firm is one of the largest and oldest international management consulting firms. It serves senior management of business and institutional organizations by developing strategies and action plans for all management functions critical to the success of an enterprise. Headquartered in New York, it serves clients throughout the world from offices in the United States, Europe, Latin America, the Middle East, and Tokyo.

Booz Allen has had more than 10,000 clients, including business and government organizations in 72 countries, more than 70 of the largest 100 companies in the world, over half of the world's 100 largest banks, and more than 400 of the 500 largest industrial corporations in the United States.

Background Desired

Political science, international affairs, economics, area studies, accounting, finance, marketing, industrial management, previous business experience, and an M.B.A. or Ph.D.

Deloitte & Touche

> One World Trade Center
> New York, NY 10048
> (212) 669-5000

or

200 Renaissance Center
16th Floor
Detroit, MI 48243

This consulting firm operates in the following fields: information technology, financial information management, health care, manufacturing, financial services, public utilities, and federal, state, and local government. It has 121 offices in the United States and 625 offices in 103 countries.

Background Desired

Finance, health care, accounting, economics, research, information management, an M.B.A. and previous experience in any of the fields for which you are applying.

Ernst & Young

787 Seventh Ave.
New York, NY 10019
(212) 773-3000

Ernst & Young is a full-service professional firm with 125 offices in the United States serving clients of all sizes in all industries and in 650 offices in more than 100 countries. Areas of practice include information technology consulting, human resources consulting, management consulting, executive search, accounting and auditing, financial planning and control, international tax services, and entrepreneurial services. Two companies, Arthur Young and Ernst & Whinney, merged to form this company.

Background Desired

Accounting, finance, information systems, human resources and personnel work, and an M.B.A. or Ph.D.

Hill and Knowlton

420 Lexington Ave.
New York, NY 10017
(212) 697-5600

Hill and Knowlton, through its acquisition of Gray International, Carl Byoir and Associates, and other public relations firms, has become one of the leading international public relations firms in the world. It has more than 1,000 clients, serving 25 percent of the world's largest companies, and has 65 offices in 25 countries. Among its locales are Canada, Latin America, Africa, Europe, the Middle East, Asia-Pacific, Australia, and New Zealand.

Hill and Knowlton also offers a management consulting service. In addition to general counseling and media relations assistance, the firm provides communications strategy development, public relations program planning, lobbying, and editorial support for corporate publications.

Background Desired

Advertising, public relations, ability to write, international relations, area studies and language, economics, and publications.

A.T. Kearney Inc.

222 South Riverside Plaza
Chicago, IL 60606
(312) 648-0111

Kearney assists industrial, commercial, and government clients in more than 90 countries to improve their overall effectiveness. Its areas of practice include marketing strategy, information management and technology, executive search, environmental policies, organization effectiveness, and litigation support.

Background Desired

Marketing, finance, environmental studies, information technology, and an M.B.A. or Ph.D.

Arthur D. Little Inc.

Acorn Park
Cambridge, MA 02140

This is one of the more diversified management consultants. Its functions include electronics, economic development, education, food, engineering, health care, and banking and insurance.

Background Desired

Economics, economic development, finance, accounting, education, and health care, depending on which aspect of the company's work you are applying for. A Ph.D. or M.B.A. is preferred.

Louis Berger International

> 100 Halsted St.
> East Orange, NJ 07019

This firm has been involved at one time or another in transportation and urban planning in the Middle East, environmental planning and water resources in the United States, railroads in Africa, information systems in Iran, and agricultural improvements in Central and South America.

Background Desired

Economics, urban and social planning, architecture, economic development, engineering, area studies, and world resources. A Ph.D. is preferred.

McKinsey and Company

> 55 East 52nd St.
> New York, NY 10022
> (212) 446-7000

McKinsey is an international consulting firm specializing in problem solving and program implementation for corporate and, to a lesser extent, government institutions. Founded in 1926, it now has 51 offices in 26 countries serving organizations in both industrial and developing nations.

Its clientele consists of organizations in all types of industry — manufacturing, automotive, transportation, banking, energy, healthcare, insurance, retailing, public utilities, and public and nonprofit sectors. About 38 percent of its work is in the United States, 48 percent in Europe, and the balance in Japan, Australia, Canada, and Latin America.

Background Desired

Research, administration, area studies, economics, marketing, finance, accounting, previous business experience, and an M.B.A. or Ph.D.

Organization Resources Counselors, Inc.

> 1211 Avenue of the Americas
> New York, NY 10020

ORC concentrates its efforts on human relationships in organizations. Drawing on its knowledge of personnel practices of many overseas companies, ORC offers counseling to organizations with large numbers of third-country and foreign national employees. It also conducts seminars and training courses in the United States and abroad dealing with current aspects of international employee relations activities.

Background Desired

International affairs, personnel studies, psychology, and business administration.

KPMG Peat Marwick

> 767 Fifth Ave.
> New York, NY 10153
> (212) 758-9700

Peat Marwick is an international professional firm that provides accounting, auditing, tax, and management consulting services through a worldwide family of partnerships with more than 300 offices in 82 countries. Consulting services include information systems, financial management, employee benefits, compensation and personnel, and executive search needs of clients.

Background Desired

Accounting, finance, human resources, information systems, and a CPA or M.B.A.

Price Waterhouse

> 1251 Avenue of the Americas
> New York, NY 10020
> (212) 819-5000

This organization provides auditing and accounting services to large and small businesses, government, nonprofit organizations, and individuals. In addition, it has a consultant wing that provides help in product development and pricing analyses for business, health-care pension, and employee benefits development and evaluation.

Overall, Price Waterhouse Management Consulting Services provides client management with business advice to improve productivity, profitability, and competitive position. Its clients include advertising agencies, banks, brokerage and investment houses, chemical companies, computer and business equipment manufacturers, engineering and construction services, insurance companies, petroleum companies, paper companies, retail businesses, and utilities. It has 460 offices in 110 countries.

Background Desired

Accounting, finance, administration, and public relations.

Towers Perrin

> 245 Park Ave.
> New York, NY 10167
> (212) 309-3400

This management consultant company was established by combining three independent consulting firms: Cresap, Tillinghast, and TPF and C. Its technical resource groups monitor economic, legal, and regulatory developments worldwide; and its computer resource groups design and modify information management systems and other computer programs. The firm has a staff of 5000 located in 69 cities throughout the world. Its areas of practice are: actuarial services, employee benefits, human resources management, operations, strategy and organization, life and health insurance, property and casualty insurance, and management services. Because this firm advertises its ability to quickly assemble professionals with various skills in every large foreign city, it would seem that most hiring abroad is of foreign nationals and that opportunities for Americans are fewer than you might want.

Background Desired

Computer work, engineering, economics, law, administration, and public relations.

GOVERNMENT CONTRACTORS

Known fondly in Washington, DC as "beltway bandits," on account of their proximity to the capital city and dependence, in some respects, on the government system for survival, government contractors keep much of the wheels and cogs of certain government agencies in operation. Essentially, government agencies like the U.S. Agency for International Development, the Environmental Protection Agency, the Department of Energy, and the Department of Defense contract a large portion of their projects to consulting firms known as government contractors.

Each year, hundreds of multimillion dollar contracts are awarded to these "beltway bandits" to carry out tasks in line with the objectives of the particular government agency. The scope of projects is vast. A book called *INTERNET Profiles: International Development Contractors and Grantees* (obtainable from Network for International Technical Assistance, Incorporated, P.O. Box 3245, Chapel Hill, NC 27515 (919) 968-8324) lists organizations that conduct government tasks related to international development. Some of the organizations listed in this book are nonprofit as well. Each entry includes a description of the company and a list of the government contracts for which it has carried out tasks. It also includes a listing of Canadian organizations.

Projects range in scope from economic development in Eastern Europe, privatization in Africa, public health in Asia, and coal bed methane control in China to computer support or systems development.

If you are unable to get into the foreign service or land a job with the federal government directly, this is a great way to get involved with international affairs in Washington and abroad. (A number of these contractors place people overseas for organizations such as the Agency for International Development.) The reason that this may be an easier way to get involved in foreign affairs is that you do not have to go through the elaborate bureaucratic steps that are entailed in becoming a civil servant. Just apply directly to the corporation that supports projects in your area of interest. Remember, too, that all of these contracts are won by these consulting firms through competitive bidding. Aside from persons with technical skills relevant to the project activities, there is a need for managers, marketers, and proposal writers.

Below is a list of a few of the many government contractors in *INTERNET Profiles*:

Abt Associates
Applied Management Sciences
Development Alternatives
Development Associates
Devres, Incorporated
Pragma Corporation
Price Waterhouse
Washington Consulting Group

POLITICAL RISK ANALYSIS

International crises in Iraq, Central America, Eastern Europe, and almost everywhere on the globe, have provided impetus for the growth of political risk analysis consultants. Many of these companies were started by and are staffed with former American military and government officials.

The general function of these firms is to assess the risk to business ventures in various parts of the world. It is an important service to many corporations because of the access it sometimes provides them to foreign leaders and to sensitive — and possibly secret — information that the firms hope to gain from consultants formerly employed in government service.

All of these firms put a premium on many years of top-level government service in U.S. foreign-oriented agencies, on area studies, and on languages. For lower-level professional jobs, economics, finances, political science, administration, publications, and public relations are desirable. The role of these organizations can be summarized by the motto of one of them: "Use us and you'll never be bothered by an Iran again."

The following are some of the prominent consultants in this growing field:

Control Risks Ltd.

> 8200 Greensboro Dr.
> McLean, VA 22101

This is a British firm that goes beyond politics and economics in its work. Starting with security problems for companies operating abroad, it now deals with a whole spectrum of risk factors. According to published reports, this firm states that its consultants have been involved in 100 kidnapping negotiations. At one time, and perhaps now as well, it has been retained by Lloyd's of London to handle ransom negotiations.

International Business Government Counsellors

> 818 Connecticut Ave., NW
> 12th Floor
> Washington, DC 20006

IBGC was founded by former CIA director William Colby. The main business of the firm is political assessment, and it focuses primarily on Latin America and Canada.

Kissinger Associates (KA)

> 350 Park Ave.
> New York, NY 10022

Unlike most of the other consultants in this field, which are forthcoming with information on their functions, Kissinger Associates is reluctant to provide information on its work. What follows, accordingly, has been obtained from other consultants and from newspaper articles that may or may not have been authorized.

KA's clients are mostly multinational corporations. By the early 1990s they included Arco, Chase Manhattan Bank, Merck, American Express, Coca-Cola, and Volvo. The company advises on foreign as well as economic policy, and is said to give introductions overseas to its clients, although members of Kissinger Associates appear not to accompany clients on their travels. Countries are often ranked in terms of stability for specific clients. For Arco, KA's contribution has been geared toward preventive measures rather than toward increasing trade. Sometimes, as with Merck, an analysis from KA is used to confirm the firm's own findings and instincts.

Multinational Strategies, Inc.

> 67 Irving Place
> New York, NY 10003

In its brochure, this organization states that its priority is to anticipate changes in the foreign environment. Clients are advised how these changes affect their operations and, more importantly, how to take advantage of them. In its risk assessments, Multinational Strategies watches more than 75 countries and dozens of world markets annually. Problems are identified, predictions made, and solutions formulated.

Safeer Company

> 1627 K St., NW
> Washington, DC 20006

Safeer (the Persian word for ambassador) was founded by Richard Helms, former director of the CIA. He has generally been a consultant on the tangled politics of the Middle East for Bechtel and other clients.

A few other consultants should be mentioned:

1. International Relations Consultants (IRC Group)
   1150 17th St., NW
   Washington, DC 20036
   Started by former diplomats Donald McHenry and Willian van den Heuvel.
2. Consultants International Group, Inc.
   1616 H St., NW
   Washington, DC 20006
   Headed by Gerard Smith, former ACDA director.

Finally, a consortium (not by any means small) consisting of Lehman Brothers Kuhn Loeb in New York (George Ball, former under secretary of state), Warburg

Paribas in London, and Lazard Frères in Paris and New York (Frank Zarb, former federal energy administrator), offers sophisticated financial advice to developing countries.

INTERNATIONAL BANKING

Until recently, international banking was one of the best sources of jobs for students of international affairs. Beginning in the 1960s, international earnings of some banks grew faster than their domestic earnings, and as this happened, these banks turned increasingly to schools of international affairs for their young talent.

Is this trend likely to continue? Not for the immediate future. After many developing countries defaulted on their loans, international earnings of lending banks plummeted. As a result, major losses in international loans have been incurred since 1987. This in turn led to a sizable cut in the recruiting of internationally trained graduating students as well as a reduction in size of the international divisions of some troubled banks.

As for the future, opinions vary. Banks are rescheduling their loans and as the creditor-debtor relationship is stabilized, recruiting may increase again. On the other hand, some students who lived through the crash of 1987 now find themselves less interested in a career either on Wall Street or in a bank.

According to some economists, the days of large-scale bank lending to developing countries are at an end. Amounts of loans to these countries may permanently level off or decline as the International Monetary Fund resumes its old role as a major source of such financing.

Because of future uncertainties, you should inform yourself about international banking prospects when you start your job hunt. A placement office or university instructor in banking subjects should be a good source of this information. Also get copies of the latest annual reports of the large banks, such as Citibank and Chase Manhattan, and compare their current and past international earnings.

What Kinds of Banks Offer the Best Chances for International Work?

You should focus your job hunt on the following:

Large American Banks

Citibank, Chase Manhattan, Bank of America, and Chemical Bank are all heavily involved in international business. In addition to commercial functions, some of them have taken on investment functions.

U.S. Branches of Foreign Banks

This is a growing source of jobs, whether or not commercial banks reduce their international hiring. The increasing number of these banks, such as the Swiss Bank and the Bank of Tokyo, stems in part from legislative changes that make it easier for foreign banks to do business in New York, and also from an increase in investments by foreign companies in American manufacturing concerns.

If you are interested in the investment side of banking, include investment banks, such as Goldman Sachs and Salomon Brothers, in your job search. These banks provide financing for businesses by floating their stocks and bonds. They are less visible than other banks because they usually do not deal directly with the public.

Savings banks offer fewer opportunities for you because of the lack of international content of most of their work. The same holds for savings-and-loan associations, many of which are also in bankruptcy.

Overseas Assignments and Languages

Only in the case of the largest commercial banks, such as Bank of America, Citibank, and Chase Manhattan, is a substantial part of your career likely to be spent overseas. In other cases, you will ordinarily do your international work at U.S. headquarters.

For this reason, language proficiency is particularly valued at the largest banks, where assignments abroad are expected, or at American branches of foreign banks.

Entry-Level Jobs

Your initial assignment in international commercial banking is liable to be full-time academic course work in the case of the largest institutions, or academic work mixed with on-the-job training in the case of smaller institutions.

In both cases, the thrust of your training will be to acquaint you with procedures and problems in the evaluation of applications for loans. Since credit analysis is the heart of much commercial banking, there will be stress on accounting procedures, problems of finance, and money and banking practices.

When training is over, you may be assigned as a loan investigator or credit analyst, depending on the credentials you bring with you. After some years of creditable performance, you may reasonably expect to become a branch bank manager.

An M.B.A. is not necessarily the best degree to get for international work at a bank. If you have a masters degree in international affairs, or the equivalent from one of the schools mentioned in Chapter One, and have taken the accounting-finance courses suggested for business, you will often fare better than with the M.B.A. — except at investment banks. These banks still prefer the M.B.A.s, since ordinarily business school graduates will have had more intensive training in finance and investment.

The happy fact is that commercial banks are usually more flexible about the background required of applicants than are businesses. This flexibility extends beyond the conventional accounting-finance courses to include economics and a general international affairs background — depending on the bank. Entry-level jobs in major banks for those with an M.B.A. or M.A. in international affairs pay $40,000 or more.

Which Banks Require What Background?

The flexibility of background requirements often varies in proportion to the size of the bank and the comprehensiveness of its training program. Citibank and Chase Manhattan, which offer extensive training programs, are more relaxed on the academic qualifications of candidates than are the smaller banks with limited training facilities.

In other words, even if you have not taken accounting and finance courses, you may still be given serious consideration by the largest financial institutions. The theory on which these banks operate is that it is easier to teach finance and accounting to applicants who have an international affairs background than it is to teach international affairs to students equipped with the basic technical courses in banking. A few other banks, such as Chemical Bank, will accept an economics background in lieu of banking courses.

Many large banks publicize their interest in finding the best "human being" rather than the graduate with the best technical background. They will send campus recruiters who majored in English or biology, perhaps to deemphasize the importance of conventional accounting and finance studies. Still, when you look at the statistics of those hired by these banks, you will find that the large majority of successful candidates have had courses in finance and accounting. Smaller banks may be forgiven for requiring that you have technical banking course before they will interview you. Since they do not have the training facilities of the largest banks, they want you to be fully productive as soon as you come on board.

Note: Many of you who are attracted to international banking because of the possible availability of jobs may not belong in this career. Before you blithely scramble into position, be sure you know what you're doing. And that means, as we have seen, find out — through reading, experimenting, and talking with friends and relatives in banking — what it's like and whether it's right for you.

B.A. — M.A. — M.B.A. — Ph.D.? A Summary

For international business the optimum degrees, in order of preference, are:

1. M.B.A., or M.A. in international affairs with accounting and finance courses. Your chances increase if you select your targets as indicated earlier in this chapter.
2. B.A. For lower-level jobs.
3. Ph.D. Be prepared to answer the question "Why are you applying for a business job when you seem to have prepared yourself for teaching or research?"

For international commercial banking they are:

1. M.A. in international affairs with accounting and finance courses.
2. M.B.A. Ranks first for investment banking.
3. B.A. As above.
4. Ph.D. As above.

The rest of this chapter is devoted to a listing of some major banks, primarily commercial, with international interests.

BankAmerica

World Banking Group
BankAmerica
P.O. Box 37000
San Francisco, CA 94137

BankAmerica Corp., which owns the Bank of America, recently merged with Security Pacific Corporation to become one of the largest banks in the United States. As a result, it will be undergoing some restructuring for the next few years. Nonetheless, BankAmerica Corp. has offices in more than 35 countries. Retail banking services to the individual remain the largest area of its business, but the bank increasingly services businesses and institutions.

The bank has built a vast global network of branches, subsidiaries, affiliates, and representatives throughout the world. In 1991, 36 percent of BankAmerica Corporation's net income came from overseas. Latin American and the Caribbean provided half of that income, followed by Europe, the Middle East, Africa, and Asia. Overall, 19 percent of the bank's loans are international.

Background Desired

Usually accounting and finance, but economics is also acceptable, and occasionally a background limited to general international studies.

Bank of Boston

> 100 Federal St.
> Boston, MA 02110

The Bank of Boston, formerly called the First National Bank of Boston, is New England's only global bank. The international activities of this bank account for a substantial share of total corporate earnings. Several thousand employees work in the bank's international network in 25 countries. Branches, offices, and wholly owned subsidiaries are located in Europe, Asia, and especially Latin America. Most kinds of financial assistance are offered to overseas customers as well as to U.S. clients: export and import financing, project financing, foreign exchange, letters of credit, and money transfer operations.

Background Desired

Banking and finance, economics, and area studies (Latin America).

Bank of New York

> 48 Wall St.
> New York, NY 10286

The Bank of New York Company is the 16th-largest bank holding company in the United States. It provides a complete range of banking and other financial services to corporations and individuals worldwide through its five basic businesses: *Corporate Banking, Retail Banking, Securities Processing, Trust and Investment Management*, and *Financial Market Services*. Its foreign activities consist of banking, trust, and securities processing services provided to customers outside the United States, principally in Europe and Asia.

Background Desired

Banking, finance, and economics, in addition to international studies.

Bankers Trust

> International Banking Department
> Bankers Trust Company
> One Bankers Trust Plaza
> New York, NY 10006

This is one of the nation's largest banks, with assets of more than $20 billion. From its first international offices established in the 1920s in London and Paris, it now has a network of branches, subsidiaries, and representative offices throughout the world. Sixty percent of Bankers Trust's earnings come from activities outside the United States.

Background Desired

Accounting and finance studies and/or economics, plus international affairs.

Brown Bros. Harriman and Company

> 59 Wall St.
> New York, NY 10005

Brown Bros. Harriman has provided a full range of commercial banking services for more than 150 years. It is also an investment manager and adviser, corporate finance specialist, securities broker, short-term money investor, foreign exchange adviser, and investment research house.

Its *International Banking Department* helps American corporations with their international expansion plans, aids foreign interests with direct investment in the United States, and provides them with international financial assistance. Though committed to correspondent banking relationships abroad, Brown Bros. Harriman is directly involved in offshore money and capital markets through its London affiliate and a branch office in the British West Indies. In Zurich a wholly owned subsidiary serves investment clients throughout Western Europe.

Background Desired

An M.B.A., preferably with a specialty in finance or banking.

Chase Manhattan

> One Chase Manhattan Plaza
> New York, NY 10081

The Chase Manhattan Corporation is the holding company of the Chase Manhattan Bank. The corporation has assets of about $100 billion and employs more than 42,000 people in 60 countries. Its major components are:

1. *Global Private Banking* serves individual clients through a network of banking and trading locations in more than 20 countries around the world. Included

in its services are portfolio management, trust and estate planning, and deposit and credit services.

2. *Global Corporate Finance* has four regional sectors — North America, Asia-Pacific, Europe, and the Western Hemisphere — through which it helps clients with cross-border and in-country transactions.

3. *Global Risk Management* provides services related to foreign exchange, derivative products, financial and energy futures, and banking services to the security industry.

Chase has one of banking's most complete training programs, combining on-the-job experience with classroom instruction. Rigorous training in academic subjects pertinent to banking lasts up to a year. Because of the demanding nature of the work, some students do not finish the program, either by their own choosing or at the request of the bank. Those who do finish the work find themselves desirable commodities on the job market should they wish to leave Chase. Smaller banks without training facilities often try to hire these Chase trainees, who on graduation need no further training to be fully productive.

Background Desired

General international background, plus finance and accounting or economics.

Chemical Bank

> 270 Park Ave.
> New York, NY 10017

The name "Chemical" comes from the company's original purpose when it was founded in 1824, the manufacture of chemicals. Since then, Chemical has emerged as the "complete" bank for the consumer, and is now the second largest bank in the United States, thanks to its merger with Manufacturers Hanover Corporation.

Latin America is the bank's oldest international market, with the result that today there is a broad market penetration in every major country in the area. Its first European branch, in London, opened in 1960, and the company's business in Western Europe has developed rapidly. Although the bank has emphasized business with multinational companies in Europe, its relationships with indigenous companies in the area have grown. Asia and the Middle East are becoming increasingly important to Chemical; in Africa, its business is conducted primarily through a network of correspondent banks. Its first African office was opened in the Ivory Coast.

Background Desired

Banking and finance or economics, plus international affairs.

Citicorp and Citibank

University Relations — MA Recruiting
Citibank
578 Lexington Ave.
12th Floor
New York, NY 10043
(212) 559-1000

Citicorp is a global financial services organization with a staff of 82,000 serving individuals, businesses, governments, and financial institutions in more than 3,300 locations in 92 countries throughout the world.

At the end of 1990, Citicorp instituted a "Five Point Plan" designed to restore the company's earnings' momentum and increase its capital strength. Two key objectives of the Five Point Plan are building core businesses and developing a strong customer focus.

Citicorp's core franchises are its global consumer business and its global finance business, both of which serve customers in the world's developing and developed markets alike.

1. *Global Consumer* business serves 13.8 million households through 1,666 offices in 37 different countries. In addition to branch banking, Global Consumer includes the Citibank Private Bank, the mortgage business, and insurance and credit card businesses outside the United States.
2. *Global Finance* operations serve corporations and financial institutions in both the sophisticated capital market economies of Japan, Europe, and North America and in more than 60 of the world's developing economies, where banking services tend to be traditional and based in local currency. Citibank has a longstanding presence in many markets around the world. In 1991, it celebrated 75th anniversaries in a number of Latin American countries, and in 1992 it is celebrating its 90th anniversary in Asia. Global Finance businesses serve both local and multinational customers, including governments and other financial institutions, and provide transactional as well as corporate finance services.

An interesting sidelight on Citibank's global impact: In Germany its name has been changed to KKB. It is the first bank to have a standardized name throughout Europe as part of a Pan-European marketing effort.

Management Associate positions are available to upcoming graduates in most parts of the world. A Management Associate (MA) would be initially assigned to a function or business area in which one has demonstrated an interest and ability and where there is a defined business need.

MAs may be hired into a program lasting anywhere from 3 to 24 months, depending on the business. During that time, they may rotate through a number of functional areas and/or businesses where they gain hands-on experience.

At the completion of the program, MAs may be actively involved in identifying their next position.

Citibank's Summer Associate (SA) Program is viewed as an entree to its MA Program. All candidates for SA positions must be one year away from graduation.

All candidates must be presently authorized to work in their desired country on a permanent basis.

Background Desired

An M.B.A. is most helpful. Otherwise a general international background with some economics will probably get you an interview, but accounting-finance studies combined with international training will get you a more serious hearing.

Continental Illinois Corporation

> International Banking Department
> Continential Illinois Corporation
> 231 South La Salle St.
> Chicago, IL 60697

CI Corp is a bank holding company and *Continental Bank* is its main subsidiary. The corporation operates 126 units in 39 countries.

Through its *International Banking Department*, Continental acts as a multinational bank, attracting deposits, making loans, and providing other financial services to promote trade and investment. Its network of branches and subsidiaries extends to Europe, Asia, Latin America, Africa, and Australia. Lending officers provide international services to U.S. and foreign customers; they also travel to various parts of the world to sell bank services to corporations and governmental entitites. The International Banking Department also operates domestic subsidiaries in New York, Los Angeles, and Houston that specialize in international trade and overseas financing. The New York unit includes one of the major foreign exchange trading operations in the world.

Background Desired

Banking and finance subjects, or economics, plus international affairs.

French-American Banking Corporation

> 200 Liberty St.
> New York, NY 10005

This corporation is a wholly owned American subsidiary of the Banque Nationale de Paris. With its $25 billion in assets and about 2,000 branches, agencies, affiliates, and representative offices in 60 countries, the BNP is the largest French and European bank and one of the largest banks in the world.

It works closely with foreign governments and European and American companies, offering all of them a full range of loan, investment, and correspondent banking services. It focuses particularly on financing foreign trade and is active in the Eurocurrency market.

Background Desired

Banking, finance, accounting, and economics, plus international affairs. An M.B.A. is preferred.

Goldman Sachs

> 85 Broad St.
> New York, NY 10004

Goldman Sachs is one of the world's leading international investment banking firms, providing a variety of financing services to corporations, government, and investors around the world. It has 14 offices in the United States, London, Tokyo, and Zurich.

Goldman Sachs raises capital in the United States and overseas for governments, their agencies, and U.S. and foreign corporations. It uses the following major capital markets for international borrowers: the U.S. long-term public bond market; private placement with U.S. institutional investors; the commercial paper market; the international capital market, the largest segment of which is the Eurobond market; and project financing.

Background Desired

Finance, accounting, banking, and economics. An M.B.A. is preferred.

HSBC Group

> HSBC Holdings
> 1 Queens Road Central
> Hong Kong

In 1991, the Hong Kong and Shanghai Bank and its subsidiaries were reorganized under a new holding company, HSBC Holdings. With consolidated assets of more than $160.5 billion, it is one of the largest and most strongly capitalized banking organization in the world, and provides a comprehensive range of financial services — commercial banking, merchant banking and capital markets, consumer finance, securities, investment, and insurance — through an international network of some 1400 offices in more than 50 countries. Among the cities in which HSBC operates are Beirut, Bogota, Buenos Aires, Caracas, Frankfurt, Hong Kong, Jakarta, London, Madrid, Manila, Nairobi, Nassau, Panama City, Paris, Rio de Janeiro, São Paulo, Seoul, Singapore, Sydney, and Tokyo.

Background Desired

Banking, finance, accounting, and economics. An M.B.A. is preferred.

Marine Midland Bank

One Marine Midland Center
Buffalo, NY 14240

or

HSBC Holdings, Inc.
Group Head Office
1 Queens Road Central
Hong Kong

Marine Midland Bank is the principal entity in the Hong Kong and Shanghai Banking Corporation (HSBC). In addition to a broad range of credit services, international activities include money management services covering foreign exchange, Eurodeposit business, and other money market instruments. An international treasury services group provides custom counseling on all corporate money matters.

Background Desired

Banking and finance and economics, plus international affairs.

J.P. Morgan and Co.

60 Wall St.
New York, NY 10260-0060

J.P. Morgan is the holding company for subsidiaries engaged globally in providing financial services to corporations, governments, institutional investors, private firms, and nonprofit organizations. One of its subsidiaries is Morgan Guaranty Trust Co. J.P. Morgan has 11 principal offices in major cities in Europe, 9 in the Asia-Pacific region, and 4 in Latin America. It also manages the Euroclear system, which is the largest international clearance and settlement organization linking participants from 63 countries to 27 securities markets around the world.

Background Desired

Banking, finance, and economics. An M.B.A. is preferred.

Morgan Guaranty Trust Company

23 Wall St.
New York, NY 10015

Morgan Guaranty is a wholly owned subsidiary of J.P. Morgan and Company. The bank is the fourth largest in the United States in terms of assets, but it has fewer customers than any other large bank because it is a "corporate" bank — its clients are predominantly corporations and institutions. Only a few individuals — in the United States and abroad — with substantial income and assets are serviced. Recently it has moved into investment banking.

Its offices are in London, Paris, Brussels, Antwerp, Amsterdam, Frankfurt, Düsseldorf, Munich, Zurich, Milan, Rome, Tokyo, Hong Kong, Singapore, and Nassau. It has representative offices in Madrid, Beirut, Sydney, Jakarta, Kuala Lumpur, Manila, São Paulo, and Caracas.

Its *International Banking Division* is organized by area as well as by specialized departments, such as Foreign Exchange, International Money Management, Commodities and Export, and International Currency and Eurocurrency Trading.

Background Desired

Banking, finance, and economics. An M.B.A. is preferred.

Philadelphia National Corporation

P.O. Box 7618
Philadelphia, PA 19101

or
Philadelphia International Bank
180 Maiden Lane
New York, NY 10038

The *International Banking Group* of the corporation engages in foreign banking and international financing activities, including making loans to foreign banks, governments, and multinational corporations; letter-of-credit financing; foreign exchange trading; and related financial services. Besides its head offices in Philadelphia, the group maintains offices in Nassau and Luxembourg, and representative offices in London, Manila, São Paulo, Panama City, Tehran, and Sydney.

The Banking Group includes not only the international division of the Philadelphia National Bank but also two wholly owned subsidiaries of the bank: the *Philadelphia International Bank*, headquartered in New York, which provides international banking services to foreign and multinational clients; and the *Philadelphia International Investment Corporation*, headquartered in Philadelphia, which engages in foreign investment and financing activities.

Background Desired

Banking, finance, and international relations, with economics.

Wells Fargo International Trade Services Group

420 Montgomery St.
San Francisco, CA 94163

Wells Fargo International Trade Services Group is a wholly owned subsidiary of Wells Fargo in California. It provides complete international commercial banking facilities. These services include receiving deposits from those living outside the United States and from those in the United States if the funds are used for international purposes. The International Trade Services (ITS) Group handled more than 200,000 overseas banking and currency exchange, trade financing, and payment transactions for California clients in 1991. In conjunction with the Hong Kong and Shanghai Banking Corporation Ltd. (HBSC), clients have access to 1,000 branches overseas and 400 Wells Fargo correspondent banks. ITS issued more than $1.5 billion letters of credit and other trade commitments in 1991.

Background Desired

Banking, finance, and/or economics, plus international affairs.

Following is a more complete listing of banks, primarily commercial with international interests, as well as a list of major foreign banks located in New York. As indicated earlier, these banks should be a major target for those of you who have international training, language proficiency, and accounting-finance courses.

Other International Banks in New York, Washington, DC, and Canada

Bank of Montreal

Bank of Nova Scotia

Export-Import Bank of the United States (See page 77.)

Federal Reserve Bank (New York)

Federal Reserve Bank (Washington) (See page 111.)

Kuhn Loeb

Lehman Brothers

National Bank of North America

Republic National Bank of New York

United States Trust Company of New York

White Weld & Company

Major Foreign Banks in New York

Algemene Bank Nederland N.V.

Allied Irish Banks Ltd.

Atlantic Bank of New York

Banca Commerciale Italiana

Banca Nazionale Del Lavoro

Banco di Napoli

Banco di Roma

Banco di Sicilia

Banco do Brasil Sociedade Anonima

Banco Popular de Puerto Rico

Bank Hapoalim, B.M.

Bank Leumi Trust Company of New York

Bank of Montreal Trust Company

Bank of Tokyo Trust Company

Banque Nationale de Paris

Barclays Bank International, Ltd.

Barclays Bank of New York

Bayerische Vereinsbank (Union Bank of Bavaria)

Canadian Bank of Commerce/Trust Company

Crédit Commercial de France

Crédit Lyonnais

Crédit Suisse

Credito Italiano

Dai-Ichi Kangyo Bank, Ltd.

Daiwa Bank Trust Company

Deutsche Bank AG

European-American Bank and Trust Company

French-American Banking Corporation

Fuji Bank and Trust Company

Habib Bank, Ltd.

Hong Kong & Shanghai Banking Corporation

Industrial Bank of Japan

Israel Discount Bank of New York

Korea Exchange Bank

Lloyds Bank International, Ltd.

Mitsubishi Bank, Ltd.

Mitsui Bank, Ltd.

National Bank of Pakistan

National Westminster Bank, Ltd.

Nippon Credit Bank, Ltd.

Philippine National Bank

Royal Bank of Scotland, Ltd.

IBJ Schroder Bank and Trust Company

Standard Chartered Bank, Ltd.

State Bank of India

Sumitomo Bank, Ltd.

Swiss Bank Corporation

Toronto Dominion Bank and Trust Company

Toyo Trust and Banking Company, Ltd.

UBAF Arab American Bank

UMB Bank and Trust Company

Union Bank of Switzerland

United Bank, Ltd.

Westdeutsche Landesbank Girozentrale

Yasuda Trust and Banking Company, Ltd.

Regional Banks in the United States

In addition to the Philadelphia National Corp., Continental Illinois Corp., and Bank of Boston mentioned previously, there are a large number of regional banks with active international interests:

California	First Interstate Bank of California 707 Wilshire Blvd. Los Angeles, CA 90017
	Security Pacific National Bank 333 South Hope St. Los Angeles, CA 90071
	Wells Fargo Bank 420 Montgomery St. San Francisco, CA 94163
Connecticut	Connecticut National Bank 777 Main St. Hartford, CT 06115
Florida	Southeast First National Bank of Miami 100 South Biscayne Blvd. Miami, FL 33131
Illinois	First National Bank of Chicago One First National Plaza Chicago, IL 60670
	Harris Trust and Savings Bank 111 West Monroe St. Chicago, IL 60690
	Northern Trust Company 50 South La Salle St. Chicago, IL 60675
Massachusetts	Shawmut Bank of Boston One Federal St. Boston, MA 02211
Minnesota	Norwest Bank Sixth and Marquette Minneapolis, MN 55479
North Carolina	Nations Bank Charlotte, NC 28255
	Wachovia Bank and Trust Co. P.O. Box 3099 Winston-Salem, NC 27150

Ohio	Ameritrust Company 900 Euclid Ave. Cleveland, OH 44101
	National City Bank National City Center Euclid and Ninth Sts. Cleveland, OH 44114
Pennsylvania	Fidelity Bank Broad and Walnut Sts. Philadelphia, PA 19101
	First Pennsylvania Bank 1500 Market St. Center Square Building Philadelphia, PA 19101
	Mellon Bank Mellon Square Pittsburgh, PA 15230
	Pittsburgh National Bank Fifth Ave. and Wood St. Pittsburgh, PA 15222
Texas	Nations Bank 901 Main St. Dallas, TX 75202
Washington	Seafirst Bank 701 Fifth Ave. Seattle, WA 98104
Wisconsin	First Wisconsin National Bank of Milwaukee 777 East Wisconsin Ave. Milwaukee, WI 53202

9

NONPROFIT ORGANIZATIONS

We now temporarily abandon the world of profit-making for the world of non-profit organizations. Compared to the standardized job-seeking procedures in business and banking, and especially to the competitive application process of the U.S. government, nonprofit organizations operate informally. There are a diversity of application forms, and sometimes there are no forms at all.

WHAT IS A NONPROFIT ORGANIZATION?

The U.S. government and the United Nations are not run for profit, but they are public enterprises and their size and importance warrant separate consideration. What we are now considering are the myriad organizations in the private sector to which profit making is irrelevant and indeed impossible, considering their functions, such as helping refugees, making the public aware of foreign policy issues, helping American students traveling abroad, family planning, placing foreign students in American homes and schools, arranging study trips to Russia, analyzing issues before the General Assembly, researching and promoting human rights, supporting community development in African nations, exhibiting art from Southeast Asia.

All of these organizations service people in various ways and are intended to enhance the public good. Some have consultative status with the United Nations and are known as NGOs (nongovernment organizations); a few cooperate with the U.S. government on some of its minor functions, such as hosting foreign officials in the United States. Others operate without relationship to either the government or the United Nations.

A few of these organizations are large (the Ford Foundation); many are so small that their offices are cubbyholes, open only part time and staffed by volunteers.

If you are out for personal profit, you will hardly be attracted to organizations that make none. Except for the largest of these organizations, the entry salaries are about the lowest you will find on the international totem pole (fortunately, mid- and top-level positions offer respectable salaries). In close competition for the dubious award of poor initial reimbursement are the publishing and journalism jobs. (More about this in Chapter Ten.)

However, if you are service-oriented and wish to work on behalf of people and worthwhile ideas — or if you are turned off by the competitive rat race around you, disturbed by the bureaucracy of the United Nations and the government, and willing to accept a lower salary in return for job satisfaction — the nonprofit world may be right for you.

Don't be thrown off by the opprobrious appellation "do-gooder," which you may hear about employees of nonprofit organizations. The term conjures up an image of idealistic, but disorganized, woolly-minded, and inefficient individuals. Not necessarily so. Many employees of these organizations are hardheaded administrators, economists, scientists, and sociologists who "do good" in the best sense of the term.

The funding of these organizations is often precarious. Many of them depend on private donors who, in a down stock market, pull their purse strings tight. Corporate donors may also be less generous in a recession. Lack of financial support in trying times often results in budget cuts and curtailed projects for which you may be admirably qualified. Job possibilities, then, may depend not only on the size of the organization, but also on the state of the economy and particularly the state of business — an ironic dependence if the business world has turned you off from the beginning.

You may notice that quite a few nonprofit organizations seem to have overlapping functions. Some of them seek "to increase understanding among peoples," and this phrase appears again and again in the description of functions publicized by their public relations officials. You will also notice that several organizations are involved with "global interdependence," others with "hemispheric solidarity," and many seem concerned with economic development in Latin America, population problems, and environmental issues. There is undoubtedly duplication. Still, the enormity of the job to be done in increasing both understanding and development may justify the number of organizations in these fields. The question of efficiency of operations (couldn't the job be better done by combining all these smaller organizations into one master conglomerate?) can reasonably be posed. That the question arises at all highlights the state of the nonprofit organization today: its independence and goodwill plus a certain amount of inefficiency and lack of discipline.

Since very few of these organizations have branches overseas, work will almost always be at U.S. headquarters. Business trips abroad for short-term conferences or consultation take place only with the largest nonprofit organizations, and even then only occasionally.

Because travel is rare, language fluency is seldom needed. An exception exists in the case of some headquarters jobs involving research from original sources, where translation ability may be required. A background in area studies, however, may be at a premium in nonprofit organizations geared to a particular region, such as the Asia Society, the Citizen Exchange Council, or the Center for Inter-American Relations.

Internships

If you cannot find a paying job in a nonprofit organization, you may wish to consider an internship in this field. Voluntary work is a valuable way of gaining experience and may subsequently lead to a job. If you decide to go the internship route, consult the *International Directory for Youth Internships*, a compilation of internships with the United Nations, its specialized agencies, and nongovernmental organizations, available at the Council on International and Public Affairs, 777 U.N. Plaza, New York, NY 10017.

*   *   *

The nonprofit organizations listed below are the most important with international interests. They are grouped under the following headings: Foreign Affairs (p. 229); Area Interests (p. 252); Educational, Cultural, and Exchange (p. 271); Economics and Economic Development (p. 282); Environment, Energy, and Population (p. 292); Business and Labor (p. 301); Relief, Rehabilitation, Health, and Human Rights (p. 307); Organizations that Work for Peace (p. 321); and Others (p. 325). Organizations and centers attached to universities, such as the Economic Growth Center at Yale and the Research Institute on International Change at Columbia, are not included here because any jobs that may open up will probably be filled from within.

For each organization we will list some of the qualifications usually desired of an applicant should a job opening occur. (Some organizations may depend on volunteers with few, if any, jobs ever available. Still, if motivated and qualified, do not hesitate to apply.) Any necessary academic degree will be noted. If not noted, a B.A. or M.A. is acceptable, depending upon the type of job applied for. Organizations marked with an asterisk (*) are relatively large and are more likely to have a job opening from time to time. Check addresses before you write or visit, since there is much movement, especially among the smaller of these organizations. They can pass out of existence with alarming frequency. For a complete listing of nongovernment organizations that have consultative status with the Economic and Social Council of the U.N., consult *Non-Governmental Organizations at the United Nations: Identity, Role, and Functions*, by Pei-Heng Chiang. Although the book was written in 1981, it is still useful and can be found in the U.N. library in New York. A list of directories of various types of nonprofit organizations is found in the Bibliography.

FOREIGN AFFAIRS

American Political Science Association

> 1527 New Hampshire Ave., NW
> Washington, DC 20036

This is an organization for students and professors interested in the study of government and politics. It publishes the *American Political Science Review*, a quarterly journal of scholarly articles and book reviews in political science, including international affairs.

Background Desired

International relations, editing skills, and administrative experience. An M.A. or Ph.D. is preferred.

Carnegie Council on Ethics and International Affairs

> 170 East 64th St.
> New York, NY 10021

The Carnegie Council, formerly the Council on Religion and International Affairs, was established in 1914 by Andrew Carnegie. Since its beginning it has acted to support its strong belief that ethics, as informed by moral and religious traditions, is an integral component of any policy decision. The interrelationship of ethics and foreign policy is thus a unifying theme of all Carnegie Council programs, which include seminars, discussions, lectures, and the publication of books, pamphlets, newsletters, case studies, and an annual journal, *Ethics and International Affairs*. The Carnegie Council also hosts an Education and Studies program, a Leadership program, and Asian programs.

Background Desired

International affairs, conference and seminar organizing, and publishing. M.A. preferred.

Council on Foreign Relations, Chicago*

>116 South Michigan Ave.
>Chicago, IL 60603

The council engages in a program of foreign policy seminars, briefings, study groups, conferences, and publications designed to serve its large constituency in the Chicago area. It generally gives priority to issues of international economic policy.

Among the council's program are an annual conference on a specialized international topic, a noon lecture series, a lecture forum subscription series, a women's luncheon forum supplemented by evening meetings, a secondary-school program of seminars and workshops for teachers, and a corporate service program. In summary, the council aims to increase the Chicago public's awareness of international issues.

Background Desired

International relations, foreign policy, economics, economic development, and conference and seminar organization. An M.A. or Ph.D. is preferred.

Center for Strategic and International Studies*

>1800 K St., NW
>Suite 400
>Washington, DC 20006

Once affiliated with Georgetown University, the CSIS is now independent. It employs a full-time staff of 150 and more than 60 interns. Its mission is to advance the understanding of emerging world issues in the areas of international security, politics, economics, and business. It has 12 program areas, 6 regional and 6 functional.

CSIS maintains ties with institutions in countries as diverse as Venezuela, Poland, Malaysia, and South Africa. CSIS outreach to the Pacific region is amplified by the Pacific Forum's regional network, which links 20 Asia-Pacific research institutes. CSIS publications — and there are many — are designed to shed light on a special problem by defining its origins, importance, possible evolution, and policy options.

Background Desired

International affairs, regional studies, economics, business, research ability and experience, and administration. An M.B.A. or Ph.D. is desirable.

Council on Foreign Relations, New York*

58 East 68th St.
New York, NY 10021

The origins of the council lay in the disappointment of its founders in what they considered a lack of understanding of international affairs in the United States. Its membership of several thousand persons throughout the country is made up of individuals with special interest and experience in international problems.

In order to increase the awareness of Americans of the importance of international issues, the council conducts meetings to give its members an opportunity to talk with knowledgeable U.S. and foreign officials. It does not take any position on questions of foreign policy.

The studies program of the council explores questions of international importance through individual scholarly research by its professional staff and through study groups and conferences involving members and nonmembers. Since 1922 the council has published the quarterly journal *Foreign Affairs*.

The *Committees on Foreign Relations* are another important facet of the council. Thirty-seven of these committees, located in as many U.S. cities, schedule meetings from time to time on problems of international relations. The purpose of this program is to help develop in important U.S. communities a nucleus of informed opinion on current issues of international affairs. The committees are almost always run by volunteers, but even if involvement in a local committee may not bring a job, it does provide contact with individuals who have similar interests.

Background Desired

International affairs, foreign policy, economics, and area studies. A Ph.D. is preferred for scholarly research. For some administrative jobs, a B.A. suffices. For *Foreign Affairs*, editing.

Council on International and Public Affairs

777 U.N. Plaza
Suite 9A
New York, NY 10017
(212) 972-9877

This organization, formerly called Conference on World Affairs, seeks to "promote the study of the problems and affairs of the peoples of the United States and other nations of the world through conferences, research, publications, and other means."

The council operates in four main areas: (1) improvement of college and university instruction so that the policy analysis skills of students can be strengthened and applied to important public issues; (2) increase of citizen participation in world affairs; (3) an international literature and arts program to strengthen "world cultural literacy of Americans and other peoples"; and (4) a program in international science and technology.

Background Desired

International relations, publishing, communications, and conference and seminar organization. An M.A. or Ph.D. is preferred.

Foreign Policy Association*

> 729 Seventh Ave.
> New York, NY 10019
>
> or
>
> 1800 K St., NW
> Washington, DC 20006

FPA has as its purpose the development of an "informed, thoughtful, and articulate public opinion on international affairs." FPA provides informational and educational materials and television programs, and sponsors meetings designed to increase American interest in foreign policy issues. Its *Great Decisions Program* and briefing book involves thousands of people, mainly at the secondary and university level, in discussion groups on world affairs throughout the country. Through Great Decisions ballots and meetings in Washington, FPA's national participants make their views known to governmental policy makers. FPA also publishes a *Headline* series and *Foreign Policy Briefs*, kits with briefing cards on current world problems that are used by voter groups and political candidates.

Background Desired

International relations, foreign policy, economics, area studies, communications studies and experience, and public relations. An M.A. or Ph.D. is preferred for most jobs.

Fund for Democracy and Development

> 2033 M St., NW
> Washington, DC 20036

The fund was established to mobilize private aid for humanitarian purposes in the former Soviet Union. Former President Nixon is honorary chairman of the fund, and former Vice-President Mondale is co-chairman.

Background Desired

Soviet studies, international affairs, relief, and philanthropy.

Institute of Current World Affairs

The Crane Rogers Institute
4 West Wheelock St.
Hanover, NH 03755

The institute (also known as the Crane-Rogers Foundation) provides a limited number of long-term fellowships to persons of exceptional ability to enable them to work on foreign or problem areas of significance to the United States.

Background Desired

Administration, area studies, and international relations. If the job is an administrative one, a B.A. may be acceptable.

Institute of Defense Analysis*

400 Army-Navy Dr.
Arlington, VA 22202

IDA aims to promote national security by conducting studies and analyses on matters of interest to the U.S. government. Originally, IDA's research was done almost exclusively for the Department of Defense; in this role it came under attack from students in the 1960s because of its assistance to the military during the Vietnam War. Now there has been some broadening of its role and it assists other government agencies in problems of significant national and international interest. IDA's program includes science and technology, systems evaluation, communications research, foreign affairs, and social studies.

Background Desired

Science, military technology, foreign policy, national security, computer science, international relations, and economics. A Ph.D. is preferred.

Institute for Democracy in Eastern Europe

>48 East 21st St.
>3rd Floor
>New York, NY 10010

IDEE is dedicated to promoting independent social movements in Eastern Europe. It publishes *Uncaptive Minds*, a quarterly publication that provides information and opinions on political and social affairs in Eastern Europe. A recent edition included such articles as "Ukraine: What Kind of Independence," "Poland: The First Free Parliament," and "Estonia, Latvia, Lithuania: Starting Anew Amidst the Rot of the Old."

Background Desired

Eastern European studies, political science, and international affairs.

Institute for East West Security Studies

>360 Lexington Ave.
>New York, NY 10017

The Institute for East West Security Studies provides a forum for experts from multiple disciplines to examine issues such as economic reform and democratization in Eastern Europe and the former Soviet Union; Western assistance to the region; and political, military, and environmental security. The Institute has an office in Prague.

Background Desired

Eastern Europe or Soviet studies, security studies, and economics.

Kettering Foundation*

>200 Commons Rd.
>Dayton, OH 45459

The Kettering Foundation conducts both theoretical and operational research in the practice of politics at the community, national, and international levels. The object of the Foundation's work is the development of new ways to address fundamental problems in politics. Its particular focus is on the resources the public brings to bear in meeting its responsibilities in politics. The Foundation's efforts are concentrated in the area of international affairs, public policy, public–government relationships, community politics, and public leadership education. It has sponsored programs of nongovernmental diplomacy among such regions as the United States and the former Soviet Union and China, and conducted a national assessment of how citizens, the press, and officials respond to major policy issues. The Foundation's work is carried out by staff, associates, student research assistants, and international scholars-in-residence.

Background Desired

International relations, economics, economic development, Third World country studies, communications, teaching, and educational studies. An M.A. or Ph.D. is preferred.

National Committee on American Foreign Policy

232 Madison Ave.
New York, NY 10016

The National Committee "seeks to stimulate informed interest in and concern for the serious problems confronting the U.S. in its foreign relations." To this effect, it holds discussion meetings almost every month, sponsors symposia on foreign policy questions, and publishes a bimonthly newsletter. It also organizes special study missions to countries or regions that are the focus of foreign policy issues important to the United States.

Background Desired

International affairs, foreign policy, research, administration and conference organization, and public relations.

National Democratic Institute for International Affairs

1717 Massachusetts Ave., NW
Washington, DC 20036

The NDI aims to promote and strengthen democratic institutions overseas. Working with political parties and other institutions, NDI conducts nonpartisan programs to support democratic political development in new and emerging democracies. During 1991, NDI continued its programs in Albania, Bangladesh, Bulgaria, Cameroon, Chile, Cuba, Ethiopia, Guinea, Hungary, Mexico, Namibia, Paraguay, Poland, Romania, Senegal, South Africa, Zambia, and republics of the former Soviet Union.

Background Desired

Politics and the political process, area studies and languages, administration, and public relations.

National Endowment for Democracy

> 1101 15th St., NW
> Washington, DC 20005

Established by Congress in 1983 and subject to its oversight, this organization aims to strengthen democratic institutions around the world through nongovernmental efforts.

The endowment is funding programs in five substantive areas: encouragement of strong independent trade unions and business associations, as well as cooperatives and women's and youth groups, promotion of strong political parties committed to the democratic process; education, culture, and communications (support for publications as well as other communications media and training programs for journalists); research (on "particular regions or countries where the Endowment has a special interest"); and international cooperation (encouragement of regional and international cooperation in promoting democracy).

Background Desired

Political science, economics, trade unions, communications, research, administration, business, and public relations.

National Strategy Information Center

> 140 East 56th St.
> New York, NY 10022

The objective of the NSIC is to conduct educational programs in international security affairs. It tries to encourage "civil-military partnership" in the belief that an informed public opinion is necessary to the establishment of a defense system in the United States capable of protecting the country.

NSIC carries out its program by holding seminars and conferences on national security matters, conducting workshops on geopolitics and defense budgets, and publishing books and papers to inform the public on strategy and military security.

Background Desired

National security, military studies, and research ability.

Social Science Research Council

605 Third Ave.
New York, NY 10016

Fellowships are offered for doctoral dissertation research in the social sciences to be carried out in Africa, Asia, Latin America, the Near and Middle East, or Western Europe. Programs are designed to support scholars who intend to become specialists in the area in which the research is conducted.

Background Desired

Full-time enrollment at a U.S. or Canadian university and completion of all Ph.D. requirements except the dissertation.

Twentieth Century Fund

41 East 70th St.
New York, NY 10021

The purpose of the fund is to inform and stimulate national public debate on critical issues. It sponsors individual scholars pursuing independent research efforts and also uses task forces composed of distinguished authorities to report on policy issues in the fund's research program.

The fund's research concentrates on six broad areas: (1) economics, finance, and government regulation; (2) urban affairs and poverty; (3) media and communications; (4) governance; (5) global politics and economics; and (6) U.S. foreign politics. Among some of the international subjects researched are: how domestic economic and regulatory issues are affected by the globalization of trade and financing; United States relations with Europe, Japan, and Latin Ameria; and arms control.

Background Desired

Economics, international affairs, economic development, nuclear technology, arms control, area studies, and research ability. A Ph.D. is preferred.

United Nations Association of the USA*

485 Fifth Ave.
New York, NY 10017

or

1010 Vermont Ave., NW
Suite 904
Washington, DC 20005

The philosophy of this organization is expressed in the following quote: "The United Nations is the only institution in the history of man that has become indispensable before it has become possible." Putting its faith in the United Nations, the UNA is not unwilling to admit its weaknesses, but emphasizes its strengths and potential.

UNA seeks to stimulate American public opinion in support of constructive U.S. policies in the United Nations. It tries to develop new ideas on how to make the United Nations more effective, and provides American citizens with factual information on current U.N. issues through its information, research, education, and community action programs.

UNA conducts a variety of programs. Its *Policy Studies Program* brings together independent panels of experts in specific fields to apply their knowledge to controversial international programs. The *Economic Policy Council* examines international economic issues and their impact on U.S. relations with industrialized and developing countries. The *Public Information Service* works with the media and Congress, trying to get across to the American public objective information about the United Nations and its activities.

UNA is the official coordinating body for the annual observation of National United Nations Day, on October 24. Although headquartered in New York, UNA has a Washington office that feeds information on the United Nations to Congress and the Executive Branch.

Background Desired

International organizations, international relations, economics, disarmament and military technology, public relations, research ability, and publications experience. An M.A. or Ph.D. is preferred.

World Affairs Councils

These councils exist in most major U.S. cities. In general, their function is to help Americans gain a better understanding of significant issues in U.S. foreign policy and to stimulate informed citizen participation in world affairs. At one time directly connected with the Foreign Policy Association, these councils are now independent and provide their own funding and programming. Most of the councils depend to a large extent on volunteers, although there are a few paid positions in the largest councils.

Background Desired

International affairs, economics, foreign policy, and occasionally area studies. A B.A. may be acceptable.

How to Apply

A list of councils and related community organizations follows. If you are interested in working for a specific council, contact it at the address indicated.

World Affairs Councils and Related Community Organizations

Alabama	Executive Director Alabama World Affairs Council CIS, Auburn University Montgomery, AL 36193-0401 (205) 271-9391
Alaska	Executive Director Alaska World Affairs Council 524 W. Fourth Ave., Suite 204D Anchorage, AK 99501 (907) 276-8038
	President Juneau World Affairs Council P.O. Box 201 Juneau, AK 99802 (907) 586-2763
	President World Affairs Council of Sitka P.O. Box 798 Sitka, AK 99835 (907) 774-5533
Arizona	Executive Director World Affairs Council of Arizona 6850 East Main St. (Ramada Valley HO) Scottsdale, AZ 85251
California	President World Without War Council 1730 Martin Luther King Jr. Way Berkeley, CA 94709 (415) 845-1992
	Department of Political Science California State University at Chico Chico, CA 95929
	President Los Angeles World Affairs Council 900 Wilshire Blvd., Suite 230 Los Angeles, CA 90017 (213) 628-2333

President
World Affairs Council of the Monterey Bay Area
2951 Peisano Rd.
Monterey, CA 93953
  (408) 375-4804

Director
World Forum of Silicon Valley
990 Blair Court
Palo Alto, CA 94303
  (415) 321-3828

Chairman
World Affairs Council of the Desert
P.O. Box 1928
Rancho Mirage, CA 92270
  (619) 325-9317

President
World Affairs Council of Inland Southern California
Riverside Community College
4800 Magnolia Ave.
Riverside, CA 92506
  (714) 682-4505

President
World Affairs Council of Sacramento
650 University Ave., Suite 102E
Sacramento, CA 95825
  (916) 929-4570

Executive Coordinator
World Affairs Council of San Diego
635 C St., Suite 400
San Diego, CA
  (619) 235-0111

Executive Director
World Affairs Council of Northern California
312 Sutter St., Suite 200
San Francisco, CA 94108
  (415) 982-2541

Executive Director
World Affairs Council of Orange County
P.O. Box 1926
Santa Ana, CA 92702
  (714) 835-2564

Colorado

Executive Director
Colorado Springs World Affairs Council
P.O. Box 608
Colorado Springs, CO 80901
  (719) 633-2011

Director
Rocky Mountain Forum on International Issues
University of Denver
Denver, CO 80208

Program Chairman
IIE/Denver World Affairs Council
700 Broadway, Suite 112
Denver, CO 80203
  (303) 837-0788

Connecticut

Executive Director
World Affairs Center of Greater Hartford, Inc.
770 Asylum Ave.
Hartford, CT 06105
   (203) 549-7121

Executive Director
The Forum for World Affairs
5 Landmark Square, Suite 105
Stamford, CT 06901
   (203) 356-0340

Delaware

Treasurer
World Affairs Council of Wilmington
900 Market Street Mall
Wilmington, DE 19801
   (302) 421-7937

District of Columbia

Executive Director
ACCESS
1730 M St.
Washington, DC 20036
   (202) 785-6630

International Director
Am. Ass'n. of Community Colleges and Jr. Colleges
One Dupont Circle, Suite 410
Washington, DC 20036
   (202) 293-0200

Acting Executive Director
American Association of Retired Persons
601 E. St., NW
Washington, DC 20049
   (202) 434-2000

President
American Foreign Service Association
2101 E St., NW
Washington, DC 20037
   (202) 338-4045

President
Atlantic Council of the United Staes
1616 H St., NW
Washington, DC 20006
   (202) 347-9353

Director of Communications
Center for Strategic and International Studies
1800 K St., NW, Suite 400
Washington, DC 20006
   (202) 887-0200

Director, School Programs
Foreign Policy Association School Program
1726 M St., NW
Washington, DC 20036
   (202) 293-0046

Executive Director
General Federation of Women's Clubs
1734 N St., NW
Washington, DC 20036
   (202) 347-3168

Deputy Executive Director
League of Women Voters of the U.S.
1730 M St., NW — 10th Floor
Washington, DC 20036
(202) 429-1965

President
Meridian House International
1630 Crescent Place, NW
Washington, DC 20009
(202) 667-6800

Executive Director
National Council of World Affairs Organizations
1726 M St., NW
Suite 800
Washington, DC 20036
(202) 293-1051

Director, Washington Office
National Council of World Affairs Organizations
1726 M St., Suite 800
Washington, DC 20036
(202) 785-4703

Executive Director
National Council Returned Peace Corps Volunteers
2119 S St., NW
Washington, DC 20006
(202) 462-5938

President
Overseas Development Council
1717 Massachusetts Ave., NW, Suite 501
Washington, DC 20036
(202) 234-8701

President
The Middle East Institute
1761 N St., NW
Washington, DC 20036
(202) 785-1141

President
World Affairs Study Program
1630 Crescent Place, NW
Washington, DC 20009
(202) 667-6800

Executive Director
World Federalist Association
418 Seventh St., SE
Washington, DC 20003
(202) 546-3950

President
Youth for Understanding International Exchange
3501 Newark St., NW
Washington, DC 20016
(202) 966-6808

Florida

Miami Council on World Affairs
P.O. Box 8123
University of Miami
Coral Gables, FL 33124
(305) 284-4303

President
Naples Council on World Affairs
P.O. Box 1434
Naples, FL 33939
(813) 774-7847

Executive Director
Florida International Alliance
400 South Atlantic, Suite 104
Ormond Beach, FL 32074
(904) 672-3874

Sahlman Company
609 West Horatio
Tampa, FL 33606
(813) 251-4242

Georgia

Executive Director
The Japan-America Society of Georgia, Inc.
225 Peachtree St., NE, Suite 801
Atlanta, GA 30303
(404) 524-7399

President
The Southern Center for International Studies
320 West Paces Ferry Rd., NW
Atlanta, GA 30305
(404) 261-5763

President
Savannah Council on World Affairs
P.O. Box 10231
Savannah, GA 30326

Hawaii

President
East-West Center
1777 East-West Rd.
Honolulu, HI 96848
(808) 944-7100

Executive Director
Pacific and Asian Affairs Council
2999 Kaala Street
Honolulu, HI 96822
(808) 941-6066

Illinois

Continuing Ed. in International Affairs
University of Illinois at Urbana-Champaign
302 East John St., Suite 202
Champaign, IL 61820
(217) 333-1465

President
Chicago Council on Foreign Relations
116 South Michigan Ave.
Chicago, IL 60603
(312) 726-3860

President
Peoria Area World Affairs Council
Illinois Central College
East Peoria, IL 61635

Whiteside Forum 150
P.O. Box 51
Morrison, IL 61270
  (815) 654-4419

World Affairs Council of Central Illinois
P.O. Box 2233
Springfield, IL 62701
  (217) 744-8953

Director of Public Affairs
The Union League Club
65 West Jackson Blvd.
Chicago, IL 60604
  (312) 427-7800

World Affairs Council of Effingham County
P.O. Box 1137
Effingham, IL 62401
  (217) 342-9211

Peoria Area World Affairs Council
305 W. Cruger #5
Eureka, IL 61530
  (309) 467-3721

West Central Illinois Council of World Affairs
23 Leland Ave.
Jacksonville, IL 62650
  (217) 245-4381

President
Quad Cities World Affairs Council
2401 11th St.
Molie, IL 61265
  (217) 333-1465

President
World Affairs Council of Mount Vernon
Box 907
Mount Vernon, IL 62864-0907
  (618) 244-5871

Chairman
World Affairs Conference of North Western Illinois
Rock Valley College
Rockford, IL 61101
  (815) 226-2600

Indiana

Executive Director
Social Studies Development Center, Indiana U.
2805 East Tenth St.
Bloomington, IN 47405
  (812) 335-3838

Vice President
Indiana Council on World Affairs
Union Building, Room 574
620 Union Drive
Indianapolis, IN 46202
  (219) 274-6999

Director
Indiana Council on World Affairs
Institute of Transnational Business
Ball State University
Muncie, IN 47306
   (317) 285-5207

Iowa

Executive Director
Iowa City Foreign Relations Council
120 International Center
Iowa City, IA 52242
   (319) 335-0335

President
Quad-Cities World Affairs Council
2623 Fair Ave.
Davenport, IA 52803
   (319) 324-5722

President
Quad-Cities World Affairs Council
RR# 3, Box 336A
Muscatine, IA 52761
   (319) 263-8250

Project Coordinator, Midwest Program
The Stanley Foundation
216 Sycamore
Muscatine, IA 52761
   (319) 264-1500

Executive Director
Louisville World Affairs Council
International Center, U. of Louisville
Louisville, KY 40292
   (502) 588-6602

Louisiana

Director
Foreign Relations Association of New Orleans
611 Gravier St., 408 International Building
New Orleans, LA 70130
   (504) 523-2201

Maine

Administrative Director
World Affairs Council of Maine
U. of Southern Maine
96 Falmouth St.
Portland, ME 04103
   (207) 780-4551

Maryland

Executive Director
Baltimore Council on Foreign Affairs
World Trade Center, Suite 312
Baltimore, MD 21202
   (301) 727-2150

Executive Director
Association for International Practical Training
320 Park View Building, 10480 Little Patuxent Pkwy.
Columbia, MD 21044-3502
   (301) 997-2200

Massachusetts

Executive Director
World Affairs Council of Boston
22 Batterymarch St.
Boston, MA 02109
  (617) 482-1740

Executive Director
World Affairs Council of Western Mass., Inc.
P.O. Box 4234
Springfield, MA 01101-4234
  (413) 733-0110

Michigan

Chairperson
Center for Peace and Conflict Studies
5165 Gullen Mall
Detroit, MI 48202
  (313) 577-3468

President
Economic Club of Detroit
920 Free Press Building
Detroit, MI 48226
  (313) 963-8547

Director
Detroit Council for World Affairs
Center for Peace and Conflict Studies
5229 Cass Ave., Room 101
Detroit, MI 48202
  (313) 577-3453

Executive Director
World Affairs Council of Western Michigan
1607 Robinson Rd., SE
Grand Rapids, MI 49507
  (616) 458-9535

Minnesota

Executive Director
Minnesota International Center
711 East River Rd.
Minneapolis, MN 55455
  (612) 625-0842

Mississippi

Special Assistant to the Governor
Governor's Office
P.O. Box 139
Jackson, MS 39205
  (601) 359-2971

Missouri

Executive Director
International Relations Council
210 Westport Rd.
Kansas City, MO 64111
  (816) 531-0089

Executive Director
World Affairs Council of St. Louis
212 North Kings Highway
St. Louis, MO 63108
  (314) 361-7333

New Hampshire

President
New Hampshire Council on World Affairs
11 Rosemary Lane
Durham, NH 03824
  (603) 862-1683

New Jersey

Executive Director
School of American and International Studies
Ramapo College
505 Ramapo Valley Rd.
Mahwah, NJ 07430
   (201) 767-3293

New Mexico

President
Santa Fe Council on Foreign Relations
P.O. Box 1223
Santa Fe, NM 87501
   (505) 982-4931

New York

Executive Director
Buffalo Council on World Affairs
Pitt Petri Building, Suite 213
864 Delaware Ave.
Buffalo, NY 14209-2008
   (716) 883-0547

Executive Vice President for Programs
AFS Intercultural Programs, Inc.
313 East 43rd St.
New York, NY 10017
   (212) 949-4242

President
Citizen Exchange Council
12 West 31st St., Fourth Floor
New York, NY 10001
   (212) 643-1985

Assoc. Dir.: Internatl. Programs
Council on Foreign Relations
58 East 68th St.
New York, NY 10021
   (212) 734-0400

President and Executive Director
Council on International Educational Exchange
205 East 42nd St., 16th Floor
New York, NY 10017
   (212) 661-1414

President
Foreign Policy Association
729 Seventh Ave.
New York, NY 10019
   (212) 764-4050

Executive Director
International Christian Youth Exchange (ICYE-US)
134 West 26th St.
New York, NY 10001
   (212) 206-7307

Executive Vice President
National Jewish Community Relations Advisory Council
443 Park Ave. South
New York, NY 10016
   (212) 684-6950

President
The American Forum, Inc.
45 John St., Suite 1200
New York, NY 10038
  (212) 732-8606

Vice President
The Asia Society
725 Park Ave.
New York, NY 10021
  (212) 288-6400

Coordinating Director Outreach Services
The Japan Society, Inc.
333 East 47th St.
New York, NY 10017
  (212) 832-1155

North American Director
The Trilateral Commission
345 East 46th St.
New York, NY 10017
  (212) 661-1180

Director
World Affairs Council of Long Island
Southampton Campus of Long Island University
Southampton, NY 11968
  (516) 283-4000

President
Syracuse World Affairs Council
RFD 2
Lafayette, NY 13084
  (315) 473-8741

Executive Director
Lake Placid Council on Foreign Relations
P.O. Box 845
Lake Placid, NY 12946

North Carolina

Executive Director
World Affairs Council of Western North Carolina
UNC-Asheville North Carolina
c/o Dept. of Pol. Sci., Univ. of No. Carolina
One University Heights
Asheville, NC 28804
  (704) 251-6023

Executive Director
Charlotte Council on World Affairs
UNCC — Center for International Studies
Charlotte, NC 28223
  (704) 547-2442

Chairman, Executive Committee
Triangle World Affairs Council
Hamilton Hall 070A, UNC
Chapel Hill, NC 27514
  (919) 962-2211

North Carolina World Center
615 Willard Place
Raleigh, NC 27603
   (919) 834-4040

Ohio

Executive Director
Ohio Valley International Council
Ohio University, Burson House
Athens, OH 45701
   (614) 593-1838

President
Cincinnati Council on World Affairs
432 Walnut Street, #300
Cincinnati, OH 45202
   (513) 621-2320

President
Cleveland Council on World Affairs
539 Hanna Building
1422 Euclid
Cleveland, OH 44115-1901
   (216) 781-3730

Executive Director
Columbus Council on World Affairs
Two Nationwide Plaza, Suite 705
Columbus, OH 43215-3840
   (614) 461-0632

Executive Director
Dayton Council on World Affairs
P.O. Box 9190
Wright Brothers Branch
Dayton, OH 45409
   (513) 229-2319

Oklahoma

Coordinator
International Visitor's Council
P.O. Box 1373
Norman, OK 73070
   (405) 321-5644

World Affairs Forum Chair
International Council of Tulsa
616 South Boston Ave., Suite 616
Tulsa, OK 74119
   (918) 584-4685

Oregon

Executive Director
World Affairs Council of Oregon
121 SW Salmon St., Suite 320
Portland, OR 97204
   (503) 274-7488

Willamette World Affairs Council
P.O. Box 11458
Eugene, OR 97440
   (503) 342-5625

Pennsylvania

President
World Affairs Council of Philadelphia
206 South Fourth St.
Philadelphia, PA 19106
   (215) 922-2900

President
National Council of World Affairs Organizations
3416 Brookdale Dr.
Pittsburgh, PA 15241
   (412) 835-3687

President
World Affairs Council of Pittsburgh
400 Oliver Ave.
Pittsburgh, PA 15219
   (412) 281-7970

Executive Director
World Affairs Council of Reading & Berks Co.
R.D. #1 Welsh Rd.
Reading, PA 19607
   (215) 775-3832

Rhode Island

President
World Affairs Council of Rhode Island
72 Arcade Building
Providence, RI 02903
   (401) 421-0401

South Carolina

Director
Columbia Forum on World Affairs
Institute for International Studies
University of South Carolina
Columbia, SC 29208
   (803) 777-8180

President
World Affairs Council of Charleston
2413 Briggers Hill Rd.
Charleston, SC 29487
   (803) 763-7091

Tennessee

President
World Affairs Council of Memphis
577 University
Memphis, TN 38112
   (901) 725-1056

Executive Director
Arts and Education Council
424 Georgia Ave.
Chattanooga, TN 37403
   (615) 267-1218

Texas

Executive Director
Dallas Council on World Affairs
World Trade Center, P.O. Box 58232
Dallas, TX 75258
   (214) 748-5663

Chairman
Austin World Affairs Council
P.O. Box 50237
Austin, TX 78763
   (512) 474-7550

Vice President (Adm.)
Fort Worth Council on World Affairs
309 West Seventh St., #1500
Fort Worth, TX 76102
   (817) 332-3421

Executive Director
Houston World Affairs Council
1107 Shepherd Dr.
Houston, TX 77019-3604
(713) 522-5262

Director, ICASALS
Texas Tech University
Lubbock, TX 79409
(806) 742-2218

Executive Director
World Affairs Council of San Antonio
900 Northeast Loop 410: Suite D 200
San Antonio, TX 78209
(512) 829-7381

Executive Director
East Texas Council on World Affairs
600 Green Lane
Tyler, TX 75701
(214) 597-6768

Gulf Coast Council on Foreign Affairs
8001 Palmer Highway
Texas City, TX 77590
(409) 938-1211

Vermont

Executive Director
Vermont Council on World Affairs
Trinity College
Burlington, VT 05401
(802) 863-3539

Virginia

President
Close Up Foundation
44 Canal Center Plaza
Alexandria, VA 22314
(703) 706-3300

President
World Affairs Council of Greater Hampton Rds.
6409 Eleanor Court
Norfolk, VA 23508
(804) 445-1584

Washington

Executive Director
World Affairs Council of Seattle
Madison Hotel, Suite 526
515 Madison St.
Seattle, WA 98104
(206) 682-6986

World Affairs Council of Tacoma
827 Tacoma Avenue N.
Tacoma, WA 98403
(206) 272-2216

Wisconsin

Director
Institute of World Affairs
U. of Wisconsin — Milwaukee
P.O. Box 413
Milwaukee, WI 53201
(414) 229-6094

Councils Offshore   Executive Director
                                          Ramstein Council on International Relations
                                          c/o CINCUSAFE Political Advisor
                                          APO, New York 09012

Worldwatch Institute

> 1776 Massachusetts Ave., NW
> Washington, DC 20036

Worldwatch seeks to anticipate global problems and social trends. Through its publications and research, Worldwatch focuses public attention on emerging international issues. Its concerns cover a broad area: global energy alternatives; environmentally induced illnesses; the changing status of women and its impact on society; current global trends in population growth; and economic and political discontinuities facing the world in the last years of this century. The small staff of the Institute is said to be "future-oriented."

Background Desired

Energy and environmental studies, population studies, economics, foreign policy, and research ability. An M.A. or Ph.D. is preferred.

AREA INTERESTS

Acción International

> 130 Prospect St.
> Cambridge, MA 02139

This organization specializes in research, evaluation, and implementation of development programs in Latin America. Acción focuses on the problems of low-income populations and stresses the need for self-help in local, regional, and national development plans.

Background Desired

Economic development, economics, Latin American studies, knowledge of Spanish and Portuguese, agricultural studies, and sociology.

African-American Labor Center

1400 K St., NW
Washington, DC 20005

The AALC was established by the AFL-CIO in 1964 to assist and strengthen free democratic trade unions in Africa. Major activities of the center include worker education, leadership and vocational training, cooperatives and credit unions, social services, and study and exchange programs for Africans engaged in trade unionism.

Background Desired

Trade unionism, African studies and/or experience, African languages, industrial relations, vocational training, and teaching. A B.A. is usually sufficient.

American Committee

109 11th St., SE
Washington, DC 20003

Established in 1974, this organization aims to strengthen official and public understanding of the complex overall relationship between the United States and the former Soviet Union by providing accurate information and expert analyses. The committee's work is based on the conviction that common-sense businesslike relations with Russia are essential to the interests of the United States. The nearly 500 members of the committee — Republicans, Democrats, independents — include many of the key people involved in U.S.-Soviet relations since the end of World War II.

Background Desired

Soviet studies and language, administration, and conference organization.

American Committee on Africa

198 Broadway
New York, NY 10038

The committee is devoted to supporting African people in their struggle for freedom and independence. ACOA also informs Americans about significant African issues and mobilizes public support on behalf of African freedom.

To carry out its objectives, the committee has established the *African Fund* to support African liberation movements. It also arranges meetings, conferences, and speaking tours in the United States for African representatives.

Background Desired

Public relations, fund raising, African studies and experience, and administration. A B.A. is accepted.

American Council on Germany

14 East 60th St., Suite 606
New York, NY 10022

This organization, as might be surmised from the name, seeks to promote better understanding between the United States and Germany. Drawing on resources from both countries, the council sponsors group discussions, personal exchanges, and joint working projects. In addition, it supports efforts by government, academia, and business that can yield benefits to both peoples.

The *John J. McCloy Fund*, which was a gift to the council from the German government, provides fellowships to young Germans and Americans, giving each the opportunity to work in the other country. Fellowships have been in the fields of trade unionism, journalism, state and municipal government, law, and creative writing.

Other council projects include biennial meetings of American and German leaders to examine urgent global issues, biennial meetings of American and German young adults, workshops, seminars, lectures, and programs for freshman legislators of both countries.

Background Desired

German studies and language, economics, administration, exchange program experience, seminar and conference organization, and public relations. An M.A. or Ph.D. is preferred.

American Educational Trust

P.O. Box 53062
Washington, DC 20009

American Educational Trust is a foundation incorporated in Washington, DC, by retired Foreign Service officers "to provide the American public with balanced and accurate information concerning U.S. relations with Middle Eastern States." A monthly publication, *The Washington Report on Middle East Affairs*, endorses a land-for-peace formula for the Palestine problem. It also claims to support moderate Israeli, Iranian, and Arab leaders.

Background Desired

Middle East studies and language, research capability, writing and editorial talents, and public relations.

American Jewish Committee*

> 165 East 56th St.
> New York, NY 10022

In addition to local and domestic goals, the AJC is very much involved internationally. It helps Israel's efforts to safeguard her existence; it supports the United Nations in its human rights work; it protects the rights of Jews in countries where they may be oppressed; and it assists Jews in all lands to enjoy equal status with other inhabitants in those countries.

Background Desired

International relations, Middle East studies, and human rights work. A B.A. may be accepted.

American-Mideast Educational and Training Services*

> 1100 17th St., NW
> Washington, DC 20036

AMIDEAST is what used to be known as American Friends of the Middle East. Formerly a small organization that encouraged cultural exchange between Americans and the people of the Mideast, it is now involved in all aspects of the development of human resources in the Middle East and Africa.

AMIDEAST's newest programs concern technical training in areas where rapid economic growth places a premium on management and technological skills. Under contracts with corporations and governments, AMIDEAST services help increase the reserve of trained manpower — teachers and administrators, personnel managers, pilots, accountants, computer programmers, electronics experts, and many other kinds of technicians.

Background Desired

Middle East studies and languages, business administration, vocational train-ing, personnel work, computer studies, electronics, and accounting.

American-Scandinavian Foundation

> 725 Park Ave.
> New York, NY 10021

This foundation advances cultural relations between the United States and Scan-dinavian countries. Among the programs carried out are exchange programs; publication of books and periodicals; and cultural projects such as concerts, lecture tours, and exhibitions of arts and crafts.

Background Desired

Scandinavian studies and/or languages, cultural activities, exchanged programs, and publishing skills. A B.A. may be accepted.

American Zionist Youth Foundation

> 110 East 59th St.
> New York, NY 10022

The foundation offers both summer and long-term programs to bring American youth into contact with Israel. Summer programs, for college and high-school students, range from kibbutz living to archaeology seminars to art and dance workshops. Long-term programs involve a spring semester at Tel Aviv Univer-sity and other work-study programs in Israel.

Background Desired

Middle East studies, and a strong commitment to Israel. A B.A. is accepted.

Americas Society

> 680 Park Ave.
> New York, NY 10021

In a very general way, the center works toward strengthening understanding between the United States and other nations in the Western Hemisphere. The society has a *Public Affairs Program*, which provides for seminars and conferences on current political and economic problems of the hemisphere; a *Literature Program*, which promotes the publication in the United States of Latin American and Caribbean fiction, poetry, and drama; a *Visual Arts Program*, which holds exhibits in the center's art gallery; and a *Music Program*, which brings Latin American music and performers to audiences in the United States.

Background Desired

Latin American studies and languages, cultural studies, conference organization, and museum experience. A B.A. is sometimes accepted.

Amigos de las Americas

> 5618 Star Lane
> Houston, TX 77057

Amigos has two purposes: leadership development opportunities for North American youth, and improved public health in Latin America. Through Amigos, young North American volunteers get leadership training while serving in public health projects in Mexico, the Caribbean, and Central and South America. Amigos has operated continuously since 1965 and has placed many thousands of volunteers in 13 countries in Latin America. Currently the program operates in Mexico, Costa Rica, Brazil, Ecuador, Paraguay, and the Dominican Republic.

Background Desired

Latin American studies, Spanish, health, community development, and a belief in what Amigos wishes to accomplish.

Asia Foundation*

> 2301 E St., NW
> Washington, DC 20037

The foundation aims to strengthen Asian educational, cultural, and civic activities with American assistance. It makes private American support available to Asian individuals and institutions that are helping to modernize and develop their own societies. It also encourages cooperation among Asian, American, and international organizations working toward these goals.

Background Desired

Cultural studies and experience, Asian studies, exchange of individuals, and fund raising. A B.A. is occasionally accepted.

Asia Society*

725 Park Ave.
New York, NY 10021

The Asia Society is dedicated to increasing American understanding of Asia. It is concerned with both the traditional arts and humanities, and with contemporary social, political, economic, and cultural issues.

Asia House Gallery, one of the best known of the society's programs, introduces many Americans to Asian art treasures. The *Performing Arts Program* brings to America the finest Asian theater, music, and dance. The society's *Education Program* seeks to strengthen the study of Asia throughout the curriculum of American schools at all levels.

The society also has a *Meetings and Studies Program,* which brings outstanding Asian and Western scholars, politicians, and economists before American audiences, at Asia House and elsewhere in the country. This program depends on the advice and participation of the society's *Country Councils,* each of which is composed of Asia Society members with special interest in and knowledge of an Asian country or region. There are councils for Afghanistan, Bangladesh, Burma, Cambodia/Laos, China, the Himalayas, India, Indonesia, Iran, Korea, Malaysia/Singapore, Pakistan, the Philippines, Sri Lanka, and Thailand.

Background Desired

Asian studies, cultural interests and experience, conference organization, business administration, education studies, and museum work. A B.A. is sometimes accepted.

Asian-American Free Labor Institute

1125 15 St., NW
Washington, DC 20005

Under policy guidance from the AFL-CIO, AAFLI encourages the development of strong, free-trade unions throughout Asia. It helps provide a framework within which Asian trade unionists can build programs and institutions suited to their needs. Help consists of funds, in some cases, as well as training programs for Asian officials of trade unions.

Background Desired

Trade union experience, Asian studies and languages, vocational training, and business administration. A B.A. may be accepted.

Asian Cultural Council

> 280 Madison Ave.
> New York, NY 10016

The council supports cultural exchange in the visual and performing arts between Asia and the United States. Fellowship awards are given in the following fields: archeology, architecture, art history, crafts, dance, film, music, painting, sculpture, and theater. These functions were taken over from the John D. Rockefeller III Fund in 1980, when the council was established.

Background Desired

Cultural studies and experience, Asian studies and languages, and exchange program experience. An M.A. or Ph.D. is preferred.

Atlantic Council of the United States*

> 1616 H St., NW
> Washington, DC 20006

The council seeks to promote ties between Western Europe, North America, Japan, Australia, and New Zealand. It fosters debates on issues of international security and political and economic problems. The objective is to identify challenges and opportunities, illuminate choices, and foster informed public debate about U.S. foreign security and international economic policies. Typical council publications include *Energy Imperatives for the 1990s* and *The Future of NATO: A European's View.*

Background Desired

National security studies, military technology, Western Europe studies, foreign policy, international relations, and Russian and communist studies. An M.A. or Ph.D. is preferred.

China Institute in America*

> 125 East 65th St.
> New York, NY 10021

The institute has a dual purpose: (1) to educate Americans in various aspects of Chinese culture; and (2) to help Chinese-Americans adjust to the life and customs of their new country. The institute operates a *School of Chinese Studies* that offers courses in Chinese history and culture especially for schoolteachers. The school also offers courses in computer programming for Chinese immigrants wishing to make a career in this field. Lectures, seminars, and conferences are held on a wide range of political, economic, and cultural subjects relating to China. Small art exhibitions are presented from time to time at the institute's gallery.

Background Desired
Chinese studies and language, teaching, administration, international relations, economics, museum work, and cultural studies. A B.A. may be accepted.

Citizen Exchange Council*

> 12 West 31st St.
> New York, NY 10001

The CEC offers opportunities to Americans to participate in intercultural programs with citizens of nations having different political and/or economic systems. Education, mutual understanding, and cooperation are the goals of CEC programs. The council emphasizes the exchange of culture, ideas, vocations, and values on a one-to-one basis. There are three facets to CEC work: *Intercultural Travel, Hospitality,* and *Special Activities* (including Russian-American exchange conferences, seminars for American citizens, and Russian-American art exchanges). The emphasis of each of the three programs is on the former Soviet Union.

Background Desired

Russian studies and language, cultural studies, and exchange programs. A B.A. may be accepted.

The Commonwealth Fund

> Harkness House
> One East 75th St.
> New York, NY 10021

Some years ago the fund established the Harkness Fellowships, under which young people of the United Kingdom, Australia, and New Zealand pursue graduate-level studies in the United States. In 1987 there were 22 Harkness Fellows, 16 from the United Kingdom, from Australia, and from New Zealand.

Background Desired

Administration, education, and knowledge of the three countries participating in the program.

Council on Hemispheric Affairs (COHA)

> 724 Ninth St., NW
> Suite 401
> Washington, DC 20001

The council brings together U.S. leaders from the academic, business, professional, and public sectors to analyze policies and problems in inter-American relations. Typical of the issues studied are the region's economic interrelationships, military assistance programs in Latin America, advancing respect for human rights, opportunities for women and minorities in Latin America, and the right of Latin American trade unions to organize and function freely. The council publishes a bimonthly report, *The Washington Report on the Hemisphere*.

Background Desired

Latin American studies and languages, economics, international affairs, industrial relations, and military technology. An M.A. or Ph.D. is preferred.

Council of the Americas*

> 680 Park Ave.
> New York, NY 10021

Though nonprofit, the council is a business organization, directed and operated by its corporate members, which acts as an interpreter of the interests and operations of U.S. businesses investing in Latin America. It seeks to increase cooperation and understanding between Latin American countries and foreign investors. Toward these ends, the council (1) provides for a direct dialogue between Latin American government officials and U.S. corporate executives; (2) coordinates the work of its member companies in sponsoring managerial education and grass-roots self-help in Latin America; (3) encourages direct dialogue between U.S. corporate executives and officials of the U.S. government concerned with Latin America; and (4) exchanges information on Latin American social, economic, and political development among its members.

Background Desired

Latin American studies and languages, economics, business, administration, finance, and marketing. A B.A. may be accepted.

Eisenhower World Affairs Institute

918 16th St., NW
Washington, DC 20006

The Eisenhower World Affairs Institute conducts educational and leadership development programs to strengthen democratic institutions in the United States and around the world. Institute programs include leadership studies, public affairs dialogues, scholarships, and college support programs. The current focus of the institute is the economic and political restructuring of Eastern Europe.

Background Desired

Russian studies, conference and seminar organizing, writing skills, and administration.

English-Speaking Union of the United States

16 East 69th St.
New York, NY 10021

The function of the ESU is to "further peace, mutual understanding, trust, and friendship with the English-speaking people of the world." Its activities include administering exchange scholarships and travel grants, scheduling speakers, and printing pamphlets and newsletters.

Background Desired

English and Commonwealth studies, experience in exchange programs, and experience in organizing lectures and seminars. A B.A. may be accepted.

European Communities Press
and Information Office*

1 Dag Hammarskjold Plaza
New York, NY 10017

As its name indicates, the ECPIO provides information about the European community. It publishes a monthly magazine and periodic brochures and provides groups with speakers. It creates exhibits about the European community for conferences and seminars. It issues press releases to the media and provides films for conferences and classrooms.

Background Desired

Communications, Western Europe studies, and economics. A B.A. is sometimes accepted.

Foundation for Middle East Peace

> 555 13th St., NW
> Washington, DC 20004

The foundation's aim is to promote peace in the troubled Middle East. It has published three books on facing the PLO question, Israel's West Bank settlement policy, and the Lebanese experience.

Background Desired

Middle Eastern studies and languages, public relations, publications, and administration.

Fund for a Free South Africa

> 729 Boylston St., Fifth Floor
> Boston, MA 02116

This charitable organization was started in 1986 by a group of South African exiles living in the United States. It was established to support the movement for a democratic nonracial South Africa. It has a field representative with an office in South Africa.

Background Desired

Studies and/or experience in African affairs with particular emphasis on South Africa.

German Marshall Fund of the United States

> 11 Dupont Circle, NW
> Washington, DC 20036

The purpose of the fund is to assist individuals and organizations in the United States, Europe, and elsewhere to understand and resolve contemporary and emerging problems common to industrial societies. It operates both domestically and internationally.

The fund was started as a gesture of gratitude from the German government for the help given Europe by the Marshall Plan. It has a wide variety of programs that focus on exploring changing U.S.-European economic roles; improving U.S. competitiveness, supporting political, economic, and environmental reform in Central and Eastern Europe; and building U.S.-European environmental partnerships. They have provided grants to give Polish environmental nongovernmental organizations start-up funds; to train Romanian lawyers to defend victims of human rights violations; and to video successful small manufacturing networks in Italy and Denmark.

Background Desired

European studies, tariffs and trade, industrial relations, business administration, and economics. An M.A. or Ph.D. is preferred.

Institute for Policy Studies

> 1601 Connecticut Ave., NW
> Washington, DC 20009

The 28-year-old Institute for Policy Studies is composed of scholars and activists that challenge politicians and prepare alternative directions to achieve real security, economic justice, environmental protection, and grassroots political participation. Through working groups and informal alliance, this institute focuses on themes such as the impact of the new globalized economy on the United States, the special role of women in developing countries, the role of the United Nations in Global Security Arrangements, and a new understanding of equity and human rights.

The *Latin American Program* of the institute examines hemispheric relations with the goal of establishing an improved relationship between the hemisphere's two continents.

Background Desired

Latin American studies and languages, international relations, economics, and conference and seminar organizing. An M.A. or Ph.D. is preferred.

International Defense and Aid Fund
for Southern Africa

> Cannon Collins House
> 64 Essex Rd.
> London, England N18LR

The fund aims to make the outside world aware of the evils of apartheid in South Africa. It pays for the legal defense of thousands of prisoners accused of political crimes, and aids their families if they become destitute.

Background Desired

Knowledge of South Africa, law, and public relations.

Japan Productivity Center

> 3-1-1 Shibuya, Shibuyaku
> Tokyo, Japan

> or

> 1729 King St., Suite 100
> Alexandria, VA 22314

The JPC sends teams of businessmen and government officials to the United States for observation and study tours. The professional program is arranged by the JPC with the help of community organizations. The latter arrange for home hospitality and for team participation in community activities. The JPC is also active in various training and research activities in Japan, including receiving study teams from abroad, and in hosting events to introduce Japanese productivity activities to management, labor, universities, and productivity organizations outside Japan.

Background Desired

Japanese studies and language, exchange program experience, and business administration. A B.A. may be accepted.

Middle East Institute*

> 1761 N St., NW
> Washington, DC 20036

The institute was founded in 1946 to increase understanding between the people of the Middle East and the United States. Obviously, there are many different ways of approaching this type of goal, and the institute focuses on the following: a rather complete library on Middle East documentation; publication of the *Middle East Journal*; conferences, seminars, and lectures; a business advisory service for businesses interested in trade expansion; and a language training program.

Background Desired

Middle Eastern studies and languages, communications and journalism, research ability, economics, business administration, library science, and seminar and conference organization. An M.A. or Ph.D. is preferred.

National Committee on U.S.-China Relations*

> 777 U.N. Plaza
> New York, NY 10017

The National Committee believes that increased knowledge of China and U.S.-China relations is essential to international understanding and the effective conduct of U.S. foreign policy. This belief is carried out through a program of educational, cultural, civic, and sports exchanges with the People's Republic of China and through educational activities enhancing such exchanges. Conferences, meetings, and information services are other adjuncts of the committee's activities. Many high-level delegations of Americans have been invited for study tours of China and many Chinese cultural and sports attractions — dance groups, a table-tennis team, an acrobatic troupe, and a gymnastics team — have toured the United States under the auspices of the committee.

Background Desired

Chinese studies and language, cultural and educational exchange experience, communications, and public relations. An M.A. or Ph.D. is preferred.

Near East Foundation*

> 342 Madison Ave., Suite 1030
> New York, NY 10173

This is one of the oldest U.S. organizations involved in technical assistance and rural development overseas. Although it emphasizes the Near East area, it is also involved in parts of Asia and Africa. The NEF invests its resources in trained U.S. technicians who set up overseas projects that benefit people in that area.

Among the kinds of work performed are vocational training of young people, helping farmers by introducing crops suited to special weather conditions and by making available superior breeds of livestock, and helping villages by training teachers and showing people how to control diseases.

Background Desired

Middle East, Asian, and African studies and languages, economics and economic development, agricultural economics, health studies, nutrition, community development, and teaching. An M.A. or Ph.D. is preferred.

North American Congress on Latin America (NACLA)

> 475 Riverside Dr., Suite 249
> New York, NY 10115

NACLA publishes a bimonthly magazine, *Report on the Americas*, which focuses on the political economy of the Americas. Each issue usually features a single country with the aim of putting into perspective U.S. relations with that country.

Background Desired

Publications, writing, editing, and Latin American studies.

Operation Crossroads Africa*

> 475 Riverside Dr.
> New York, NY 10115

Operation Crossroads Africa arranges work camps, study tours, and other projects for North American college students in African countries during the summer months. Eight to ten Americans, an Operation Crossroads leader, and African volunteers live in a rural community in Africa on a project that usually requires vigorous physical labor: digging foundations, hauling water, mixing cement. Crossroads offers an intense cross-cultural and educational experience and, at the same time, an opportunity to make a contribution to community development in Africa.

Background Desired

If applying for leadership in one of the groups, African studies and language, community development, economic development, sociology, and leadership training or potential. A B.A. usually suffices.

Opportunities Industrialization Centers International

> 240 West Tulpehocken St.
> Philadelphia, PA 19144

OIC International contributes to the development of Third World nations, primarily in Africa, through the establishment of training programs needed by each country. Technical training given includes vocational training (building trades, auto mechanics, drafting, and arts and crafts); agricultural training; and business management development, including small business development. Since 1970, more than 20,000 individuals have completed the above training programs. OIC International also develops training institutions in the developing world. Twenty-three institutions are currently in operation.

Background Desired

African studies, economics and economic development, teaching (for teaching jobs), administration, and public relations (for office work).

Partners of the Americas

> 1424 K St., NW
> Washington, DC 20005

This organization fosters a closer relationship between the people of the United States and the people of Latin America by means of self-help projects. Partners works on technical assistance programs related to agriculture and rural development, cultural exchange, natural resource management, training, and health. A "partnership" links a state in the United States with a country or an area in Latin America — e.g., Kansas with Paraguay, New Jersey with Haiti, and Missouri with Para, Brazil. One example of how the partnerships work: To build a school, one partner contributes the land and labor, and the other provides the equipment or funds. Forty-five U.S. states are paired with thirty-one regions of Latin American and the Caribbean.

Background Desired

Latin American studies and languages, economic development, exchange program experience, public relations, and administration. A B.A. is often adequate.

Technoserve

148 East Ave.
Norwalk, CT 06851

Technoserve attempts to improve the long-term economic and social well-being of people in the developing world by fostering the development of small- and medium-scale enterprises. Technoserve works primarily in Latin America and Africa in the rural agricultural sectors to provide technical and managerial training. In Kenya, for example, Technoserve helped the low-income members of a farming cooperative increase their food production by introducing modern techniques of herd and range management.

Background Desired

Agriculture, farming, economics and economic development, African studies, and languages.

Tinker Foundation

55 East 59th St.
New York, NY 10022

The foundation attempts to "create a climate of better understanding between the peoples of the United States and Ibero-America, Spain, and Portugal." A sampling of subjects for which grants have been given are a two-year grant to enable the American Field Service to establish a two-way exchange program of high school teachers from Argentina, Brazil, Colombia, and the United States; the purchase of a liberal arts library for the Bilingual Institute of Biscayne College; defraying the travel costs of Latin American participants to a meeting of the Atlantic Conference sponsored by the Chicago Council on Foreign Relations; an award to the Department of Agricultural Economics of Cornell University to work on the economic and social aspects of agricultural development in the Mexican tropics; and an award to Johns Hopkins University to support its Latin American Diplomats Program.

Background Desired

Latin America studies and languages, educational and cultural studies, knowledge of exchange programs, and administration. An M.A. or Ph.D. is preferred.

Trade and Economic Council

> 805 Third Ave.
> New York, NY 10022

This organization of American and Russian business-related enterprises is devoted to facilitating trade expansion between the two countries. It draws its authority from a government-to-government protocol and its effectiveness from the support of the governments and business people of both countries. The council has the dual responsibility of market development and individual trade facilitation for members. Through a binational board of directors, it works to develop new business projects to meet the special conditions of U.S.-Russian trade. It provides a full range of trade-assistance services for members through its New York and Moscow offices, both of which maintain binational staffs of trade and economic specialists. In addition, the council offers its members complete business support facilities to handle day-to-day dealings in both countries.

Background Desired

Economics, trade, Russian studies and language, and business administration.

Trilateral Commission*

> 345 East 46th St.
> New York, NY 10017

The commission is an organization of distinguished individuals from North America, Western Europe, and Japan who aim to (1) enhance cooperative relations among these three industrially advanced areas of the world; (2) analyze major issues affecting the three regions; (3) develop practical proposals on questions of mutual interest; and (4) obtain endorsement of these proposals from influential citizens of the three areas. Most recently, the topics of an annual meeting included: Japanese developments and their international implications, the future of the international economic order, and Asian-Pacific Regional developments in a global context.

Background Desired

Research ability; Japanese, West European, or Russian studies; economics; international affairs; and administration. A Ph.D. is preferred.

United Board for Christian Higher Education in Asia

475 Riverside Dr.
New York, NY 10027

The United Board financially assists more than twenty Asian academic institutions. It supports mainly academic programs that encourage community responsibility and national leadership.

Background Desired

Asian studies, education, languages, community development, and public relations.

United States–Japan Foundation

145 East 32nd St.
New York, NY 10016

This is an American organization that supports education and exchanges between the United States and Japan.

Background Desired

Japanese studies and language, education, public relations, and administration.

EDUCATIONAL, CULTURAL, AND EXCHANGE

Academy for Educational Development*

1255 23rd St., NW
Washington, DC 20037

The AED helps schools and colleges, governmental agencies, and other educationally oriented institutions to improve their present plans and develop future programs. The academy provides advisory and staff services to these organizations and conducts in-depth research designed to make education more effective. Its international functions include assisting the development of educational and social programs in foreign countries.

Background Desired

Teaching, educational studies, economics, and administration. An M.A. or Ph.D. is preferred.

American Council on Education*

One Dupont Circle, NW
Washington, DC 20036

The ACE's function is to extend the range and enhance the quality of higher education in the United States. It acts as a coordinating council among the national educational associations, and provides a center of communication between the academic community and the federal government in matters of higher educational policy.

The ACE has some international functions as well, which are carried out by an *Overseas Liaison Committee*, the *International Education Project*, and the *Council for International Exchange of Scholars*. The committee provides a means of communication between the higher education professionals in the United States and the academic communities in Africa, Asia, Latin America, the Caribbean, and the Pacific. The *Rural Development Network*, a major committee program, promotes the exchange of information among researchers and professionals active in rural development.

The International Education Project tries to enlarge the constituency and resource base of international education and international studies. Much of the project's work is done through task forces that explore subjects such as transnational research and language and library resources. The council for International Exchange of Scholars recommends senior scholars for university lecturing and postdoctoral research under the Fulbright-Hays program.

Background Desired

Teaching experience and courses on education, economics, and area studies. A Ph.D. is preferred.

American Field Service* (AFS)

313 East 43rd St.
New York, NY 10017

The AFS offers an opportunity for students between the ages of 16 and 18 to live for a summer or a year with families of different cultures. American students are sent abroad, and foreign students are welcomed to the United States. Since it was founded, more than 180,000 students have been placed worldwide. Abroad, AFS works with hundreds of local committees in 50 countries on 6 continents. For 19 years, AFS has also offered opportunities for teachers to come to the United States to teach.

If you connect the American Field Service with ambulances during the first World War, you are on the right track. The AFS was started as a volunteer ambulance service for the French army in 1914. The American-French understanding that resulted from this association led to scholarships for American students at French universities. From there AFS broadened its activities to include its present concentration on the high school student.

Background Desired

International relations, area studies, languages, cultural studies, and student counseling. A B.A. is accepted.

American Forum for Global Education

> 45 John St., Suite 1200
> New York, NY 10038

The forum was formed in 1988 by the merger of the Center for War/Peace Studies and the National Council on Foreign Languages and International Studies. Currently, the task of the forum is to effect profound change in schools, colleges, and universities. Clearly, its emphasis is to increase the content of foreign languages and internationalism in the curriculum of American schools, so that students will have a better knowledge of the world and its people.

Background Desired

Education, international affairs, languages, and area studies.

Boy Scouts of America

> 345 Hudson St.
> New York, NY 10014

The *International Divison* of the Boy Scouts participates in international activities by arranging the following services for visiting foreign scouts: visits to the National Office of the Scouts and to its National Training Center; consultations with leaders of the National Office; and contacts with local Boy Scout groups.

Background Desired

Boy Scout training and some interest in international affairs. A B.A. is accepted.

Carnegie Corporation*

437 Madison Ave.
New York, NY 10022

This corporation is a philanthropic foundation created by Andrew Carnegie that is primarily interested in education and in certain aspects of governmental affairs. Grants for projects are made to colleges, universities, and professional associations. Approximately 7 percent of the income is allocated to educational endeavors in British Commonwealth areas.

Recently Carnegie has been studying restructuring the Russian defense industry, and means of facilitating the shift from military to civilian production.

Background Desired

Commonwealth and Russian studies, program and grants experience, economics, and education. A Ph.D. is preferred.

Council on International Educational Exchange
(CIEE)* (Also see pages 9, 30)

205 East 42nd St.
New York, NY 10017

The council's members are U.S. academic institutions and national organizations that send American students abroad or bring foreign students to the United States. It maintains staffs in New York and 23 other U.S. cities as well as in France and Japan.

Student travel services available to individuals and groups include authorization of the International Student Identity Card, group air charters, student railpasses, car plans, and publications. The council also administers a small exchange program for students on the high school level, and publishes the annual *Student Travel Catalog* with details on work, study, and travel abroad.

Background Desired

International studies, administrative ability, travel background, and experience in exchange programs. A B.A. may be adequate.

Council for International Exchange of Scholars

3007 Tilden St., NW
Washington, DC 20008

The council, which is administered by the American Council on Education, is a private agency cooperating in the administration of Fulbright-Hays grants for American University lecturers and advanced research scholars to study and work abroad.

Background Desired

International relations, exchange program experience, and administration. An M.A. or Ph.D. is preferred.

Eisenhower Exchange Fellowships

> 256 South 16th St.
> Philadelphia, PA 19102

This organization provides for travel and observation in the United States for foreign individuals who have demonstrated leadership potential in their own countries. Programs in the United States are developed on the basis of the professional interests of the fellows.

Background Desired

Experience in exchange programs and international studies. A B.A. may be accepted.

Experiment in International Living

> Brattleboro, VT 05301
>
> or
>
> 1015 15th St., NW
> Suite 750
> Washington, DC 20005

The EIL focuses on cross-cultural communication with the belief that living with foreign people is the best way to understand their culture. Thousands of young Americans "experiment" annually by living with foreign families, and many foreigners live with American families. The EIL also has the School for International Training, which offers undergraduate and graduate courses and degrees in language teaching and world issues.

Background Desired

Experience with exchange programs, teaching, and languages. A B.A. is sometimes adequate.

Foreign Student Service Council

> 2337 18th St., NW
> Washington, DC 20036

The programs of this council are designed to give the university-level foreign student an understanding of the U.S. government and an introduction to people in Washington, DC. A member of COSERV, a national organization that coordinates services to students and visitors from abroad, the council offers three-day hospitality stays with American life and customs. The council also issues a quarterly newsletter.

Background Desired

Experience in organizing hospitality programs and seminars and general international relations. A B.A. is adequate.

Girl Scouts of the United States

> International Department
> 830 Third Ave.
> New York, NY 10022

                              or

> 132 Ebury St.
> London SWI W9QQ
> England

This organization's *International Department* assists in developing programs for international visitors. Assistance includes home hospitality and opportunities to observe Girl Scout activities.

Background Desired

Exchange program experience and a background in the Scouts. A B.A. is usually adequate.

Institute of International Education (IIE)*

> 809 U.N. Plaza
> New York, NY 10017

The IIE is a leading organization in the field of educational and cultural exchange. It administers scholarships and fellowships for foreign students and arranges for their admission to U.S. colleges and universities. It also services U.S. students, screening applicants for Fulbright grants for overseas study. Among its other functions are organizing travel, study, internships, and research programs for U.S. and foreign leaders and specialists; providing information and advice on higher education in the United States and abroad to individuals and institutions throughout the world; planning itineraries and providing hospitality for foreign students and leaders in the United States; and conducting seminars and conferences on major issues in international education.

The IIE purposes can vary from the institutional development of a university in an emerging nation to multinational corporate staff development, and from short-term training to long-term research on world food needs.

Its overseas educational advising centers are located in Hong Kong, Indonesia, Mexico, and Thailand and its project management offices are located in Egypt, Ethiopia, and Sri Lanka.

Background Desired

Educational studies, economics, area studies, experience in exchange programs, and administration. A B.A. is sometimes adequate.

International Association of Economics and Management Students (AIESEC)*

> AIESEC U.S. National Committee
> 135 West 50th St., 20th Floor
> New York, NY 10020

> or

> AIESEC International
> Rue Washington, 40-BTE 10
> B-1050 Brussels, Belgium

AIESEC (the acronym of the original French title of this organization, Association Internationale des Etudiants de l'Economie et de la Commerce) is a student organization whose major activity is the exchange of students between member countries on a work-traineeship basis. Traineeships — in all parts of the world — are in the field of management for such areas as hospitals, public and university administration, development corporations, city government, and businesses. The traineeship is usually taken during the summer but can last up to 18 months. Each student receives a stipend to cover living and incidental expenses; transportation expenses are not paid.

Background Desired

For both national and international headquarters staff, campus experience with AIESEC, program coordination, finance, and management. Work toward a B.A. usually suffices if you are applying for a traineeship.

AIESEC operates on a decentralized basis, with offices on the campus of many large American universities. Find out if there is a local representative on your campus.

International Student Service (ISS)*

> 356 West 34th St.
> New York, NY 10007

The ISS offers its services to all students and trainees from abroad. Among the services provided are meeting students at port of entry, facilitating student-community contacts, administering the *International Camp Counselor program*, and sponsoring programs of educational travel.

Background Desired

Exchange program experience, international relations, and languages. A B.A. is usually accepted.

International Youth and Student Movement for the United Nations (ISMUN)

> ISMUN Secretary General
> Palais des Nations
> CH-1211 Geneva 10, Switzerland

The aims of ISMUN, as stated in its 1975 constitution, are "to work with young people and students for the aims and ideals of the United Nations . . . to strive for national liberation . . . for peace and disarmament . . . against imperialism, colonialism, neocolonialism. . . ." In addition, ISMUM desires to work with students and young people in order to promote through research greater knowledge of the United Nations.

Background Desired

International relations, international organizations studies, economics, and experience in youth movements. A B.A. may be accepted.

Metro-International Student Center

285 West Broadway, Suite 450
New York, NY 10013

Metro-International coordinates citywide services and programs for foreign students in the New York area. It has put out a housing guidebook and "Living in New York" booklets to help foreign students adjust to the city, and provides students with orientation sessions and opportunities to become involved with the local community. Metro has held seminars that focus on business and foreign policy and homelessness. It also organized a global classroom program and has worked on the New York City marathon.

Background Desired

Counseling, job placement, education, international affairs, area studies and languages, and knowledge of New York.

National Association for Foreign Student Affairs

1860 19th St., NW
Washington, DC 20009

NAFSA serves as a source of professional training and as a spokesman for international educational exchange programs in government and academic circles. It supports research and developmental projects, issues numerous publications on international educational interchange, and conducts conferences and workshops in this field.

Background Desired

Educational exchange, student personnel work, international relations, conference and seminar organizing, communications, and public relations. A B.A. may be accepted.

North American Students Association

23 Bloomsbury Square
London WC 1, England

This association finds university placement in England for Canadians and Americans. Its general aim is to link North Amerian students with their counterparts in Europe or on American campuses. The association also provides a social and cultural program to promote a greater understanding of the member countries involved.

Background Desired

English, American, or Canadian citizenship and knowledge of exchange programs. A B.A. is usually accepted.

Phelps Stokes Fund (PSF)

> 10 East 87th St.
> New York, NY 10028

The PSF creates educational opportunities for blacks, American Indians, and poor whites in the United States. Similarly, African education is a primary concern, and PSF programs have been broadened to include funding of emerging colleges in the Caribbean.

The fund provides opportunities for Americans to meet with Africans: American scholars are sent to African institutions, and African professors serve as visiting faculty at American colleges and universities. In addition, interest-free emergency loans are given to African students in American colleges. Much research has also centered around the state of African education.

Background Desired

African studies and languages, educational studies, exchange program experience, and administration. An M.A. or Ph.D. is preferred.

Putney Student Travel

> Hickory Ridge Rd.
> Putney, VT 05346

PST arranges travel plans and tours for teenage students. Most of the destinations are in Europe, although travel is also arranged on other continents.

Background Desired

To be a tour guide: international affairs, a good knowledge of Europe and its languages, and administration. A B.A. is accepted.

Sister Cities International

> 120 S. Payne St.
> Alexandria, VA 22314

SCI aims to foster better international cooperation and understanding through sister city relationships between cities in the United States and other nations. The national concept of sister cities was launched in 1956, when President Eisenhower called for massive exchanges between Americans and foreign peoples. Today hundreds of U.S. cities are said to carry out "meaningful exchanges" with their affiliates in more than 85 nations.

Background Desired

International relations and interests, language knowledge, administration, public relations, and particularly an interest in the sister city concept.

U.S. English

> 818 Connecticut Ave., NW
> Washington, DC 20006

This organization, started by former Senator S.I. Hayakawa of California, aims to establish English as the official language of the United States, and to expand opportunities to learn English. Since 1983, 14 more states have made English their official language.

Background Desired

Public relations, administration, political science, teaching, and belief in the aims of U.S. English.

World Education, Inc.

> World Education
> 210 Lincoln St.
> Boston, MA 02111

This organization uses special techniques developed in India for teaching illiterate villagers in several dozen countries to read and write. Central to the technique is the use of reading materials that help villagers with their work. World Education's projects reflect the priorities and needs of their learners. Their projects have included promoting economic opportunities for women in Mali, the careful use of pesticides in Indonesia, and nonformal education projects in Thailand and Bangladesh.

Background Desired

Teaching, education, area studies in the Third World, and languages.

Note: A directory of interest to those looking for jobs in education is: *Who's Doing What? A Directory of US Organizations and Institutions Educating about Development and Other Global Issues*, 2nd edition. Joelle Danant, ed. New York: National Clearinghouse on Development Education, American Forum for Global Education, 1991.

ECONOMICS AND ECONOMIC DEVELOPMENT

Agricultural Development Council

> 725 Park Ave.
> New York, NY 10021

Concern about inadequate food supplies for rapidly growing populations in Asia led John D. Rockefeller to organize the ADC in 1953. The organization is involved in research and training to provide the manpower needed to help Asian countries use their agricultural resources more effectively. Although the initial impetus was toward Asia, the ADC is also involved to a limited extent in other areas of the world. The council pursues its goals through fellowships to Asian students for travel and study, grants for Asian research projects, publications, and meetings.

Background Desired

Economics, economic development, Asian studies and languages, agricultural economics, and administration. A Ph.D. is preferred.

American Economic Association

> 2014 Broadway
> Suite 305
> Nashville, TN 37203-2418

Founded in 1885, the American Economic Association encourages economic research and publication. More than 50 percent of the association's members are from academic institutions and 35 percent from business and industry. Among the journals that AEA publishes are the "American Economic Review" and the "Journal of Economic Abstracts." Of great interest to readers of this book, AEA also publishes a bimonthly listing of job vacancies called *Job Openings for Economists (JOE)*.

Background Desired

If you apply, you might do well to have some economic background. Also be prepared to couch the language of economics in the simplest of terms and concepts. An M.A. or Ph.D. is preferred.

American Enterprise Institute for Public Policy Research*

1150 17th St., NW
Washington, DC 20036

The institute is a center for the study of problems in economics, foreign policy, law, and government. It fosters research, analyzes public policy proposals, and identifies and presents varying points of view on the issues studied. To achieve this objective, it commissions scholars to undertake original research and publishes their findings. It sponsors conferences and debates on these issues and makes the proceedings available to the public. This procedure is designed to bring about a broader understanding of controversial issues.

Background Desired

Institute personnel function in the following capacities, each of which defines the kind of background desired: seminar programs, health policy, economic policy, legal policy, government regulation, foreign and defense policy, and research on advertising. For the internationally trained student, foreign policy analysis, economics, international relations, and area studies provide a desirable background. A Ph.D. is preferred.

Brookings Institution*

1775 Massachusetts Ave., NW
Washington, DC 20036

Brookings is devoted to research and education in economics, foreign policy, government, and the social sciences. Its main purpose is to bring knowledge to bear on current and emerging public policy problems facing the United States. It organizes conferences and seminars on these issues and publishes its findings for the public.

Its activities are carried out through three research programs: *Economic Studies*, *Governmental Studies*, and *Foreign Policy Studies*. It also has an *Advanced Study Program* and a *Publications Program*. In all these activities, Brookings acts as an independent analyst and critic.

Background Desired

A Ph.D. is preferred, since Brookings requires proven excellence in scholarship, research ability, international relations, foreign policy analysis, area studies, and economics.

Committee for Economic Development (CED)

> 477 Madison Ave.
> New York, NY 10022

CED's purpose is "to propose policies that will help to bring about steady economic growth at high employment and reasonably stable prices, increase productivity and living standards, provide greater and more equal opportunity for every citizen and improve the quality of life for all." Most of the trustees of this organization are businesspeople and educators.

The CED develops recommendations for business and public policy. Among the international issues considered by CED have been international trade, the world monetary system, and global energy policy.

Background Desired

Research, economics, and economic development. A Ph.D. is preferred.

Conference Board*

> 845 Third Ave.
> New York, NY 10022

This is a research organization concerned with economic trends and management practices. Major areas of research in the international field are international economics, international operations management, financing overseas operations, export management, investment climate analyses, compensation of third-country nationals, and industry-government relations.

Background Desired

International economics, finance, business administration, and trade. A Ph.D. is usually required.

Council on Economic Priorities

> 30 Irving Place
> New York, NY 10003

This organization publishes a paperback, *Shopping for a Better World*, a guide to corporate responsibility, with information on policies and practices of U.S. companies with respect to pollution control; treatment of minorities; and doing business in South Africa, China, Libya, and other countries in which civil rights are abused. Similar books on companies in Japan, England, and other countries are now being undertaken.

Background Desired

International affairs, regional studies, business, economics, environmental studies, administration, and research.

Ford Foundation*

> 320 East 43rd St.
> New York, NY 10017

One of the largest foundations in the world, Ford gives funds for educational, developmental, research, and experimental efforts designed to produce significant advances in selected problems of national and international importance such as urban and rural poverty, human rights and governance, and education. Much of its overseas effort is concerned with economic development, and substantial programs of developmental assistance are in effect in many developing nations. It has 16 overseas offices in the less-developed world and one in Japan. Even though in recent years Ford has reduced its staff, vacancies still arise in the economic and economic development fields.

Background Desired

Economics or economic development combined with an area studies and language background (Latin America or Africa or Asia or Middle East). Sometimes, also, there are vacancies for those with communications experience. An M.A. or Ph.D. is preferred.

Institute for International Economics

> 11 Dupont Circle, NW
> Washington, DC 20036

This institute was created by the German Marshall Fund of the U.S. (see page 264). It focuses on issues it considers likely to confront policymakers over the medium term. On the institute's agenda are issues such as international monetary affairs, trade, investment, energy, commodities, and North-South and East-West relations.

Background Desired

Economics, finance, trade, banking, area studies, economic development, and energy. A Ph.D. is usually needed, except for administrative positions.

International Center for Development Policy

> 731 Eighth ST., SE
> Washington, DC 20003

The ICDP is a nonpartisan foreign policy organization focused on relations with Asia, Africa, Latin America, and the former Soviet Union. The center conducts programs of research, publications, and overseas travel, and hosts foreign visitors to inform the press, Congress, U.S. government officials, and the public of the impact of American policies abroad.

Background Desired

Regional studies, economics, foreign policy, and international affairs.

International Center for Law in Development

> 777 United Nations Plaza
> New York, NY

The International Center for Law in Development is a nonprofit organization that works with lesser developed countries' nongovernmental organizations to help develop alternative, people-centered strategies of development. It supports projects that develop legal strategies to help those who are displaced by development projects; projects that inform workers; and those that develop more effective, equitable, and participatory systems for the introduction of hazardous products and technologies in the workplace and environment.

Background Desired

Human rights, alternative development, rural development, and area studies.

International Development Research Center

P.O. Box 8500
Ottawa, Canada K1G 3H9

The center was set up by Canada and is dedicated to "initiate, encourage, support, and conduct research into the problems of the developing regions of the world, and into the means for applying and adapting scientific, technical, and other knowledge to the economic and social advancement of those regions." Regional offices are located in Singapore, Bogotá, Dakar, Beirut, and Nairobi, indicating the areas of greatest interest to the center.

The professional staff is made up of citizens of many countries, including the United States.

Background Desired

Agriculture and nutrition sciences, information activities, population and demography studies, social sciences, international relations, Third World area studies, and economics. An M.A. or Ph.D. is preferred.

International Economic Policy Association

1400 I St., NW
Washington, DC 20006

The association analyzes U.S. and foreign government policies affecting international trade, aid, investments, finance, and taxation. Courses of action are recommended as a result of these evaluations. The guiding philosophy of IEPA is that freedom in economic enterprise is necessary to ensure political liberty. Its membership consists of business organizations, to which the results of these studies are submitted.

Background Desired

International business, economics, trade, finance, and taxation. An M.A. or Ph.D. is preferred.

International Voluntary Services (IVS)

> 1424 16th St., NW
> Washington, DC 20036

IVS does in a private capacity what the Peace Corps does for government. It recruits American youth for person-to-person work in developing countries. It has developed teams in education — teaching English and teaching in English. Its volunteers have also been successful in community development projects both rural and urban. The idea behind the IVS is that nongovernmental personnel can have a greater impact in working with foreign people than can government employees, who often are suspect for their official affiliations.

Background Desired

Teaching, community development, and a service ideal. A B.A. is often adequate.

National Bureau of Economic Research*

> 269 Mercer St.
> New York, NY 10003
>
>   or
>
> 1050 Massachusetts Ave.
> Cambridge, MA 02138

The bureau is one of the largest economic research organizations in the world. It works on economic problems of domestic as well as international importance. The results of its research are issued in the form of scientific reports entirely divorced from recommendations on policy. In this way the bureau aims to provide well-researched documentation on important problems, objectively presented as a basis for discussion by policymakers.

Among the subjects of an international nature previously undertaken have been (1) the effect of world commodity prices on U.S. manufacturing prices; (2) multinational firms; (3) alternative trade strategies and employment; (4) U.S.-USSR scientific and technical programs of cooperation; and (5) the international transmission of inflation through the world monetary system.

Background Desired

Research ability, economics, world resources, energy and environmental studies, and trade. A Ph.D. is preferred.

Overseas Development Council*

1717 Massachusetts Ave., NW
Washington, DC 20036

The ODC seeks to increase American understanding of the economic and social problems confronting the developing countries of the world. Through research, conferences, and publications, this organization seeks to make the American public, businesses, and policymakers aware of the importance of development and developing countries to the United States.

Among the subjects researched by the ODC are the United States and Third World development, international economic systems, alternative development strategies and basic human needs, a global approach to energy, world hunger and food scarcity, and private organizations and development. Visiting fellows from business, government, and universities regularly participate in the work of the ODC.

Background Desired

Third World area studies, economic development, public relations, and conference and seminar organizing. An M.A. or Ph.D. is preferred.

Rockefeller Brothers Fund

1290 Avenue of the Americas
New York, NY 10020

The Rockefeller Brothers Fund makes grants under the theme of global interdependence — one world. Under this theme there are two major components: sustainable resource use and world security. In addition, the fund focuses on New York City, the well-being of the nonprofit sector, education in the United States, and South Africa. Grants are regularly given to projects in East Asia, East-Central Europe, and countries of the former Soviet Union.

Background Desired

Economics, economic development, Third World area studies, business administration, world resources, environment, and population. A Ph.D. is preferred.

Rockefeller Foundation*

1133 Avenue of the Americas
New York, NY 10020

In addition to involvement in a great number of national projects, the foundation also funds many projects of an international nature. Among its international concerns are the conquest of hunger, problems of population, the quality of the environment, and university development. A random sampling of projects undertaken by the foundation show that it has funded (1) an increase of agricultural productivity among small landowners in El Salvador; (2) an experimental program to increase the productivity of disadvantaged Asian rice farmers; (3) research on the formulation of population policy in Chile; (4) research on the motivation for delayed marriage of Hong Kong women; (5) support costs of East Asian graduate scholars at the University of Nairobi; and (6) staff development at the University of Zaire.

The foundation also invites about 80 scholars and artists each year to spend four weeks in residence at its Bellagio Study and Conference Center at Lake Como, Italy, to enable them to work on a book or other creative undertaking.

Background Desired

Economics, economic development sociology, Latin American, Asian, or African studies and languages, population studies, education, and teaching. A Ph.D. is preferred.

Society for International Development

> 1401 New York Ave., NW
> Washington, DC 20005

The society provides a forum for the exchange of ideas, facts, and experiences among all those professionally concerned with the problems of economic and social development in modernizing societies. To this effect, the SID publishes the *International Development Review*, which presents opinions and comments of scholars and practitioners in the field. It also holds conferences on the regional and international level. Sponsors of SID comprise many national banks in various parts of the world, and its members include such diverse organizations as Planned Parenthood, the OECD, and banks, development bodies, research organizations, and foundations in many countries.

Background Desired

Economics, economic development, Third World area studies, sociology, and conference organization. A B.A. may be accepted.

TransCentury

> 1901 Fort Meyer Dr.
> N. Arlington, VA 22209

TransCentury is composed of a consulting firm, TransCentury Corporation, and a foundation, the New TransCentury Foundation, that are often under contract with the U.S. Agency for International Development. The corporation is a research and operations firm that has expertise in a wide range of areas including international development, investment, and procurement. The foundation promotes democratic and innovative social development, particularly in the areas of human resource development. One form that the assistance takes is the development in Africa, Asia, the Middle East, and Latin America in fields like agriculture, education, health, management, and business. None of these positions is with TransCentury. The foundation usually provides a preliminary screening of applicants and sends the résumés of the most qualified to the agency with the vacant position.

Background Desired

Job placement work, Third World area studies, economic development, economics, finance, and administration. (This background is applicable for work with TransCentury and also for the type of jobs listed in the *Job Opportunities Bulletin*.) A B.A. may be accepted.

Trickle Up Program

> 54 Riverside Dr. PHE
> New York, NY 10024

TUP creates new opportunities for employment among the low-income populations of the world with grants assigned to people in many countries in the Caribbean, Central and South America, Asia, and Africa. If a group of five or more people in a developing country wish to invest 1,000 or more hours of their time, they can apply for a TUP grant of $100 to initiate a profit-making enterprise of their own. TUP has had extraordinary success in helping low-income populations to become self-supporting.

Background Desired

Masters in International Affairs, small business development, and experience overseas.

How to Apply

Unlike most nonprofit organizations, TUP uses the greater part of its donated funds for its program and very little for administration. For this reason, there are seldom any jobs available. But do write if you are particularly interested in the aims and work of this organization — or wish to do volunteer work.

Volunteers in Technical Assistance

> 1815 North Lynn St., Suite 200
> Arlington, VA 22209

VITA is an organization working on international development. It makes available to individuals and groups in developing countries information and technical resources aimed at fostering self-sufficiency. It places special emphasis on agriculture and food processing, renewable energy applications, water supply and sanitation, housing and construction, and small-business development. It has a documentation center of specialized technical material.

Background Desired

Economics, development, agriculture, energy and environment, water supply, engineering, housing, administration, and business.

ENVIRONMENT, ENERGY, AND POPULATION

Center for Marine Conservation

> 1725 De Sales St., NW
> Washington, DC 20036

The Center for Marine Conservation (formerly the Center for Environmental Education) is dedicated to protecting marine wildlife and their habitats and conserving coastal and ocean resources. The center also supports major international efforts to protect all wildlife species threatened by international trade. Programs include conducting policy-oriented research, educating the public, and supporting domestic and international conservation programs. For example, in the Caribbean the center helped to set up a sanctuary for the critically endangered humpback whales.

Background Desired

Environmental studies, world resources, population and demography, and economic development. An M.A. or Ph.D. is preferred.

Environmental Defense Fund

257 Park Ave. South
New York, NY 10010

The EDF aims to make the world and its citizens aware that environmental problems can no longer be limited to one country but must be seen as global. The EDF links science, economics, and law to create innovative, economically viable solutions to today's environmental problems. It aims to halt ozone depletion, stop acid rain, save tropical rain forests, clean up toxic wastes, protect Antarctica, and safeguard wildlife and habitats. The EDF is now working to ensure that the public's demand for constructive action is not diverted by political maneuvers but is translated into corrective action.

Background Desired

Environmental studies, law, experience, and motivation, as well as public relations and conference organization.

Environmental Mediation International

43 Florence St.
Ottawa, Ontario
Canada K2P 0W6

EMI was established in 1978 to encourage mediation for settling disputes involving environmental, natural resource, and health problems. It conducts training programs in conflict management and has held seminars for officials from developing countries. One of EMI's efforts has been to assess the attitudes of U.S. and Canadian interests in the aftermath of the International Court of Justice decision fixing boundaries on the Gulf of Maine.

Background Desired

Environmental studies and experience, law, administration, public relations, and seminar organization and planning.

Family Care International

588 Broadway
Suite 510
New York, NY 10012

Family Care International was established in 1987 to develop creative and practical solutions to health and family planning problems affecting women in the developing world. It helps governments and nongovernmental organizations develop community-based programs on topics such as safe motherhood. It has held workshops in 45 countries and provided technical assistance to several countries, including Mexico, Kenya, and Ghana.

Background Desired

Public health and women's studies.

Greenpeace

> 1436 U St., NW
> Washington, DC 20009

Greenpeace is dedicated to preserving the earth. It works to stop the threat of nuclear war; protect the environment from nuclear and toxic pollution; stop the threat of global greenhouse warming and ozone layer destruction; and halt the slaughter of whales, dolphins, seals, and other endangered animals. It has offices in 26 countries throughout the world, primarily in Europe and Latin America.

Background Desired

Environmental studies, international affairs, and legal studies.

International Institute for Environment and Development

> 27 Mortimer St.
> London W1A 4QW
> England

Among the institute's concerns have been habitat and the U.N. conference on this subject, compiling the most accurate information available on the environment, publishing a newsletter on world environment matters, the law of the sea, the World Food Conference, analysis of the energy crisis, and establishment of an international environmental fellowship program.

The IIED devotes much of its time to two special priorities: making environmental issues known to a wider citizen audience and attempting to ensure that commitments entered into by governments are in fact implemented.

Background Desired

Environmental studies, research ability, economics, economic development, energy studies, population and demography, and Third World area studies. A Ph.D. is preferred.

International Planned Parenthood Federation/ Western Hemisphere

902 Broadway
New York, NY 10010

IPPF/WH includes 46 private family-planning associations in North and South America and the Caribbean. Members are local, grassroots, autonomous associations providing family planning and related health services according to local law and custom. Together, IPPF/WH's members have created the largest network of family-planning services in the western hemisphere. IPPF/WH is one of six regional divisions of the International Planned Parenthood Federation, located in London, England.

The IPPF has offices in Beirut, Colombo, Kuala Lumpur, London, Nairobi, New York, and Tokyo. All of them assist family-planning associations in their areas. In addition, IPPF has several regular publications: the monthly *International Planned Parenthood News* and two specialist bimonthly publications, the *Medical Bulletin* and *Research in Reproduction*. The central and regional libraries of the IPPF are an important source of information on all aspects of human fertility and contraception.

Background Desired

World resources, population studies, research, public relations, sociology, regional studies, and family planning. A B.A. is sometimes accepted.

Natural Resources Defense Council*

40 West 20th St.
New York, NY 10168

or

1350 New York Ave., NW
Washington, DC 20005

or

71 Stevenson St.
San Francisco, CA 94105

The NRDC attempts to protect America's endangered natural resources and to improve the quality of the human environment. It combines legal action, scientific research, and citizen education in an environmental program. NRDC's major involvements are in the areas of air and water pollution, energy policy, nuclear safety, natural resource management, and the international environment.

The international functions of NRDC have been increasing. Together with the Sierra Club and other environmentally conscious organizations, NRDC helps plan national positions on the environment for use by U.S. representatives at international conferences.

NRDC has put special emphasis on Africa and Southeast Asia because of the extreme environmental stresses operating there and because many of the world's poorest countries are in those areas. It is working with the African Development Bank on the first debt-for-conservation swap in Africa. It has expanded its work in Asia by establishing an NRDC on-the-ground representative in Indonesia. And in recent years one of its major goals has been to influence the U.S. Agency for International Development to become a leader in providing the "right kinds" of energy assistance. Owing principally to a series of NRDC lawsuits, all of U.S. AID's loans and grants are now subject to strict environmental assessement requirements to guard against projects that might cause environmental harm.

Background Desired

Environmental studies, world resources, energy, public relations, and area studies, particularly Africa. An M.A. or a Ph.D. is usually needed.

Nature Conservancy

> 1815 North Lynn St.
> Arlington, VA 22209

The Nature Conservancy's mission is to preserve plants, animals, and natural communities that represent the diversity of life on earth and protect the lands and water that they need to survive. To date the Nature Conservancy has protected 5.5 million acres in the United States and Canada. It has assisted numerous partner organizations in Latin America and the Caribbean and Pacific.

Background Desired

Environmental studies.

Negative Population Growth

P.O. Box 1206
Teaneck, NJ 07666

This organization has three aims: (1) to educate the American public to the social cost of a growing population; (2) to find incentives that will motivate Americans to limit their fertility; and (3) to get the U.S. government to adopt policies that will brake population growth in this country as an example to other countries. Its international aims include U.S. aid for population control programs in other countries, restrictions on immigration into the United States, and formation of a special U.N. agency to work toward the reduction of world population.

Background Desired

Population studies and experience, economics, sociology, international affairs, public relations, and advertising.

Pathfinders Fund

Nine Galen St.
Suite 217
Watertown, MA 02172-4501

Established in 1957, Pathfinder promotes and supports population and family-planning activities in less developed countries, primarily by making grants to institutions, governments, organizations, and individuals in those countries. Pathfinders Fund seeks innovative ways and techniques to make fertility services more effective, less costly, and more readily available so that population growth may be controlled. It has overseas regional offices in Mexico City, Istanbul, and Nairobi and country offices in Jakarta, Lima, Karachi, Lagos, and El Salvador.

Background Desired

Population studies and experience, medicine, sociology, area studies and languages, and economic development.

Population Council*

One Dag Hammarskjold Plaza
New York, NY 10017

The functions of the council are to conduct research and provide professional services in the broad field of population, encompassing development issues and population policies; investigate into a safe and effective means of birth planning; and design, implement, and evaluate programs to provide birth planning services and information.

The council is in contact with institutions overseas having similar interests. Occasionally it provides financial support for the work of institutions and trains professionals in specialized areas of population studies. The council also distributes publications and information on population matters to interested professionals.

Background Desired

Demography studies, medicine, biology, public relations, publishing, and research ability. An M.A. or Ph.D. is preferred.

Population-Environment Balance

> 1325 G St., NW
> Washington, DC 20005

This organization works to obtain an "effective" immigration policy to include a legal immigration ceiling of 200,000, which is "approximately the same number of people who voluntarily leave the United States every year."

Background Desired

Economics, experience with immigration and immigrants, environmental studies, and statistics.

Population Institute*

> 110 Maryland Ave., NE
> P.O. Box 96872
> Washington, DC 20077-7550

The philosophy of the institute is that continued world population growth threatens resources, destroys the environment, and degrades human life. The institute approaches this problem by trying to bring about a change in attitudes of individuals as well as of societies.

Its *Communication Center* helps the television industry try to create a turnabout on population issues. It is responsible for many population articles in newspapers and magazine and works with national education leaders to promote population programs in the media.

The institute seeks to draw attention to those developing countries where the problems of overpopulation are most critical. They publicize the issue, develop the leadership required to overcome overpopulation, and address the developing world's needs for voluntary birth control.

Background Desired

Population and demographic studies, world resources, journalism, Third World area studies, economics, economic development, and public relations. An M.A. or Ph.D. is preferred.

Rainforest Alliance

> 1133 Broadway
> New York, NY 10010

The Rainforest Alliance is dedicated to the conservation of the world's tropical forests. The primary mission of the Rainforest Alliance is to develop and promote economically viable and socially desirable alternatives to tropical deforestation. These alternatives are designed in concert with local peoples to develop forest products and businesses that offer long-term, stable income for people living in or near tropical forests. The Rainforest Alliance also educates the public about tropical conservation.

Background Desired

Environmental science, biology, international affairs, development studies, and area studies.

Sierra Club*

> 730 Polk St.
> San Francisco, CA 94109
>
> or
>
> 625 Broadway
> New York, NY 10010

The slogan of the club is, "Not blind opposition to progress, but opposition to blind progress." This pretty well defines the attitude and activities of this environmentally conscious organization. It helped bring the National Park Service and the Forest Service into existence; it played a leading role in the establishment of many national parks; it tries to curtail overcutting in forests and to keep the wilderness in its natural state. The International Office of this organization works closely with the United Nations on international activities pertaining to the environment.

Background Desired

Environmental studies, world resources, international organization studies, and international relations. A B.A. may be accepted.

World Environment Center

> 419 Park Ave. South
> Suite 1404
> New York, NY 10016

The World Environment Center serves as a bridge between industry and government aimed at strengthening environmental management and industrial safety worldwide through the exchange of information and technical expertise. WEC has explored how environmental needs can best be served by U.S. expertise, and helped open an environmental center in Budapest. WEC has worked worldwide in many countries, including Thailand, Turkey, Indonesia, and Pakistan.

Background Desired

Environmental studies, development studies, and area studies.

World Resources Institute

> 1709 New York Ave., NW
> Washington, DC 20006

The WRI, a center for policy research, seeks to address a fundamental question: How can people and nations meet their basic needs and economic requirements without undermining the natural resources and environmental quality on which life depends? The WRI brings together leading thinkers from many fields and nations to study this question and to create policy options for the future. Through its research it provides information about global resources and environmental conditions. In order to increase public awareness, it publishes a variety of reports, and holds conferences and seminars.

Background Desired

Ecology, international affairs, economics, public relations, and research.

World Wildlife Fund

> 1250 24th St., NW
> Washington, DC 20037

This organization, which now includes the former Conservation Foundation, works to preserve wildlife by making modest investments of time and money in the activities of private conservation organizations, international agencies, and national governments. Among its accomplishments have been helping to create 437 national parks in countries including Kenya, Nepal, and Peru and pioneering debt-for-nature swaps in Ecuador and the Philippines. In more than 30 countries, World Wildlife Fund staff teaches local people to use alternative fuels and trains and equips rangers, guards, and anti-poaching teams.

Background Desired

Ecology, area studies, research, science, biology, zoology, and public relations.

Zero Population Growth

> 1400 16th St., NW Suite 320
> Washington, DC 20036

Here is yet another population-oriented nonprofit organization. ZPG maintains that unlimited population growth is threatening the quality of life of future generations and the planet's natural resources. It advocates a world with reproductive rights and the availability of effective contraception. It also considers urban blight, poverty, and the depletion of resources as additional results of uncontrolled population increase.

Background Desired

Population studies, labor relations, economics, and labor economics. A B.A. may be accepted.

BUSINESS AND LABOR

Amalgamated Clothing and Textile Workers Union

> 15 Union Square
> New York, NY 10003

This association has an international program that works toward "international labor unity." It has supported labor organizations in other countries and has sent funds to workers hit by natural disasters in various parts of the world. Amalgamated has been active in preventing unrestricted imports of textiles, and has also been instrumental in getting voluntary quotas imposed on some competitive Asian countries.

Background Desired

Trade unionism experience and motivation, industrial relations, economics, Asian studies, trade, and textiles. A B.A. is adequate if you have any of the above.

American Federation of Labor — Congress of Industrial Organizations*

> Department of International Affairs
> AFL-CIO
> 815 16th St., NW
> Wasington, DC 20006

The AFL-CIO's *Department of International Affairs* recommends foreign policy positions to trade union leadership and the rank and file. Among the international issues covered by this department are AFL-CIO policy toward the International Labor Organization, the International Confederation of Free Trade Unions, and other international labor organizations; the need for strong U.S. defenses; the nonexistence of trade unions and the exploitation of labor in communist countries; and the Arab-Israeli conflict.

The AFL-CIO is in contact with the embassies of foreign governments in an effort to promote better understanding of the American labor movement. The Department of International Affairs also furthers AFL-CIO policies through publications, conferences, orientation of foreign visitors, and trade union missions overseas.

Background Desired

Trade unionism, industrial relations, international relations, area studies (particularly of East Central Europe, Russia, and China), and economics. A B.A. may be accepted.

American Institute for Free Labor Development

1015 20th St., NW
Washington, DC 20036

The institute is engaged in technical assistance for the development of the democratic trade union movement in Latin America and English-speaking Caribbean countries. The AFL-CIO sponsors the institute, which has chosen two principal means of achieving its objective: education and social projects. AIFLD also sponsors an *Agrarian Union Development Service* that helps establish agricultural credit and marketing operations for farmers.

In collaboration with Latin American trade unions, the institute teaches union members the rights and responsibilities of democratic trade unionism. Central to its social projects work is the training of trade union members to participate in national and regional economic planning leading to the economic development of Latin America.

Background Desired

Trade unionism, industrial relations, economic development, and Latin American studies and languages. A B.A. may be accepted.

Business Council for International Understanding*

420 Lexington Ave.
New York, NY 10170

The BCIU provides cross-fertilization between the foreign affairs community of the U.S. government and American business, especially companies with foreign operations or affiliates. It focuses on improving the climate for international business-government relations at the policy-making level as well as in day-to-day operations.

BCIU briefs American business people and their families who are going to be stationed abroad through seminars at the American University in Washington. Another important BCIU function is to arrange consultations and briefings for American ambassadors going overseas.

Background Desired

Business administration, international relations, area studies, seminar organization, and research capability. A B.A. is sometimes adequate.

Business Council for the United Nations

60 East 42nd St.
New York, NY 10165

Composed of nearly a hundred American corporations, BCUN was founded 30 years ago to provide a better understanding of the United Nations throughout the business community. BCUN's series of educational programs brings business leaders and U.N. representatives together in off-the-record discussions in New York and some 40 cities across the United States each year. BCUN publishes "UN Alert," for business members and "Congressional Alert" for key members of Congress, both one-page news briefs on current U.N. issues.

Background Desired

Knowledge of the United Nations and the business community, administration, and conference seminar organization.

Center for International Private Enterprise (CIPE)

1615 H St., NW
Washington, DC 20062

CIPE's central focus for the 1990s is to work with private-sector organizations and leadership to forge open-market economic systems and support the democratic political process through development of the private sector. With this aim, CIPE subsidizes 7 organizations in Africa, 6 in Asia, 13 in Eastern Europe, and 13 in Latin America and the Caribbean.

Background Desired

Business, economics, international and regional affairs, administration, and management.

International Management and Development Institute

Watergate Office Building
2600 Virginia Ave., NW
Washington, DC 20037

The purpose of the institute is to "provide education which will strengthen corporate and government management teams internationally." Put another way, it hopes to increase government and public understanding of "the international corporation as a constructive force in the domestic and world community." It works to achieve its aims through government-business training programs, executive seminars, Washington briefings, and a general education campaign geared toward government and the public.

Background Desired

International business, business administration, economics, trade, and finance. A B.A. may be accepted.

International Metalworkers Federation (IMF)

> 54 bis, route des Acacias
> CH-1227, Carouge
> Geneva, Switzerland

The IMF is an international organization of metal-workers unions. The secretariat staff has departments for research, women, youth, vocational training, and publications. In addition to these concerns, the IMF is engaged in strengthening trade unions in developing countries. To this end, it has regional representatives for Latin America, West Asia, East Asia, and Africa. These representatives channel aid from the IMF to local trade unions needing assistance.

Background Desired

Trade unionism, industrial relations, metal-work experience, economics, research, and Third World area studies. A B.A. suffices.

International Transport Workers Federation

> Maritime House
> 133-35 Great Suffolk St.
> London, SEI 1PD
> England

The ITWF is one of the most active of international trade union movements and has worked well in furthering the economic and social interests of transport workers and their national unions. It has developed a comprehensive research arm, which has studied labor legislation, collective bargaining problems, and working conditions affecting its members.

Background Desired

Trade unionism, industrial relations, transport experience (road, air, sea, railway), and labor economics. A B.A. may be accepted.

National Foreign Trade Council*

> 100 East 42nd St.
> New York, NY 10017

Sound economic growth is an objective with which it is hard to disagree, although the means of achieving such growth may be subject to a great deal of controversy. The NFTC believes that foreign trade and investment are key instruments in achieving this growth; it further believes that close coordination of U.S. domestic and international economic policies is required to establish a favorable climate in which international business can operate to make effective use of these instruments. Specifically, the council performs research, issues documentation and policy statements, and holds conferences and seminars to make its point of view known.

Background Desired

Business administration, economics, trade, finance, and conference and seminar organization. A B.A. may be accepted.

Young Presidents Organization

> 451 South Decker
> Suite 200
> Irving, TX 75062

YPO is an educational association for chief executives who become presidents of their companies before age 40 — a key membership requirement. Its main purpose is to help members become better presidents through education and an exchange of ideas.

With memberships in more than 30 countries, YPO is an international organization. In addition to those in the United States, chapters are located in Europe, Canada, Japan, Mexico, Korea, Australia, and the Caribbean. To fulfill the educational purpose of the organization, seminars, conferences, and major meetings (called Universities for Presidents) are held each year. Both a quarterly magazine and a monthly newsletter, which feature reports on a wide range of subjects of interest of YPOers, are published.

Background Desired

Business administration, educational studies, teaching, and seminar conference organizing. A B.A. may be accepted.

RELIEF, REHABILITATION, HEALTH, AND HUMAN RIGHTS

American Council for Nationalities Service

95 Madison Ave.
New York, NY 10019

For 75 years this organization has promoted understanding and cooperation between the many nations and racial groups in the United States. ACNS monitors and reports on the refugee situation worldwide and promotes public policy to help immigrants. Through its local affiliates it assists immigrants to adjust to American life and become participating citizens. Assistance provided to immigrants covers finding jobs, learning English, reuniting their families, and generally helping them adjust to the eccentricities and ordinary customs of American life. ANCS also brings to light the rich contributions that immigrants make to the United States. ACNS offices are located in large American cities.

Background Desired

International relations, area and language studies, counseling, job placement, and social work. A B.A. is sometimes adequate.

American Friends Service Committee (AFSC)

1501 Cherry St.
Philadelphia, PA 19102

The AFSC was founded in 1917 by American Quakers to provide conscientious objectors to war with an alternative to military service, such as aiding civilian victims during war. Its work began with relief and medical services during World War I, then broadened to include an emphasis on nonviolent solutions to international conflicts. Conferences and seminars involving individuals of many nations are held frequently in order to increase understanding among all nations. In addition, in various countries of Africa, Asia, Latin America, and the Middle East, AFSC workers conduct programs of social and technical assistance "to enable people to discover and utilize their own power and resources." AFSC has international headquarters in Philadelphia and about 15 regional offices across the United States.

Background Desired

More than any particular curriculum or even experience, the service ideal is required of applicants for jobs. The AFSC expects its employees to be dedicated to the principles and work of the Friends. In addition, a background in international studies is helpful. A B.A. is adequate.

American Near East Refugee Aid

> 1522 K St., NW
> Washington, DC 20005

This organization was established by Americans concerned about the plight of the Palestinians. It provides assistance to education, health services, and community development projects among Palestinians primarily on the West Bank and in the Gaza Strip.

Background Desired

Health care, community development, education, Middle East studies, Arabic language, and public relations.

Amnesty International*

> 322 Eighth Ave.
> New York, NY 10001

Though writing letters, holding publicity campaigns, sending missions and observers, and publishing special reports, Amnesty International works to gain the freedom of prisoners of conscience and protect and preserve basic human rights. It also seeks humane treatment for all prisoners and detainees. In 1977 it won the Nobel Peace Prize. Since Amnesty International was founded, in 1961, it has worked on behalf of 25,000 prisoners.

Background Desired

International relations work and studies, and in particular a commitment to human rights activities. A B.A. is adequate.

Bread for the World

> 802 Rhode Island Ave., NE
> Washington, DC 20018

This organization seeks to eliminate hunger in the world. It successfully lobbied Congress to establish a four-million-ton wheat reserve against world famine.

It mobilizes public support for right-to-food resolutions to be passed by Congress. Although it does not distribute food, it is an effective lobbying force in alleviating world hunger. Volunteer interns are welcome.

Background Desired

Nutrition, public relations, administration, knowledge of developing areas and their food needs, and lobbying. A B.A. is usually adequate.

CARE (Cooperative for American Relief Everywhere)*

> 660 First Ave.
> New York, NY 10016

CARE was established to help the needs of millions of people left destitute in Europe after World War II. The founders were 22 American cooperative, relief, religious, refugee, and labor organizations.

CARE's initial efforts were centered around food packages. It has since moved into an additional type of aid with its self-help programs around the world. Partnership programs in nutrition, development, private enterprise development, and health are now a key feature. CARE also helps victims of natural disasters, such as famine, floods, or earthquakes, and victims of civil strife in all parts of the world.

Background Desired

Third world area studies and languages, nutrition, economic development, and health studies. A B.A. is adequate.

Catholic Relief Services*

> 209 West Fayette St.
> Baltimore, MD 21201

CRS is the official overseas relief and development agency of the Catholic Church in the United States. It channels foodstuffs to the world's needy. To help solve the world's food problem, it places high priority on projects designed to assist the small rural farmer, emphasizes consumer cooperatives and rural credit structures, and stresses water resource projects and agricultural training programs.

Background Desired

Social work, Third World area studies, economic development, agricultural economics, and food and nutrition studies. A B.A. suffices.

Center for Independent Living

> 2539 Telegraph Ave.
> Berkeley, CA 94704

CIL calls for an independent life-style and civil rights for disabled people. It offers attendant referrals, housing searches, employment services, deaf and blind services, independent living skills, peer support, and advocacy. CIL has helped people from Nicaragua, Jamaica, and the Virgin Islands start centers for the disabled.

Background Desired

Occupational therapy, public relations, knowledge of Latin America and the Caribbean, and Spanish. A B.A. is acceptable.

Church World Service*

> 475 Riverside Dr.
> New York, NY 10027

The CWS, which represents most of the Protestant denominations, has a relief and rehabilitation aim of feeding the hungry and resettling refugees, and a long-range aim of "development of people and peace in our time." Its programs operate in all areas of the world and its representatives are stationed on all continents. Its work in general is similar to that of CARE and Catholic Relief Services.

Background Desired

Area studies, international relations, social work, nutrition, economic development, agricultural economics, and, above all, the service ideal. A B.A. is adequate.

Committee on Migration and Refugee Affairs

> c/o American Council of Voluntary International Action
> 200 Park Ave. South
> New York, NY 10003

This committee, which operates under the auspices of the American Council of Voluntary Agencies for Foreign Service, has a Refugee Resource Center, which employs Joint Voluntary Agencies Representatives (JVAR) to help in refugee resettlement.

The JVAR office assists U.S. government officials in the processing of refugees for resettlement in this country, and represents voluntary agency concerns in the countries of first asylum, where refugees are selected for the U.S. program.

Background Desired

Work with refugees, knowledge and language of the countries from which refugees have fled as well as countries of first asylum. A B.A. is acceptable if combined with area knowledge.

Defense for Children International — U.S.

> 210 Forsyth St.
> New York, NY 10002

DCI — U.S. is a national child advocacy organization dedicated to protecting children everywhere. It is a grassroots human rights organization operating much as Amnesty International does for political prisoners and Oxfam for the starving. DCI — U.S. is part of the Swiss-based Defense for Children International, recognized as the world's foremost children's rights organization.

Background Desired

Human rights, social work, international affairs, administration, and public relations.

Food First

> 145 Ninth St.
> San Francisco, CA 94103

Food First is a project of the Institute for Food and Development Policy, founded in 1975 as a research, documentation, and education center. It believes hunger is spreading throughout the world not because of overpopulation, floods or droughts, or the economic underdevelopment of Third World people. Hunger, according to Food First, results from people being cut out of control over their food-producing resources. From the village level to the highest levels of international trade, fewer people are making the decisions about the use of their food resources. Food First addresses itself to this problem by trying to educate the public about the causes of and solutions to hunger. In addition to focusing on famine, Food First educates people on the toxic effects of chemical-intensive agriculture and the destructive effects of export-oriented development strategies and mega-dam projects. Food First has published books including *Aid as an Obstacle* and *Circles of Poison*.

Background Desired

Economics, economic development, research, public relations, education, nutrition, and community development. An M.A. is preferred.

Freedom from Hunger Foundation

1644 DaVinci Court
Davis, CA 95617

"Feed a man a fish and he will eat for a day. Teach him to fish and he will eat for a lifetime." This Chinese proverb expresses the philosophy of the Freedom from Hunger Foundation. Instead of providing food for hungry people, it offers programs of education and self-help designed to give them the knowledge and tools to improve their own lives.

Background Desired

Nutrition, agriculture, economics, economic development, and Third World area studies.

Freedom House

48 East 21st St.
New York, NY 10010

Freedom House was started to combat totalitarianism and strengthen democratic institutions and the right of individuals to free choice. The organization issues an annual report that evaluates the state and degree of freedom in every country in the world. Freedom House also holds conferences on issues revolving around freedom and publishes a bimonthly magazine, *Freedom at Issue*, as well as a number of books.

Background Desired

Dedication to the ideal of freedom, ability to organize conferences, and research capabilities. A B.A. may be accepted.

Fund for a Free South Africa (FreeSA)

729 Boylston St., Fifth Floor
Boston, MA 02116

FreeSA is a foundation that was started in 1986 by a group of South African exiles living in the United States. The fund was established to assist the oppressed majority in South Africa and to support the movement for a democratic, nonracial South Africa. FreeSA provides financial and technical assistance to organizations working in the areas of education, health care, labor, women, and youth.

Background Desired

South Africa, economics, finances, labor, health care, and development.

Human Rights Watch

485 Fifth Ave.
New York, NY 10017

or

1522 K St., NW
Suite 910
Washington, DC 20005

Human Rights Watch monitors the human rights practices of governments, protesting murder, "disappearances," torture, imprisonment, psychiatric abuse, censorship, and deprivation of political freedom. Annually, more than 100 investigative missions are sent out to gather current information on human rights in more than 60 countries.

This organization links 6 existing Watch committees: *Helsinki Watch, Americas Watch, Asia Watch, Africa Watch, Middle East Watch*, and the *Fund for Free Expression*. In Kenya, *Africa Watch* publicized the efforts of lawyers, clergy, and others to challenge the one-party rule and dictatorial government.

Background Desired

Area studies, languages, law, administration, foreign policy and international affairs, and a strong belief in the purposes and activity of this organization.

Institute of Rural Reconstruction (IRR)

> 475 Riverside Dr.
> Room 1270
> New York, NY 10115

The Institute of Rural Reconstruction helps villagers from lesser developed countries overcome poverty, hunger, and disease through a four-fold integrated program that increases the power of rural people to improve their education, livelihood, wealth, and government on a lasting basis. It is headquartered in the Philippines with affiliated rural-reconstruction movements in Africa, Asia, and Latin America.

Background Desired

Economic development, health care, agriculture, and African, Asian, or Latin American studies.

International Center for Research on Women (ICRW)

> 1717 Massachusetts Ave., NW
> Washington, DC 20036

The International Center for Research on Women focuses on the dual economic and family responsibilities of most women in Africa, Asia, and Latin America. Established in 1976, ICRW conducts research and makes policy recommendations, provides technical services, and educates people worldwide about the contributions of women to economic development.

Background Desired

Development studies, women's studies, area specialization, education, and public policy.

International League for Human Rights*

> 432 Park Ave. South
> New York, NY 10016

The league does in the international field what the American Civil Liberties Union does domestically: protect civil rights of individuals wherever they are being violated. This organization is devoted wholly to the task of advancing human rights throughout the world.

International League activities include: (1) supporting all U.N. efforts on behalf of human rights; (2) gathering facts on human rights violations and intervening directly with governments; (3) protesting political trials; (4) assisting political prisoners; (5) aiding refugees and exiles; (6) participating in international meetings on human rights; (7) providing counsel to governments; and (8) printing bimonthly news bulletins and other publications.

Background Desired

Interest in civil rights and international relations. A B.A. suffices sometimes.

International Red Cross*

> 7 Avenue de la Paix
> Geneva, Switzerland

> > or

> American Red Cross
> 2025 E St., NW
> Washington, DC 20006

The International Committee of the Red Cross acts as a neutral intermediary in time of conflict to protect victims of war in accordance with the Geneva Convention. The *League of Red Cross Societies*, another part of the International Red Cross, coordinates the efforts of member societies in meeting the needs of victims of natural disasters and refugees from war situations. Through special missions, the loan of experts, seminars, and publications, the league helps national societies to expand and improve their programs of disaster relief, nursing, blood donations, and public relations.

The *American Red Cross*, one of the more advanced of the league's members, helps meet emergency needs of victims of disaster, gives assistance to sister societies in extending their programs, and provides opportunities for officials of other countries to study American Red Cross programs.

Background Desired

International relations and the service ideal. A B.A. is usually adequate.

International Rescue Committee*

> 386 Park Ave. South
> New York, NY 10016

The IRC is in the forefront of all refugee crises. In 1991, IRC medical, public health, and sanitation teams provided life-saving assistance to 800,000 Kurdish refugees. In Sudan, where famine is imminent, IRC has expanded its program to help prevent epidemics and malnutrition.

Financial aid, counseling, and resettlement services are provided also for refugees from the former Soviet Union and Eastern Europe, as well as from Afghanistan, Central America, the Caribbean, Ethiopia, Mozambique, Liberia, Vietnam, and Costa Rica.

IRC has 12 offices in the United States and 19 offices overseas.

Background Desired

Area studies and languages, work with refugees, and social work. A B.A. sometimes suffices.

Robert F. Kennedy Memorial Center for Human Rights

> 132 East 33rd St.
> Seventh Floor
> New York, NY 10016

The Robert F. Kennedy Memorial Center for Human Rights was established in 1988 to promote the work of the RFK Human Rights Award recipients. The center has helped gain the release of political prisoners in South Korea, supplied medical books and journals to Poland's first independent medical library, and contributed to the International Human Rights Law Group on the Chilean electoral process.

Background Desired

Human rights, international affairs, and area studies.

Medical Aid for El Salvador

> 6030 Wilshire Blvd.
> Suite 200
> Los Angeles, CA 90036

As its title suggests, this organization supports humanitarian aid, rather than military aid, to El Salvador.

Background Desired

Administration, Spanish, knowledge of El Salvador, and a belief that medical aid should replace military aid.

National Council for International Health

1701 K St., NW Suite 600
Washington, DC 20006

The mission of NCIH is to improve health worldwide by increasing U.S. awareness and response to international health needs. NCIH has identified three priority areas for its work: information, education, and policy (to provide a forum for international health policy discussions).

Background Desired

Medicine and health, public relations, administration, and education.

NEST Foundation (New El Salvador Today)

P.O. Box 411436
San Francisco, CA 94141

NEST provides humanitarian aid to communities in El Salvador. In areas devastated by war, NEST is helping with women's health care, education and cooperative projects, the reconstruction of villages, skills training for orphans, human rights and legal assistance, and environmental education and sustainable agriculture. NEST is expanding its program to provide technical assistance and access to credit. It is placing emphasis on projects that support long-term community self-sufficiency, environmental and economic sustainability, and leadership and skills development, especially for women.

Background Desired

Public relations, communications and writing skills, and belief in NEST's work in El Salvador.

Nicaragua Medical Aid

1400 Shattuck Ave.
Suite 7-125
Berkeley, CA 94709

Nicaragua Medical Aid has airlifted medicines and medical supplies for people devastated by natural disasters, the Contra war, and the U.S. trade embargo. "Let us send life, not death" describes the purpose of this organization.

Background Desired

Knowledge of Central America, belief in the functions of NMA, administration, public relations, and Spanish.

Operation Exodus

> 99 Park Ave., Suite 300
> New York, NY 10016-1599

Operation Exodus is a special campaign of the United Jewish Appeal in partnership with Jewish federations throughout the United States to aid Russian Ethiopian Jewish immigrants. UJA and the federations meet humanitarian needs in Israel, the United States, and around the world.

Background Desired

Israeli studies, fund raising, and public relations.

Oxfam-America

> 26 West St.
> Boston, MA 02116

Oxfam (Oxford Committee for Famine Relief) provides direct relief as well as long-term development assistance in Africa, Asia, and the Caribbean. Field directors employed by Oxfam encourage projects in which local people do the work, make the decisions, and take charge of their own development. Projects are in the fields of nutrition, health, agriculture, and family planning. Oxfam also produces and distributes educational materials on issues of hunger and development in industrialized countries. There are seven autonomous Oxfam organizations throughout the world.

Background Desired

Economic and community development, health care, agriculture, nutrition, languages, and area studies in the developing world.

PLAN International, or Childreach
(formerly Foster Parents Plan)

> 155 Plan Way
> Warwick, RI 02886-1099

Childreach, a program of PLAN International, seeks foster parents in developed countries as sponsors for needy children and their families in developing countries. Current programs operate in more than 23 countries in Latin America, Asia, and Africa in the areas of health, education, family income, and community development. Seventy percent of PLAN International's expenditures are for its overseas programs and services and six percent for development education in the United States and an intercultural communications program.

Background Desired

African, Asian, or Latin American studies with the appropriate language, plus the service ideal. Social work experience is also useful, as is some background in nutrition, medical services, agriculture, and vocational education. A B.A. is adequate.

Project HOPE

People to People Health Foundation
Millwood, VA 22646

Project HOPE began in 1958. Two years later the world's first peacetime hospital ship, S.S. *Hope,* sailed on her maiden voyage, bringing a cargo of health educators to developing nations requesting HOPE's assistance. With the retiring of the ship, HOPE's objective focused on health-care education at home and abroad. Health personnel in the developing world are taught modern techniques of medicine, nursing, and dentistry. Among the countries now being served by HOPE are Barbados, Belize, Brazil, Costa Rica, China, Chile, Czechoslovakia, Egypt, El Salvador, Grenada, Guatemala, Haiti, Honduras, Indonesia, Jamaica, Panama, Poland, Portugal, Swaziland, and the Southwest border area of the United States.

Background Desired

Nutrition, health care, nursing, medicine, knowledge of developing areas and their languages, and (in the U.S.) public relations and administration.

Refugees International

220 I St., NE Suite 240
Washington, DC 20002

This organization was founded in 1979 to "push the world to cope with the terrible plight of the Cambodian refugees." Since then, RI has become the "refugees advocate" for the plight of the Vietnamese boat people, the victims of the Liberian civil war, and, more recently, for the Kurds on the Turkish border.

Background Desired

Refugee problems, international affairs, and regional studies.

Save the Children Federation

> 50 Wilton Rd.
> Westport, CT 06880
>
> or
>
> 777 U.N. Plaza
> New York, NY 10017

Founded in 1932 to help Appalachian victims of the Depression, Save the Children is a pioneer in community-based development programs aimed at helping children by improving life in the communities where they live. It is involved in hundreds of overseas communities in 38 countries. Projects have included education and human resource development, small enterprise development, resource conservation, and refugee and disaster relief.

Background Desired

International relations, nutrition and health studies, social welfare, community development, economic development, and Third World studies and languages. A B.A. may be accepted.

World Concern

> Box 33000
> Seattle, WA 98133

This is a Christian organization that rushes aid to disaster areas while stressing self-help in the rehabilitation of people. It has 74 field workers on assignment in Africa, Asia, and Latin America. Specific projects involve agriculture, public health, water resource development, and handcrafts.

Background Desired

Agriculture, health, relief, and knowledge of developing countries and their languages.

World Rehabilitation Fund

386 Park Ave. South
Room 500
New York, NY 10016

Founded in 1955, this fund assists private voluntary organizations and governments in developing countries to establish, improve, and expand comprehensive rehabilitation services for physically and mentally disturbed people. One hundred fifty-four countries have been assisted in bringing hope and help to disabled people through the provision of artificial limbs and braces, the training of doctors and technicians, and the development of rehabilitation centers to train the disabled to help themselves. WRF also conducts national assessments of rehabilitation resources and needs, and helps to establish standards and guidelines for rehabilitation professions.

Background Desired

Medicine, administration, public relations, languages, and studies of developing countries.

ORGANIZATIONS THAT WORK FOR PEACE

Arms Control Association

11 Dupont Circle, NW
Washington, DC 20036

The ACA tries to promote public understanding of policies and programs in respect to arms control and disarmament. It aims to get public acceptance for limiting armaments and to otherwise reduce international tensions. It puts out a monthly periodical, "Arms Control Today," a product of the research conducted by the association.

Background Desired

Russian and Chinese studies, military technology, disarmament studies, and research experience. An M.A. or Ph.D. is preferred.

Carnegie Endowment for International Peace*

2400 N St., NW
Suite 700
Washington, DC 20037

Established in 1910, the Carnegie Endowment aims to promote international peace and understanding through research, discussion, publication, and education in international affairs and American foreign policy. The endowment covers military, political, and economic topics. It publishes the quarterly journal *Foreign Policy* and hosts the program *Face-to-Face*, discussions between international leaders and involved Americans. The Carnegie Endowment has organized numerous programs, including the *National Commission on America*, the *New World Project on Self-Determination*, the *Immigration Policy Project*, and a study group on nuclear weapons. In the field of international law, major activities are aimed at improving international law training in developing nations.

Background Desired

International relations, international law, foreign policy analysis, military technology, national security, international organizations, and U.N. studies. A Ph.D. is preferred.

Center for Defense Information

> 1500 Massachusetts Ave., NW
> Washington, DC 20005

The CDI is a research organization that analyzes military spending, policies, and weapons systems. The director and staff regularly present military analyses on these subjects to the Pentagon, State Department, and before congressional committees and the media. The CDI is committed to supporting an effective, but not excessive, military program, eliminating waste in military spending, and preventing nuclear war.

Background Desired

Military, science, engineering, research ability, and administration.

The Fund for Peace

> 345 East 46th St.
> New York, NY 10017

or the individual projects at:

> 1755 Massachusetts Ave., NW
> Washington, DC 20036

The fund is dedicated to "understanding and alleviating conditions which imperil human survival." The fund maintains a strong commitment to education, the preservation of human rights, the advancement of social and economic justice, and the cultivation of an open and informed society in the United States and around the world.

There are five major projects within the fund:

1. The *Center for International Policy* follows the peace process in Central America and provides policymakers and the press with analyses of the prospects for peace in that area.
2. The *Center for National Security Studies* studies the relationship between national security and civil liberties.
3. The *Institute for the Study of World Politics* supports research into current problems of arms control, Third World development, human rights, regional conflicts, and international economic issues.
4. The *National Security Archive* analyzes and disseminates recently classified government documents on contemporary national security issues.
5. *The Human Rights in the Horn of Africa Program* is concerned with building human rights capacity and supporting local groups through education and publication services.

Background Desired

With the variety of functions performed by the fund and its projects, useful backgrounds cover a broad spectrum: area studies and languages, publications, research, economics, economic development, international affairs, law, foreign policy, public relations, administration, and national security.

International Peace Academy*

777 U.N. Plaza
New York, NY 10017

IPA concentrates on teaching basic practical skills associated with the achievement of peace: conflict analysis, mediation, negotiation, and the presence of an impartial third party to prevent or limit hostilities. It cooperates with nongovernmental organizations, governments, and educational institutions throughout the world to organize courses on conflict resolution; conducts courses and seminars on its own on this theme; publishes material on peacekeeping; performs research to strengthen education and training for peace; and organizes new national committees.

Background Desired

Peace studies, conflict resolution, international organizations, administration, and seminar organization. An M.A. or Ph.D. is preferred.

The Henry L. Stimson Center

Suite 204
1350 Connecticut Ave., NW
Washington, DC 20036

The Henry L. Stimson Center is a small research and educational institute in Washington, DC, with a focus on international security and arms control issues.

Background Desired

International studies and security studies.

Peace Research Institute

25 Dundana Ave.
Dundas, Ontario
Canada L9H 4E5

The Peace Research Institute publishes the *Peace Research Abstracts Journal (PRAJ)*, which contains about 500 summaries of peace-related articles, essays, and books received by 360 universities and governments in 42 countries. It also publishes *Peace Research Reviews* that provides a literature survey of a specific topic in each issue.

Background Desired

Human rights, peace studies, international affairs, and area studies.

World Policy Institute

777 U.N. Plaza
New York, NY 10017

The purpose of the institute is to develop and implement proposals for preventing war, advancing human rights, and establishing a healthy global ecology.

The World Policy Institute, formerly the Institute for World Order, changed its name in 1982 to reflect a new emphasis on scholarly research aimed at producing policy recommendations — in the form of books, World Policy papers, and briefings — for achieving a more peaceful structure of international relations. One of its most helpful publications is *Peace and World Order Studies: A Curriculum Guide*, a comprehensive compilation of syllabi of human rights and peace-related courses. The book also contains a collection of case study articles on the history, rationale, and intellectual content of selected peace and world order programs in the United States and abroad, as well as a list of foundations that provide seed money to faculty developing human rights and disarmament courses. A recent publication is *Post-Reagan America*.

Background Desired

Interest in peace studies, international studies, ecology and environment, and economics. A B.A. is adequate for some administrative and public relations jobs.

Others

There are many other organizations that work for peace and arms control, and against a nuclear buildup. The backgrounds these organizations find desirable include international affairs, public relations, lobbying, fund raising, military and Russian studies, weapons technology, and, above all, belief in arms control. Among these groups are:

1. SANE-Freeze

> 1819 H St., NW
> Suite 640
> Washington, DC 20006

Lobbies for arms control and against nuclear proliferation.

2. Council for a Livable World

> 100 Maryland Ave., NE
> Washington, DC 20002

> or

> 11 Beacon St.
> Boston, MA 02108

3. Clergy and Laity Concerned

> 198 Broadway
> New York, NY 10038

Has many grassroots chapters.

4. World Federalists Association

> 418 7th St., SE
> Washington, DC 20032

Also works on Law of the Sea and U.N. reform.

5. National Peace

> 110 Maryland Ave., NE
> Washington, DC 20002

Research on conflict resolution.

6. Center for War/Peace Studies

> 218 East 18th St.
> New York, NY 10003

Also research and educational work on Law of the Sea and U.N. reform.

7. Center for Defense Information

> 1500 Massachusetts Ave., NW
> Washington, DC 20036

Supports a strong defense but monitors the military for excess spending.

8. Washington Peace Center

> 2111 Florida Ave., NW
> Washington, DC 20008

9. Physicians for Social Responsibility

> 639 Massachusetts Ave.
> Cambridge, MA 02139

OTHER NONPROFIT ORGANIZATIONS

American Council of Learned Societies (ACLS)

> 228 East 45th St.
> New York, NY 10017-3398

This council, composed of national scholarly organizations concerned with the humanities, administers programs of fellowships and grants designed to advance research in the following fields, among others: area studies, languages, economics, and political science.

Most of the council's work related to international and foreign area studies is carried out by committees appointed jointly with the Social Science Research

Council. There are now 11 joint area studies committees. Of these, the *Joint Committee on Chinese Studies* and the *Joint Committee on Eastern Europe* are administered by the ACLS.

Background Desired

Applicants for jobs should have a background in area studies, languages, and sometimes administration and public relations. Applicants for grants should have a Ph.D.

American Society of International Law

2223 Massachusetts Ave., NW
Washington, DC 20008

This society fosters the study of international law and promotes the practice of international relations based on law and justice. It is a forum for the exchange of views on current international legal topics and a center for research on issues concerning international law. It publishes books and periodicals on international law and sponsors student activities in this field.

Background Desired

International law. A law degree is preferred.

Ralph Bunche Institute on the United Nations*

Graduate School and University Center
33 West 42nd St.
New York, NY 10036

This is the only American academic institution concentrating exclusively on the United Nations. For its faculty it draws on the resources of the graduate school of CUNY as well as on Columbia and New York universities. The institute emphasizes developing scholarship on the United Nations among graduate students and postdoctoral researchers. The latter are teamed up with scholars in various ways (e.g., coauthorship, panel discussions, manuscript reading). The aim is to develop not only current research and writing about the United Nations, but also a new generation of scholars dedicated to research about the world organization. The institute also carries on a program of seminars and workshops to promote understanding of the United Nations.

Background Desired

International relations, U.N. studies, conference organizing, and research. A Ph.D. is preferred.

The Christic Institute

> 1324 North Capitol St., NW
> Washington, DC 20002

This institute was founded by those who successfully pursued the Karen Silkwood and Greensboro Civil Rights cases. A previous focus of the organization was on the diversion of profits from Iran to the contras in Nicaragua. The institute's work consists of both investigation and litigation. During 1990 the Christic Institute emphasized the dangers of covert operations and drafted a set of guiding principles leading to the development of an alternative foreign policy. Their financial status, however, is presently in jeopardy. Check with the institute before applying.

Background Desired

International affairs, law, research and investigative ability, public relations, area studies, and languages.

Inter Action (formerly the American Council for Voluntary International Action)

> 1717 Massachusetts Ave., NW
> Suite 801
> Washington, DC 20036

Inter Action provides a forum for cooperation, joint planning, and the exchange of ideas and information among American voluntary agencies engaged in overseas work. Inter Action is organized as a confederation of member agencies and is governed by a board of directors composed of one representative from each member organization. It is supported by its membership.

At one time, Inter Action operated the Technical Assistance Information Clearing House under a grant from the Agency for International Development. Inter Action still publishes *Member Profiles*, which reviews the activities of American nonprofit organizations engaged in agriculture, community development, education, and health. In addition, Inter Action publishes a newsletter called *Monday Developments* that lists job openings for a variety of development organizations.

Even though Inter Action is a coalition of more than 100 private and voluntary organizations working in international relief, migration and refugee assistance, and development education on Third World issues, it does not give grants, nor does it place personnel with member agencies.

Background Desired

Overseas experience in a Third World country, public health, agriculture, forestry, water supply, construction, project management, engineering, logistics, and languages. A B.A. or M.A. in one of the fields of study pertinent to the program of the agency to which you are applying is suggested.

Federation for American Immigration Reform (FAIR)

> 1666 Connecticut Ave., NW
> Suite 400
> Washington, DC 20009

FAIR aims to tighten border controls so that illegal immigration is cut down or eliminated. The appeal it uses is that illegal immigration is taking away jobs from unemployed Americans.

Background Desired

Latin American (especially Mexican) affairs, labor relations, Spanish, and public relations.

Institute of Public Administration*

> 55 West 44th St.
> New York, NY 10036

IPA is one of the oldest centers for research, consulting, and education in public administration and public policy analysis in the United States. Its current program focuses on five areas: (1) planning and management under resource constraints; (2) stature and effectiveness of public service; (3) relationships between public and private sectors; (4) governmental structure and intergovernmental program responsibilities; and (5) international activities. On the international level IPA engages in research and provides technical and training assistance to strengthen the capacity to manage effectively. IPA has undertaken consultancies on budgeting, urban planning, and project management.

International Center*

> 119 West 40th St.
> New York, NY 10018

International Center provides assistance to international visitors facing the complexities of American life, particularly in New York City. The foreign clientele served by the center consists not only of the casual visitor but also of business people on assignment, U.N. employees, and officials of foreign diplomatic missions. Center services include social activities, tours, visits to American homes, conversational practice in English, advice and counseling, and help in locating housing.

Background Desired

International relations, languages, program organization, and knowledge of New York. A B.A. is adequate.

National Endowment for the Humanities

> 1100 Pennsylvania Ave., NW
> Washington, DC 20004

The National Endowment is a national grant-making agency supporting projects of research, education, and public activity in the humanities. The humanities include "those aspects of the social sciences employing historical or philosophical approaches," which in turn have been defined as including cultural anthropology, political theory, and international relations. Only a small part of available funds is granted in the international sector, but its existence may be of interest to those of you with an international relations background.

Background Desired

International relations and experience in obtaining grants. An M.A. or Ph.D. is preferred.

National Geographic Society

> 17th and M Sts., NW
> Washington, DC 20036

This is a scientific and educational organization for increasing geographic knowledge and promoting research and exploration in all parts of the world. The work of the society is much in evidence through its publication, *National Geographic*.

Background Desired

Geography studies, research ability, editing of articles, and environmental studies. A B.A. may be accepted.

National Service Secretariat

5140 Sherier Place, NW
Washington, DC 20016

The National Service Secretariat stimulates interest in and serves as a clearinghouse for national service throughout the world. Reflective of its overall objectives, the National Service Secretariat recently held a conference on National Youth Service: A Global Perspective, attended by representatives from 14 countries in North America, Latin America, Europe, Asia, and Africa. The representatives affirmed the benefits of national youth service as a positive instrument of youth development.

Background Desired

Economics, economic development, and generally the same background that might be offered for the Peace Corps: conservation, education, health care, and literacy training.

New York City Commission for the United Nations*

2 U.N. Plaza
New York, NY 10017

This is the result of the recognition by the City of New York that it has responsibility for establishing the best possible relationship with personnel of the United Nations and foreign diplomatic missions. The commission, therefore, helps diplomatic personnel assigned to New York with problems such as housing and schooling.

Background Required

International relations, international organization studies, and a thorough knowledge of New York and its bureaucracy. Legal background is helpful. A B.A. is adequate.

New York State Government

> New York State Education Department
> Cultural Education Center
> Washington Ave.
> Albany, NY 12210

New York and other state governments offer a variety of possible employment opportunities for those with international training. New York actually has overseas offices for its tourism and commerce departments, and in education has extensive employment in foreign languages, social studies, and bilingual education. For some years the State Education Department has maintained a network of small offices concerned directly with education about the Third World — the *Center for International Programs and Comparative Studies*, the *Foreign Area Materials Center*, and the *Educational Resources Center*.

Background Desired

While opportunities for permanent employment with these organizations are rare, they do sponsor a number of short-term projects, which may offer employment possibilities for persons skilled in education as well as international studies.

Simon Wiesenthal Center

> 9760 West Pico Blvd.
> Los Angeles, CA 90035

The center was founded in 1977 to awaken the American people to the danger they face from well-financed hate groups operating all over the country. It is dedicated to preventing another Holocaust. To this effect the center provides multimedia programs for interested parties. In order to teach young people how and why the Holocaust happened, the center carries on education programs for students in high schools and colleges. The center has international offices in Toronto, Paris, and Jerusalem.

Background Desired

Research, knowledge of the Holocaust, public relations, and education.

U.S. Committee for UNICEF*

> 331 East 38th St.
> New York, NY 10016

This organization aims to inform Americans about UNICEF and the problems of the world's children, as well as to raise funds for UNICEF. The committee produces educational material for primary and secondary schools. Major fund-raising programs include the Trick-or-Treat Halloween collections, greeting card sales, a bike-a-thon and a swim-a-thon, recycling for UNICEF, and film benefits.

Background Desired

Knowledge of UNICEF, work with children, public relations, fund-raising, administration, teaching, and educational studies. A B.A. is adequate.

United Service Organizations (USO)

> 151 West 46th St.
> New York, NY 01136
>
> or
>
> 601 Indiana Ave., NW
> Washington, DC 20004

USO, which came to prominence in World War II as a center of entertainment for the armed forces, has continued its work in peacetime. About a hundred USO centers are operated in various parts of the United States and in foreign countries where there are significant U.S. forces. These "away-from-home" centers provide social, educational, recreational, religious, and welfare services for all servicemen and servicewomen. The famous USO shows offer entertainment to patients in veterans' hospitals and to the military on active duty abroad.

Background Desired

Show business (if applying for a performer's job), and administration and organizational abilities for those in headquarters. A B.A. is adequate.

U.S. Youth Council

> 1522 K St., NW
> Washington, DC 20005

The goal of the Youth Council is to increase the participation of young people in democratic institutions, both in the United States and abroad. During the 1950s, it sponsored biracial student and youth conferences in the South. From its early days it has also brought young leaders from other countries to the

United States to examine and participate in our institutions. More currently, it has been active in helping young people in developing countries build their own representative institutions.

Background Desired

Work with students and youth, exchange program experience, and developing country studies. A B.A. suffices.

10

INTERNATIONAL COMMUNICATIONS

WHAT IS "COMMUNICATIONS"?

The term "communications" in this handbook covers print or newspaper journalism, radio and TV broadcasting, and magazine and book publishing. All three areas have certain features in common. For one thing, they pay considerably less to the beginner than government, the United Nations, business, or banking. Low salaries almost seem to be a test of motivation and dedication, qualities that are essential for most careers in communications. Small salaries may also ward off the dilettante attracted to this field by its apparent glamor, although in reality there is just as much tedium in a beginning communications career as in many others.

A second feature common to print journalism, broadcasting, and publishing is that you may have to put your international training on the back burner during the initial states of your career. The reasons for this vary by occupation. In the case of journalism and broadcasting, international news is covered mainly by the large metropolitan dailies and broadcasting stations. Reporting jobs in these organizations are practically nonexistent for the beginner. If upon graduation you apply to the *New York Times* or NBC, you will likely be advised to get a job on a small-town newspaper or broadcasting station and accumulate some experience before trying out for "the big time."

Your initial job in the boondocks may be in obits, sports, or local news, but hardly in international. After a few years you may progress to a small metropolitan paper or station where your international background will still be of peripheral interest to your employer. It is only later — with five years' or more experience — that you will be considered for a reporting job with a large metropolitan paper or station. Even then, don't expect immediate recognition of your international background. If you do land a job with the *New York Times* or Associated Press, for example, it doesn't mean you will soon be sent abroad as a foreign correspondent or even work in headquarters on international news. These jobs are plums usually reserved for those who have made names for themselves after some years in New York.

The above represents the norm for newspapers and broadcasting. As we have stressed before, there are always exceptions. If your father is the boyhood friend of the managing editor of a large paper, you may be able during your junior year to land a summer job that can blossom into a reporting job when you graduate. Or an even more unlikely event: If you have command of an exotic language at a time when a news service is desperately in need of someone with that language fluency for an overseas office, you may be hired. It would be wise to recognize, however, that the chances of this happening are slim indeed.

In the case of book publishing, you may have to put your international training on hold for quite another reason. The international business of most publishers, although growing, is still small. Accordingly, there is usually only limited value placed on your international background. Your chances improve if you apply to the following types of publishers:

1. *Firms that specialize in medical, scientific, and technical books*   These are the best-selling books overseas. The international sales of these companies may amount to as much as 40 percent of total sales.
2. *Firms that have foreign parents or subsidiaries*   These are especially good targets if some of the employees may be transferred to another part of the company from the United States.

Your entry job will most likely involve assisting in the selling, marketing, or editing of books for the American market. But even in houses where the international may only amount to a small percentage of total business, there is still international work to be done. Once you are on the payroll — even if it is on a strictly domestic job — you can probably maneuver a transfer to the international division when a vacancy arises.

The largest publishers have an International Sales Division at headquarters that is responsible for placing books of that house in the bookstores of foreign countries. Also at headquarters there is likely to be a subsidiary rights department responsible for licensing foreign rights, including translations.

The procedure for marketing books abroad depends on the size of the company. The largest companies employ agents overseas to sell their books or translation rights to foreign publishers. Smaller U.S. publishers without overseas agents may send copies of books and galley proofs to foreign publishers in order to effect sales. The annual Frankfurt and London book fairs provide occasions for book publishers of all countries to sell books they control, as well as to negotiate translation rights. In addition, there is a Children's Book Fair held every year in Bologna, Italy.

Background Desired

To prepare yourself for a long-range international career in journalism or broadcasting, take courses in journalism as well as in international affairs. Make them joint specializations. At least one journalism course should be practical; i.e., it should include exercises for covering a story and then submitting your article to a presumed editor a few hours later.

Courses in economics can be most helpful. So few economists can make their science understandable to a wide public that if you can write economics-oriented stories that are informative and enjoyable you may well find yourself a national treasure.

An internship at a local paper, wire service, or broadcasting station will also be extraordinarily illuminating. Besides, it will look very good on your résumé, even if the experience does not lead to a job upon graduation.

If you can't find a paid job and you intend to go abroad anyway, contact any of the wire services or major dailies to see if you can become a "stringer." You will not be on the regular payroll, but you can submit stories and articles and get paid for those that are accepted. Changes of being a "stringer" are obviously better if the wire service or newspaper to which you are applying does not have a regular correspondent in the country where you plan to be. This background also adds strength to your résumé.

If qualifications other than the above are needed for journalism and broadcasting, the additional background desired will be noted in individual cases. The background desired for publishing will be covered later in the chapter.

Travel Abroad and Languages

If you do land an internationally oriented job in publishing, you will usually work in the United States, with perhaps an occasional trip abroad. In contrast, foreign correspondents of the wire services and large metropolitan dailies spend the majority of their careers overseas. A tour of duty abroad may last many years, depending on the area of assignment. If you are assigned overseas, language proficiency is, of course, a great asset.

As in the other chapters, we will list only a few examples of newspapers, broadcasting stations, and publishers. Directories and reference works with more detailed listing of newspapers, periodicals, and publishers are found in the Bibliography.

PRINT JOURNALISM

Associated Press

> Personnel Department
> 50 Rockefeller Plaza
> New York, NY 10020

The AP has grown since 1848 from a small domestic staff and one lone foreign correspondent in Nova Scotia to a cadre of 3,000 reporters, editors, photographers, and staff in the United States and abroad. It is not only the oldest and largest news-gathering organization, it is also the backbone of the world's information system, reaching more than one billion people a day through 16,000 new outlets around the globe.

As Mark Twain once said, "There are only two forces that can carry light to all corners of the globe — the sun in the heavens and the Associated Press down here."

As of 1991, the AP has more than 86 foreign offices and 143 bureaus in the United States. The size of the office varies from a single correspondent in Islamabad, Pakistan, to a 120-person bureau in Washington, DC.

For employment, contact the chief of the bureau nearest to you or the AP Personnel Department in New York.

Background Desired

Writing ability, languages, economics, political science, and international affairs.

The Chicago Tribune

> Tribune Tower
> 435North Michigan Ave.
> Chicago, IL 60611

The *Chicago Trib* has more than ten full-time foreign correspondents, based in Berlin, Moscow, and London, along with other cities. In addition, it uses part-time correspondents and "stringers" for coverage in other parts of the world.

Background Desired

Writing ability, languages, journalism, international affairs, and economics.

The Christian Science Monitor

> One Norway St.
> Boston, MA 02115

The *Monitor* publishes not only daily North American editions, but also a weekly international edition, which is printed in London and distributed worldwide. The *Monitor*'s international news bureaus are located in Beijing, Bonn, Jerusalem, London, Mexico City, Moscow, Nairobi, Paris, Sydney, Tokyo, and the United Nations.

Background Desired

Writing ability, journalism, languages, international affairs, and economics.

Dow Jones Newspaper Fund

> P.O. Box 300
> Princeton, NJ 08543

The fund is a foundation that aims to encourage talented young people to enter news careers. Its programs serve the news industry by locating minority-member journalists and new editors, by encouraging excellence in journalism teaching at the high-school level, and by providing information about journalism career opportunities. The following programs cover these needs: *Editing Internship Program, Reporting Internship Program, Teacher Fellowship Program, Urban Journalism Workshops, Urban Writing Competition, Editor-in-Residence Program,* and *Career Information Program.*

Background Desired

Writing ability, journalism, languages, international affairs, and economics.

Editor and Publisher

> 11 West 19th St.
> New York, NY 10011

E and P, the weekly newsmagazine of the newspaper industry, is often referred to as the "newspaperman's newspaper." Its coverage includes activities of all departments of U.S. newspapers, including news and editorial, advertising, circulation, business, promotion, personnel, and public relations. *E and P* also publishes the *International Year Book*.

Background Desired

Public relations, advertising, journalism, and writing ability.

Facts on File

> 460 Park Ave. South
> New York, NY 10016

Facts on File publishes a reference work of world happenings that is available at schools and libraries. Weekly updating of this material is undertaken by a staff of researchers whose functions are broken down into geographic areas.

Background Desired

For research: area studies, international economics, and foreign policy.

Index on Censorship

> Scholars and Writers International Press
> 39C Highbury Place
> London N51QP England

Index on Censorship is a magazine devoted to reporting on repression around the world. It is published in London every two months and has become a source of information about writers, scholars, artists, and others suffering under regimes of the right or left. The magazine also keeps track of restrictions on the United States such as the barring of foreign writers by Washington on political grounds.

Background Desired

Writing skills, area studies and languages, editorial work, administration, and publishing.

Knight-Ridder Newspapers, Inc.

One Herald Plaza
Miami, FL 33132-1693

Knight-Ridder is an international information and communications company engaged in newspaper publishing, business news, information services, and cable television. Knight-Ridder's various information services reach more than 100 million people in 135 countries. The newspaper division has 28 daily newspapers located from coast to coast. Its range is from papers with a half million circulation (*Detroit Free Press, Miami Herald, Philadelphia Inquirer*) to those with less than 25,000 (*Boca Raton News*). Knight-Ridder has 14 foreign bureaus throughout the world and representatives for the financial news bureau in 42 countries.

Background Desired

Writing ability, journalism, languages, international affairs, and economics.

The Los Angeles Times

Times Mirror Square
Los Angeles, CA 90053

The *LA Times* covers all major areas and countries with its 19 full-time foreign correspondents: Athens, Bangkok, Bonn, Brussels, Buenos Aires, Cairo, Hong Kong, Jerusalem, Johannesburg, London, Mexico City, Moscow, Nairobi, New Delhi, Paris, Rome, Tokyo, Toronto, and the United Nations.

The *Los Angeles Times* is owned by Times Mirror, a media and information company that owns numerous newspapers (including the *New York Newsday*, the *Baltimore Sun*), magazines (like *Field & Stream, The Sporting News*), and cable television stations.

Background Desired

Writing ability, languages, journalism, international affairs, and economics.

New England Press Association

P.O. Box 820, Astor Station
Boston, MA 02123-0820

The association represents the interests of the community press of New England, whether in a small town, large town, city, suburb, or county. Its membership from the six-state area is made up of weekly, semiweekly, triweekly, and daily newspapers.

Two of the association's services are of interest:

1. NEPA arranges for newspaper leaders in New England to make study missions abroad in important countries so that on their return they can inform the American public "what people are really like" overseas.
2. NEPA has a placement service, which acts as a clearing house and registration headquarters for newspapers seeking personnel as well as for individuals looking for jobs. This service applies only to New England.

Background Desired

Writing ability, journalism, languages, international affairs, and economics.

Newsweek Magazine

> 444 Madison Ave.
> New York, NY 10022

The magazine works much the same as *Time*, described on page 343.

The New York Daily News

> 220 East 42nd St.
> New York, NY 10017

The *News* has only sporadic international coverage, but from time to time it does announce career openings for degree candidates as well as a limited number of summer internships for undergrads. Among these have been administrative assistance, sales development (training program in advertising space sales), editorial trainees (trainees rotate through various editorial activites and, usually within 18 months, receive permanent assignments in one of the paper's divisions), and staff accountants.

Although the *News* has faced several near-bankruptcies and takeovers, as of the time of writing it still appears on the newsstands daily.

Background Desired

Writing ability, journalism, languages, international affairs, and economics.

The New York Times

> 229 West 43rd St.
> New York, NY 10036

The *New York Times* has its own network of foreign correspondents in major foreign capitals and also engages in the worldwide syndication of news and features. It has a daily circulation of more than 1,000,000 and publishes 35 small city papers in Maine, the South, and California, as well as special-interest magazines such as *Family Circle*. It owns five network-affiliated TV stations and one AM-FM radio station.

Background Desired

Writing ability, journalism, languages, international affairs, and economics.

Public Relations News

> Phillips Publishers
> 7811 Montrose Rd.
> Potomac, MD 20854

PR News is geared to management and public relations executives in the United States and abroad. It provides information on all aspects of public relations and keeps its subscribers current with developments in this field.

Background Desired

Public relations, advertising, economics, writing ability, and marketing.

Time Magazine

> Time-Life Building
> Rockefeller Center
> New York, NY 10020

If you are lucky enough to get a reporting job at *Time*, whether through long apprenticeship in the provinces or through some fortuitous event upon graduation, you may not have to wait as long for an international assignment as if you were with a newspaper. Your international background may even be crucial in your hiring, and your apprenticeship at headquarters relatively short.

In addition to reporting and writing jobs, *Time* has a sizeable research staff that may be of interest to you. The magazine's research functions are broken down by geographic area, economics, and other functional subjects. There is some turnover in these jobs because promotion possibilities are limited.

Background Desired

For research: international affairs, area studies, and international economics.

United Press International

1400 I Street, NW
Washington, DC 20005

Recently rescued from bankruptcy by Saudi business money, UPI continues with its two main tasks: reporting the news for subscribers in the United States and making sure that readers outside the United States have access to the news. It has five international divisions, with headquarters in London (Europe/Africa/Middle East), Hong Kong (Far East), Buenos Aires (South America), Mexico City (Mexico/Central America/Caribbean), and Toronto (Canada). It has 90 offices abroad with a staff of about 500, including 133 overseas correspondents, engaged in international operations.

Background Desired

Writing ability, languages, journalism, international affairs, and economics.

The Washington Post

1150 15 St., NW
Washington, DC 22071-7300

The *Washington Post* has more than 17 foreign correspondents based in major capitals. The foreign bureaus are located in Beijing, Beirut, Bonn, Buenos Aires, Cairo, Caribbean/Central America, Jerusalem, Johannesburg, London, Manila, Mexico City, Moscow, Nairobi, New Delhi, Paris, Toronto, and Warsaw.

Background Desired

Writing ability, journalism, languages, international affairs, and economics.

BROADCASTING

American Women in Radio and Television

> 1101 Connecticut Ave., NW
> Washington, DC 20036
>
> or
>
> 245 Fifth Ave.
> Suite 2103
> New York, NY 10016

AWRT is a nonprofit organization of professional women in the broadcast industry and allied fields. The goals of the organization are to provide a medium of communication and exchange of ideas, to promote the advancement of women in broadcasting, and to try to improve the quality of radio and TV.

Among the services provided to members is an *International Broadcasters Program* that hosts foreign women broadcasters who wish to explore U.S. broadcasting systems and techniques. There is also an *International Study Tours Program* that provides opportunities for U.S. women in the industry to study foreign broadcast facilities and advertising methods.

Background Desired

Exchange program experience and public relations.

Board for International Broadcasting

> 1201 Connecticut Ave., NW
> Washington, DC 20036

BIB oversees the operations of *Radio Free Europe* and *Radio Liberty*. The former is beamed to the peoples of Eastern Europe and the latter to the former republics of the USSR. Together they broadcast overseas almost 1,000 program hours weekly in 22 languages. A multilingual staff of some 1,800 is employed, and an estimated daily audience of some 18,000,000 in six countries is reached. RFE/RL also engage in area and audience research.

Background Desired

Eastern European and Russian languages, translating, and research ability.

Capital Cities/ABC

> 77 West 66th St.
> New York, NY 10023

Capital Cities/ABC has three component parts:

1. The *ABC-TV Network Group* is divided into TV Stations — East (New York, Chicago, Philadelphia, Durham-Raleigh), TV Stations — West (Los Angeles, San Franciso, Houston, Fresno), Radio Stations — Group 1 (nine radio stations in New York, Los Angeles, San Francisco, Detroit, Denver, and Providence), and Radio Stations — Group 2 (Chicago, Forth Worth, Dallas, Atlanta, Minneapolis, Washington, DC).
2. The *Publishing Group* is composed of Fairchild Publications, ABC Publishing (*Modern Photography, High Fidelity, Schwann Record and Tape Guide, Musical America,* and *Automotive Industries,* among others), Agricultural Publications, and Hitchcock Publishing.
3. *Newspapers* include the *Kansas City Star-Times, Fort Worth Star-Telegram, Oakland Press,* and *Shore Line Newspaper* of Guilford, Connecticut.

Capital Cities/ABC has 20,000 full-time employees, a little more than half in broadcasting. The corporate staff amounts to about 270.

Background Desired

For broadcasting: marketing, advertising, business administration, and international affairs. For publishing: journalism, writing, and editing. For newspapers: writing ability, international affairs, economics, and journalism.

Channel 13

> 356 West 58th St.
> New York, NY 10019

Channel 13 is both a producer and broadcaster of TV programs. Its most visible producing partnership, the "MacNeil/Lehrer News Hour," is a staple of national public television. Channel 13 also has an international division that is concerned with international programming and research.

Background Desired

Area studies, research ability, and program production and planning.

Columbia Broadcasting System (CBS)

> 51 West 52nd St.
> New York, NY 10019

CBS began as a radio broadcasting service in 1927 and today operates one of the nation's top commercial TV networks, 7 TV stations, a nationwide radio network, and 21 AM and FM radio stations.

In 1987 CBS sold its magazine publishing and recorded music business. Since then it has focused entirely on its historic core business of broadcasting. Development efforts have been stepped up in all areas of entertainment programming, not only in terms of dollar investment but also in terms of innovative programming concepts and new talent. It has also increased network news through a substantial commitment to *CBS News* broadcasts in both morning hours and prime time.

Background Desired

Advertising, marketing, research, business administration, and international affairs.

Corporation for Public Broadcasting (CPB)

> 901 E St., NW
> Washington, DC 20004

The corporation is a private organization largely supported by federal funds. Its mission is to help develop an American noncommercial public radio and TV system that will "inform, enlighten, entertain, and enrich the lives of people."

Among its responsibilities are to stimulate diversity, excellence, and innovation in programs; to advance the technology and application of delivery systems; to safeguard the independence of local licensees; and to act as trustee for funds appropriated by Congress or contributed to CPB by other sources. CPB is also responsible for determining the potential audience's priority needs and interests.

Background Desired

Research ability, engineering, sampling polls and surveys, and law.

International Radio and Television Society

> 420 Lexington Ave.
> New York, NY 10170-0101

There are three educational projects under the IRTS banner:

1. *Faculty/Industry Seminars*   Here major decision makers of broadcasting and government meet with faculty members from many universities for the purpose of sharing information on developments in radio and TV.
2. *College Conference*   This is the largest of the foundation-funded projects. Panels and seminars are held for college-level juniors and seniors to provide them with an inside view of the radio and TV business.
3. *Minority Career Workshop*   This program acquaints minorities from the tristate area with the industry and provides them with a chance to interview.

Background Desired

Educational studies, seminar and conference organization, and public relations.

National Broadcasting Company (NBC) (Owned by General Electric)

> 30 Rockefeller Plaza
> New York, NY 10020

The scramble for jobs in NBC parallels that in ABC and CBS. Even those with a master's degree sometimes start as pages or tour guides and then get in line for higher-level jobs when they open up. The progression is usually from tour guide or page to desk assistant, then to research, and from there to news writing and production. NBC has a division that sells TV shows abroad and another division that prepares international reports. A third target for the internationally trained student is the NBC office that bids for contracts for installing TV stations abroad.

Background Desired

Advertising, marketing, research, business administration, and international affairs.

National Public Radio

> 2025 M St. NW
> Washington, DC 20036

NPR produces and distributes programming to almost 450 member stations nationwide using a state-of-the-art satellite system. Member stations actually broadcast NPR to the nation's radios. Although NPR concentrates on programs with national content, it does have some international programming, including "AFROPOP Worldwide," "Passage to India," and "The World of Islam."

Background Desired

Broadcasting or journalism, international relations, research ability, and area studies.

BOOK PUBLISHING

In an age when size is commonly believed to add power and profitability to an organization, publishing has experienced its share of takeovers: small publishers by large publishers and large publishers by conglomerates. In contrast, over the past few years independent bookstores have been flourishing, although they are in tough competition with chain "superstores," which are popping up all over the country. The two largest chains, Waldenbooks and Barnes and Noble (which owns B. Dalton) account for 25 to 30 percent of all book sales in the United States.

Despite these developments, many firms still exist in the publishing business, and each year many thousands of books are published. The major types of publishing are general, or "trade," books, sold in bookstores for the general reader; "mass market" paperbacks, sold in drugstores and supermarkets as well as bookstores; books for professionals, e.g., doctors or lawyers; and books for schools and colleges.

Following are the types of jobs in book publishing:

Editorial. At the bottom of this ladder is the editorial assistant, who often is 50 percent secretary and 50 percent editor's helper. Typing skills are usually required. The job may sound menial and may often be just that, but it should not be sloughed off if you are really motivated for a publishing career. In trade publishing, promotion can be rapid if your editing skills are of a high order. After that you can become an assistant editor with full-time editorial duties, then associate editor and editor with full responsibility for many manuscripts.

Designing. This job has responsibility for any artwork required, the selection of all typefaces, and the cover of the book.

Production. This covers all arrangements for composition, printing, binding, and packaging.

Marketing. This involves not only selling the book but advertising, promotion, research, and coordination of field sales managers.

Sales. This job is done by traveling representatives and people who support them from the firm's offices.

Those considering a career in publishing may wish to obtain a copy of *Who Does What and Why in Book Publishing: Writers, Editors, and Money Men* (New York: Birch Lane Press).

Publishing Courses

Since most colleges and universities don't offer a publishing major, a few institutions are now offering the next best thing — intensive, short courses that serve as introductions both to the field and to people already in the industry who can act as helpful contacts once your job search begins. Information on the two best known programs follows.

Radcliffe Publishing Course

> Radcliffe College
> 77 Brattle Street
> Cambridge, MA 02138
> (617) 495-8678

The Radcliffe Publishing Course has provided an intensive six-week introduction to all facets of book and magazine publishing since 1947. Students are taught by professionals in the industry, many of whom are graduates of the Course. The fees, which include tuition, room, and board, are rather high at about $4500. Limited financial aid is available. Applications may be filed any time after January 1 and are due by April 1. The Course runs from late June through early August.

New York University's Summer Institute in Book and Magazine Publishing

> Center for Publishing
> NYU School of Continuing Education
> 48 Cooper Square, Room 108
> New York, NY 10003
> (212) 998-7219

This seven-week program runs through the early summer and provides an overview of the book and magazine publishing industries. Lectures and training workshops are taught by publishing professionals. Admission is limited and housing and meal plans are available. NYU also offers night and weekend courses that cover the book and magazine publishing spectrum, as well as a Certificate in Book Publishing for those who complete six specified classes. Write to Certificate in Publishing at the above address for more information.

Background Desired

Unless otherwise specified, the ideal backgrounds for breaking into publishing are as follows: for editorial jobs, journalism, English, writing, and editing; for design jobs, artwork and designing; for production work, printing and typesetting; and for international work, business administration, marketing, sales, advertising, public relations, and languages (particularly French, German, and Spanish). Special backgrounds desired for individual cases will be noted.

Association of American Publishers

> 220 East 23rd St.
> New York, NY 10010

AAP is a confederation of several hundred publishers of books of all types. Its goals are to represent book publishing and educational publishing to the general public and to government, as well as to provide members with information concerning trade conditions, markets, copyright issues, manufacturing process, taxes, duties, censorship movements, government programs, and other matters of importance to publishers. The AAP also provides information on publishing as well as on occasional job leads.

Hachette Publications

> 1633 Broadway
> New York, NY 10019

> or

> 83 Avenue Marceau
> F-75783 Paris Cedex 06 France

This French organization is one of the six largest paperback book publishers in the world; it is also a leader in the consumer magazine field (*Woman's Day, Flying, Popular Photographer*).

Background Desired

Marketing, business, and French language.

Harcourt Brace Publishers

> 1250 Sixth Ave.
> San Diego, CA 92101

>> or

> 111 Fifth Ave.
> New York, NY 10011

>> or

> 6277 Sea Harbor Dr.
> Orlando, FL 32821

Harcourt Brace, along with the Neiman Marcus Group and General Cinema Theaters, is owned by General Cinema Corporation.

HB is a highly diversified organization. It is composed of five groups:

1. The *University and Scholarly Publishing Group* includes *Academic Press* (with an office in London) and the *HB International Division*, which distributes HB books and materials abroad. Publishing houses are also located in Toronto, Montreal, Australia, the United Kindom, and Japan.
2. The *Elementary and Secondary School Publishing Group* includes textbooks, audio-visual materials, psychological tests, and research into school curricula.
3. The *Periodicals and Insurance Group* includes organizations that publish farm periodicals and sell various kinds of insurance.
4. The *Psychological Corporation*, the largest for-profit publisher of educational and psychological tests in the world.
5. *Drake Beam Morin*, the largest provider of career transition, outplacement, and executive counseling services. It assists executives in 21 countries through 94 overseas offices.

Background Desired

Marketing, business administration, finance, area studies, educational studies, and public relations.

Macmillan Publishing Company

> 866 Third Ave.
> New York, NY 10022

or
Maxwell Communications Corporation
33 Holborn
London, EC1N 2NE
England

In 1991, Macmillan Publishing Company was purchased by the Maxwell Communications Corporation of London, England. Macmillan's core businesses are educational publishing, instruction, and information services.

Within educational publishing, Macmillan produces textbooks and supplementary materials for elementary, high school, college, and professional markets. The instruction group provides Berlitz language training, while Katharine Gibbs conducts office-skills training programs for many thousands of students annually. Information services are concentrated in Standard Rate and Data Service, which provides media information in published and electronic forms to the advertising industry.

Maxwell Communications Corporation also owns Fixot, a French publishing subsidiary; Panini, a group of companies headquartered in Italy that produces stickers aimed at children; and Macdonald Publishing Group of London that publishes books that range from literary biographies to paperback thrillers.

Background Desired

Marketing, business administration, publishing, music, and educational studies.

McGraw-Hill

1221 Avenue of the Americas
New York, NY 10020

McGraw-Hill has four operating segments:
1. The *Educational and Professional Publishing Segment* includes the international, education, consumer, professional-book and legal-information operations.
2. The *Financial Services Company,* including Standard and Poor's as well as international trade and logistics management services.
3. The *Information and Publications Services Company* includes construction, computer and communications, legal aerospace and defense, health-care, energy, and process-industries groups.
4. *Broadcasting Group* has a network of affiliated television stations throughout the United States.

In 1991, McGraw-Hill's revenue from foreign sources was more than 19 percent. For instance, the magazine *Business Week* was published in local languages in China, Russia, and Hungary. McGraw-Hill's *Medical Publishing Unit* has offices in 17 countries and a unit, *MMS International*, provides commentary and analysis on government security and currency markets to more than 20,000 customers worldwide.

Background Desired

Applicants are asked about experience in publishing, editing, marketing, sales, administration, international studies, or area studies. For Standard and Poor's, finance, accounting, and business administration are important.

National Geographic Society

17th and M Sts., NW
Washington, DC 20036

The *Book Service* and *Special Publications* divisions of the society prepare illustrated books ranging over a broad spectrum of interests, from ancient Greece and Rome to American inventors.

The society's cartographers are well known for the quality of their maps, and the *National Geographic Atlas of the World* is a standard reference work. The *National Geographic Magazine* is perhaps the most popular product of the society.

Background Desired

Geography, area studies, anthropology, and cultural studies.

Paramount Publishing

1230 Avenue of the Americas
New York, NY 10020

or

Paramount Communications, Inc.
15 Columbus Circle
New York, NY 10023

Paramount Publishing is owned by Paramount Communications, a global entertainment and publishing company with 12,000 employees across the globe. Formerly known as Simon & Schuster, it has worldwide publishing and distribution capabilities. Imprints include Simon & Schuster, Prentice Hall, Silver Burdett-Ginn, and Pocket Books. The Canadian office of Prentice Hall publishes original works in the educational, consumer, and business markets. In the

United Kingdon, Australia, and New Zealand, Paramount publishes academic and professional books, consumer books, and books for small children and young adults. It has subsidiaries in Brazil, Japan, Mexico, and Singapore, and offices in 17 countries including Germany, Korea, and Thailand, and co-publishes with publishers in five European countries.

Paramount has had particular success in Mexico where it publishes books in Spanish for Latin America. In the future it is focusing expansion on the markets of the Pacific Rim.

Background Desired

Business administration, marketing, international affairs, languages, and education studies.

Unipub

> 4611-F Assembly Dr.
> Lanham, MD 20706

Unipub is a central source for specialized international publications. It began as the U.S. distributor for publications of U.N. agencies, but its service has continued to expand until now it handles the output of many more organizations that publish works of international interest. Its offerings are particularly comprehensive in the fields of energy, food supply, education, environment, human rights, and economic development.

Unipub also publishes *IBID — International Bibliography, Information, Documentation*.

Background Desired

International affairs, business administration, publishing, and UN affairs.

World Trade Academy Press

> 50 East 42 St., Suite 509
> New York, NY 10017

This publishing house issues several books of particular interest to those looking for international jobs: *Looking for Employment in Foreign Countries; Directory of Foreign Firms Operating in the United States;* and *Directory of American Firms Operating in Foreign Countries*. These volumes can usually be found in any large reference library. They can be extremely helpful in identifying targets of your job search.

Background Desired

Research, business, banking, and administration.

11

TEACHING AT HOME AND ABROAD

There are two types of opportunities for those with an international background who want to teach. The first is to teach international subjects at home; the second is to teach American subjects abroad.

If you wish to teach international subjects at home, you have probably specialized in political science, international economics, languages, area studies, or history. Teaching jobs in any of these subjects are difficult to find. If you are aiming at college- or university-level teaching, a doctorate in the discipline of your choice is essential. If you are interested in junior colleges or secondary schools, an M.A. may be sufficient, although even here a Ph.D. will occasionally be needed. In any case, past instructors and any professional associations may provide good leads to the job openings that develop in your field.

In addition, contact the American Political Science Association (1527 New Hampshire Ave., NW, Washington, DC 20036) for its brochure, *Careers and Study of Political Science for Undergraduates*.

Also attend the annual conventions of the American Economic Association, the American Political Science Association, the American Historical Association, or the Association of American Geographers for contacts and possible interviews regarding available openings.

For additional help in your job search for teaching positions in the United States, write to:

American Federation of Teachers
555 New Jersey Ave., NW
Washington, DC 20001

or

National Education Association
1201 16th St., NW
Washington, DC 20036

SPECIAL TIPS

If you want to teach abroad, you must first be a teacher in the United States — or at least have the necessary credentials. It is rare indeed that you will be hired for an overseas assignment unless you have some teaching experience. Assuming, then, that you have met this requirement, two questions arise: How do I find out about overseas teaching opportunities? and How do I go about applying?

Let's look at procedures first.

When you are being seriously considered for a job, your potential employer will ask you for a copy of your dossier. Therefore, even before you start looking for a job, establish your credentials — i.e., arrange to have transcripts and letters of recommendation on file at your college placement office, or in your own possession. It is often acceptable practice to send the material yourself to an overseas school. Since it is easier to let your college take care of these administrative details, however, you will probably gratefully leave this chore in their hands.

There are three main sources of teaching jobs overseas: (1) Department of Defense Overseas Dependents schools; (2) overseas American elementary and secondary schools assisted by the Department of State; and (3) schools established by American businesses for their employees' dependents. There are other sources of jobs, however, and we will discuss these under the all-embracing "Other Opportunities."

A tour of duty abroad averages one or two years, depending on the area of assignment. In general, proficiency in the particular foreign language is not required.

Department of Defense Dependents Schools

For a list of about 250 schools abroad, write to:

Office of Overseas Dependents Schools
Department of Defense
1225 Jefferson Davis Highway
Crystal Gateway #2
Suite 1500
Arlington, VA 22202

Or write to regional offices:

DOD Dependents Schools
Pacific Region
FPO AP 98772-0005

DOD Dependent Schools
Germany Region
APO AE 09634-0005

or

or

DOD Dependents Schools
Atlantic Region
APO AE 09241-0005

DOD Dependent Schools
Mediterranean Region
APO New York 09283-0005

or

DOD Dependent Schools
Panama Region
APO AA 34002-0005

Overseas dependents schools of the Department of Defense are located in the Azores, Bahamas, Belgium, Bermuda, Cuba, Denmark, England, Germany, Greece, Iceland, Italy, Japan, Korea, Midway Islands, Morocco, Netherlands, Bahrain, Newfoundland, Norway, the Philippines, Scotland, Spain, Taiwan, Turkey, and the West Indies.

Background Desired

Among the qualifications for teaching positions are 18 semester hours in professional teacher education courses, a valid teaching certificate, and at least one year's full-time teaching experience within the past five years (practice, student, and substitute experience do not qualify).

Overseas American Schools Assisted by the Department of State

Office of Overseas Schools
Department of State
Washington, DC 20520

There are more than a hundred of these schools, which educate the dependents of U.S. government personnel stationed overseas. These schools have either binational or international student bodies.

Background Desired

Teaching, education studies, international affairs, and languages.

Schools Established by American Businesses

Write to corporate headquarters. Among such companies are:

Exxon
225 John Carpenter Freeway
Erving, TX 75062

Texaco, Inc.
1345 Avenue of the Americas
New York, NY 10105

OTHER OPPORTUNITIES

Teaching English in Japan and China

Japan

The *Japan Exchange and Teaching Program*, known as JET, recruits up to 1,000 Americans annually to teach English in Japanese schools and colleges as well as 30 to 40 Americans to work in municipal and prefectural offices in Japan. Those interested should get an application from the Japan Information Center, Consulate General of Japan, 299 Park Ave., New York, NY 10171, or from the Embassy of Japan, JET program Office, 2520 Massachusetts Ave., NW, Washington, DC 20008.

Teaching experience, though helpful, is not necessary for JET. International experience and motivation for work abroad are usually more important. Completed applications and required documentation are screened at the Japanese Embassy and selected candidates are interviewed for final selection at the embassy or consulate general.

A special organization in Japan, the Conference of Local Authorities for International Relations (CLAIR), is involved in candidate placement.

Aeon, Shinjuku Gyoen Blvd., 2-3-10 Shinjuku, Shinjuku-ku, Tokyo 160 employs 250–300 people to teach conversational English to college students, businessmen, housewives, etc. Aeon has offices throughout Japan. Applicants need neither teaching experience nor knowledge of Japanese.

China

In China the need for English language teachers is particularly great. Millions of Chinese are said to want to learn English, but the few Chinese qualified to teach it complain of small salaries compared to what they could earn in other occupations. Despite the communist slogan "A teacher is a candle, giving light to others while burning itself," few Chinese are attracted. As a result, opportunities exist for foreigners qualified to teach English.

If interested, obtain an application and a list of colleges and universities in China from the Consulate General of the People's Republic of China at 520 12th Ave., New York, NY 10036. Candidates are encouraged to submit their applications and required documentation directly to those institutions where they are interested in working.

People interested in teaching at a denominational school in China should contact the National Council of Churches, 475 Riverside Dr., New York, NY 10115.

Canal Zone Government

> Panama Canal Company
> Division of Schools
> Box 2012
> Balboa Heights
> Canal Zone

Even though American control of the Panama Canal is passing out of existence, presumably the Canal Zone government, an independent agency of the U.S. government, will continue until the twenty-first century to operate schools for its employees' dependents. These schools are on all levels: kindergarten, elementary, junior high school, senior high school, and college.

Background Desired

The Canal Zone government is one of those rare exceptions — it does not require teaching experience except for jobs at the college level.

European Council of International Schools

> 18 Lavant St.
> Petersfield, Hampshire GU32 3EW
> England

The council handles about 150 positions for teachers on the primary- and secondary-school levels. It assists in staff recruitment by working with individual schools and teachers interested in teaching posts abroad. Each February it conducts an International Staff Recruitment Center in London.

Background Desired

Teaching, international studies, languages, and M.A. in education.

International Schools Services (ISS)

> P.O. Box 5910
> Princeton, NJ 08540

The ISS provides educational services for American schools overseas. Among these services are recruitment and recommendation of personnel, curricular guidance, liaison between overseas schools and American educational resources, and consultative visits to overseas schools. It is a useful source for lists of available teaching opportunities in all overseas schools, except for Department of Defense schools, which it does not service. More than 700 schools are affiliated with ISS, in Africa, Europe, Central and South America, the Middle East, and Asia.

If you wish to take advantage of ISS facilities on your job hunt, you will have to pay a registration fee and subsequently a placement fee if you find an appropriate position with ISS assistance.

Background Desired

Teaching, academic administration work, and international affairs.

Peace Corps

> 1990 K St., NW
> Washington, DC 20526

The Peace Corps still hires teachers with experience for countries in Africa, Asia, and Latin America.

Background Desired

See Peace Corps on pages 88–89.

Overseas Colleges and Universities

Teaching opportunities with four overseas institutions should be explored:

WorldTeach
Harvard Institute for International Development
One Eliot St.
Cambridge, MA 02138-5705

WorldTeach is a nonprofit organization founded in 1986 that facilitates teaching experiences for college graduates in a half dozen countries around the world. Teachers are recruited to teach English, math, science, and sports in China, Costa Rica, Namibia, Poland, South Africa, and Thailand. WorldTeach volunteers pay a fee to cover costs of transportation, school placement, and a two to three week orientation and language training program. In return, volunteers receive housing and a modest salary.

American University of Beirut
850 Third Ave.
New York, NY 10022

Be aware of the political and miltary situation in Lebanon. Note that a Ph.D. is usually required to obtain work at this university.

Istanbul Robert Kolej
Yuksek, Okulu
Robert College
Pk 8
Bebek, Istanbul
Turkey

A Ph.D. is desirable for applicants.

American University in Cairo
866 U.N. Plaza
New York, NY 10017

A Ph.D. is usually needed to obtain work here.

Southern Center for International Studies

320 West Paces Ferry Rd.
Atlanta, GA 30305

The Southern Center is the main educational institution in the Southeast region that prepares Southern leaders for international roles. Through center programs and contacts, these leaders have opportunities to meet with international experts and decision makers from this country and abroad.

The center employs a small full-time professional and administrative staff at its Atlanta offices. In addition, fellows of the center serve as program directors and lecturers. The Atlanta offices house the center's library, country data files, and classroom.

Background Desired

Administration, education, international affairs, library science, research, seminar and conference organizing, or teaching experience depending on the kind of work for which you are applying.

Specific Locations

If you are particularly interested in the Middle East, you may wish to explore opportunities with the following:

> American-Mideast Educational and Training Services
> 1717 Massachusetts Ave., NW
> Washington, DC 20036

For positions in Greece, Turkey, and Lebanon (depending on its political situation), write to:

> Near East College Association
> 850 Third Ave.
> New York, NY 10022

Australia may be interested in applications of teachers for the primary and secondary grades. Write to:

> Victoria Teacher Selection Program
> California State University
> Hayward, CA 94542

Exchange of Positions

If you have a teaching position and wish to exchange with an overseas teacher temporarily, write to:

> Teacher Exchange Section
> U.S. Department of Education
> Washington, DC 20202

Additional Organizations and Information

For a list of agencies that assist overseas placement, or for specific job opportunities under U.S. government and foreign government programs, write to:

> Information and Reference Division
> Institute of International Education
> 809 U.N. Plaza
> New York, NY 10017

A booklet with information on agencies and organizations in almost a hundred countries that are concerned in one way or another with recuriting teaching staff may be obtained by writing to:

> National Commission for UNESCO
> UNESCO
> New York, NY 10017

If you are interested in teaching English as a second language, contact Teachers of English to Speakers of Other Languages (TESOL) at 455 Nevils Building, Georgetown University, Washington, DC 20057 for a list of institutions. Also contact the Center for Applied Linguistics, 1118 22nd St., NW, Washington, DC 20037 for information on possible opportunities.

The U.S. Information Agency may also be of help to those seeking jobs as teachers of English as a foreign language, directors of courses, and administrators in binational centers abroad. Ask for *English Teaching Programs Abroad*, a directory of binational centers. These centers work closely with U.S. Information Services posts overseas. English teaching is a major component of their cultural, educational, and information activities. Write to:

> Office of Cultural Centers and Resources
> U.S. Information Agency
> 301 Fourth St.
> Washington, DC 20547

Also, get a copy of *Opportunities Abroad for Teachers*, a booklet put out by the Department of Education that explains the Fulbright exchange program for teachers. Application procedures, awards, and arrangements with cooperating countries are covered in the booklet. Write to:

> Department of Education
> Washington, DC 20202
>
>   or
>
> Superintendent of Documents
> U.S. Government Printing Office
> Washington, DC 20402

Another book you may wish to look at is *Teachers' Guide to Teaching Positions in Foreign Countries,* compiled by H. Dilts and H. Hulleman (Box 514, Ames, IA 50010).

Most important of all is the spring 1993 edition of *Teaching Abroad,* put out by the Institute of International Education (809 U.N. Plaza, New York, NY 10017). For each country this book lists names and addresses of American and International Schools as well as teaching opportunities, qualifications to apply, benefits and salaries, date when applications are to be submittted, and names and addresses of people to contact for each school.

A small sample of the American and International Schools that were listed in the 1988 edition of *Teaching Abroad* follows:

Caribbean Area
   International School of Honduras
Europe
   American Community School, Athens
   American School of Paris
   American School of Madrid
   American School in London
   International School of Geneva
Pacific Area
   American School of Pago Pago, American Samoa
South America
   American School of Brasilia, Brazil
   Centro Boliviano Americano, Bolivia

12

INTERNATIONAL LAW

If you have a background in law and international affairs and wish to put both to use on the job market, you will find yourself in a very strong position indeed. This unusual combination provides you with one of those rare backgrounds that gives you serious consideration in the United Nations, the federal government, nonprofit organizations, businesses, banks, and the communications field, not to mention private practice — in other words, just about everywhere.

Of the two degrees — law and international affairs — you will find the former of paramount importance on the job hunt. You will ordinarily not get a professional job on the legal staff of any organization without a law degree. The addition of an international degree, even though it will not guarantee you work of an international nature, will put you on the inside track for such jobs as they develop.

If you have a law degree and are interested in a career with international overtones, you should consider seeking employment with a law firm with an international clientele or becoming part of the legal staff of a corporation with extensive overseas activities. For example, sea and air transportation legal problems often require that lawyers acting for sea and air transportation corporations or their insurers deal with questions of private international law. Such problems will frequently require foreign travel, sometimes for extensive periods of time, to deal with clients, governmental agencies, insurers, etc. Any law firm with a substantial maritime law practice will handle cases that require study of international treaties and conventions, as well as working with lawyers abroad.

Generally, a law degree takes three years and a masters of international affairs takes two. It is possible, however, to get both degrees in less time. Columbia

University, for example, has a joint program between its Law School and its School of International and Public Affairs that grants the Juris Doctor and the Master of International Affairs in four years.

A WORLD OF OPPORTUNITIES

What exactly are the career possibilities for this combined background?

United Nations

As an American looking for a legal job on the U.N. Secretariat's legal staff, you will find your chances brighter than those of Americans with only an international affairs degree who are looking for political or economic work. Jobs are few and highly competitive, but a background in public international law will improve your credentials. Because most specialized agencies in the U.N. structure have their own legal staffs, these should also be included among your targets.

Federal Government

All the foreign-oriented agencies of the U.S. government have legal divisions or General Counsel offices that will find your combined background of particular interest. The State Department even sends recruiters to some law schools in order to interview prospective candidates. Entry into the Department's Legal Adviser's office is by interview, not by written exam. Though you may make trips overseas to participate in legal negotiations undertaken by embassies, you will spend most of your time in Washington.

As for the domestic-oriented agencies, most of the large ones have legal staffs and would welcome your application. Since international work may be less important in these agencies, initially you may be assigned to domestic legal problems, but your international training can eventually be used when a vacancy calling for international know-how develops.

Federal government salaries are good but not as high as in top law firms. Competition for government jobs, accordingly, may be less keen than in the private sector.

Businesses and Banks

The largest of these organizations have their own legal division or general counsel. Others place their legal work in the hands of retained law firms.

Where businesses and banks are heavily engaged in international work, your combined background will give you a serious hearing.

Communications

The largest wire services, networks, and publishers either have their own legal staffs or contract for legal services from outside firms. Here again the combined background is a decided plus.

Nonprofit Organizations and Foundations

Only the largest of these organizations in the international field have legal staffs. The majority obtain outside legal help. Put the Ford and Rockefeller Foundations on your list of targets. Here you will find that salaries often approximate those in the private sector.

Private Practice

With your combined background, you should look at law firms with special international interests, corporations engaged in oil exploration, or companies with extensive overseas activities. The legal work you do will generally be in the field of private international law, rather than public international law, which is intergovernmental in nature. You will be dealing with cases in which, if the laws of the United States do not apply, the law applicable to the rights and liabilities of the parties will be determined either by international treaties and conventions, such as the Warsaw Convention relating to transportation by air (49 U.S.C. §1502), the Universal Copyright Convention (17 U.S.C. §104), or the convention on Ocean Bills of Lading, on which the U.S. Carriage Of Goods By Sea Act (46 U.S.C. §1300–1315) is based, or by the application of foreign law or international private law principles in courts of the United States.

U.S. Law Firms with an International Type of Practice

You will, as a rule, be permitted to practice law as such only in the courts to whose bars you are admitted to practice. Normally, you will not be allowed to practice in the courts of a foreign jurisdiction. United States law firms practicing in the fields of maritime law (admiralty), aviation law, trademark law, copyright and patent law, and licensing often represent foreign clients that are subject to the jurisdiction of courts in the United States. Many of the cases litigated in the United States arise abroad or on the high seas and require investigation outside the United States, knowledge of foreign law, and travel abroad to confer with clients and investigate the facts. A number of U.S. law firms have branch offices abroad to represent their U.S. clients and maintain liaison with their foreign clientele. In certain types of practice, such as maritime law, aviation law, copyright law, etc., there are international networks of specialty law firms which engage one another in the handling of cases. Even relatively small firms in these specialties often provide opportunities for travel and involvement with foreign law firms.

U.S. Corporations with Overseas Activities

Many U.S. corporations with extensive overseas activities maintain legal staffs abroad. Members of such staffs represent their corporations in negotiations with foreign governments, as well as with nationals of such countries. They will also deal with immigration problems of corporate employees, employment contracts, and other matters. Rarely will members of the legal staffs of such corporations be permitted to argue in the courts of the foreign country.

Members of the legal staff of the headquarters of such a corporation will supervise the legal staffs located abroad. If the corporation does not have an overseas legal staff, members of the headquarters staff may be called upon to travel abroad to represent the corporation in the same way as would a member of an outside law firm or a member of a foreign staff.

Baker and McKenzie

International Executive Offices
3900 Prudential Plaza
Chicago, IL 60601

One of the largest and most "international" of U.S. law firms is this Chicago-based firm, founded in 1949. A network of more than 40 offices in 26 countries in 6 continents makes Baker and McKenzie a truly international law firm. More than a thousand lawyers provide local, regional, and international expertise at offices in major business and commercial centers around the world. Lawyers at Baker and McKenzie possess multinational legal training and experience in both civil and common law. Many are admitted to practice in several jurisdictions and are multilingual.

Background Desired

Law degree, international affairs, area studies, and languages.

Davis, Polk, and Wardwell

450 Lexington Ave.
New York, NY 10017
(212) 450-4000

Davis, Polk is a medium-sized law firm with about 360 lawyers. It currently has U.S. offices in New York and Washington, DC, and abroad in London, Paris, and Tokyo.

The London office has three partners and eight corporate associates. The Paris office has two partners, five corporate associates, and one tax associate. The Tokyo office has two partners and two corporate associates. The U.S. legal staffs of these foreign offices are among the largest American law firms in these cities.

Associates in the firm's New York and Washington offices may seek assignments to a foreign office for periods of approximately two years. Unassigned associates are frequently sent to work in the London office for periods of up to six months.

In projects involving the London and New York offices, Davis, Polk has been involved in numerous securities offerings by U.K. companies in the United States. The Paris and New York offices of Davis, Polk have participated in the privatization of several French companies. The Tokyo office worked on the financing of Bridgestone's tender offer for Firestone, one of the largest U.S. acquisitions made by a Japanese company.

Background Desired

Law degree; international studies including languages, particularly French and Japanese; and finance.

Johnson and Gibbs

100 Founders Square
900 Jackson Street
Dallas, TX 75202
(214) 977-9000

This firm is the largest law firm headquartered in Dallas, having more than 200 lawyers. Its other offices are in Houston, Austin, and Washington, DC. All five offices provide legal services to numerous corporations having national and international interests.

The International Practice Group at Johnson and Gibbs provides international legal expertise to clients with needs falling into four categories:

1. "Outbound transactions," such as export sales, foreign distributorships or licensing arrangements, and foreign joint ventures
2. "Inbound transactions," including foreign investments and acquisitions in the United States
3. International banking and finance; i.e., representation of foreign bank offices located in Texas
4. Tax planning for multinational corporations

This firm also invites one or more foreign lawyers to join Johnson and Gibbs for periods of up to a year. In recent years lawyers from Germany, the Netherlands, Mexico, Italy, Hong Kong, China, and Argentina were employed to work with the law firm in Dallas. By the same token, lawyers of Johnson and Gibbs are sent abroad to work in legal offices in Brussels and Tokyo.

Johnson and Gibbs is also a member firm in the Pacific Rim Advisory Council (PRAC), the first multinational network of law firms with significant client interests in the Pacific region.

Background Desired

Law degree, finance, banking, investments, and international affairs.

Jones, Day, Reavis, and Pogue

> 599 Lexington Ave.
> New York, NY 10022
> (212) 326-3939

Jones, Day is an international law firm with offices located in eight major cities of the United States (New York, Washington, DC, Los Angeles, Austin, Chicago, Cleveland, Columbus, and Dallas) and five foreign cities (Geneva, Hong Kong, London, Paris, and Riyadh).

With more than 900 lawyers, Jones, Day is one of the largest law firms in the world. Its international operations span the firm's five practice groups: corporate, government regulation, litigation, real estate/construction, and tax.

Background Desired

Law degree, international affairs, area studies and languages, accounting, real estate, and business studies.

It is recommended that lawyers looking for international-type positions consult directories of law firms, such as *Martindale's*, to ascertain names of firms with offices abroad. Another source of information is the "Federal Jobs Newsletter" [(202)-393-3311], which lists not only Federal jobs but also jobs in the private sector.

One of the most helpful publications for your job hunt is the *Directory of Opportunities in International Law*, put out by the University of Virginia law school. The cost is $7 for students of the University of Virginia, $10 for other students, and $20 for the general public. Checks, made payable to John Basset Moore Society of International Law, should be sent to the society at the University of Virginia School of Law, Charlottesville, VA 22901.

BIBLIOGRAPHY

BOOKS OF GENERAL INTEREST

Beatty, Richard. *Get the Right Job in Sixty Days (or Less).* New York: Wiley, 1991.

Beckman, David, and Donnelly, Elizabeth. *The Overseas List: Opportunities for Living and Working in Developing Countries.* Bread for the World Educational Fund, 802 Rhode Island Ave., NE, Washington, DC 20018.

Boll, Carl. *Executive Jobs Unlimited.* New York: Macmillan, 1980.

Bolles, Richard. *The Nineteen Ninety-Two What Color is Your Parachute?: A Practical Manual for Job Hunters and Career Changers.* rev. ed. Berkeley, CA: Ten Speed Press, 1991.

Brown, Newell. *After College . . . Junior College . . . Military Service . . . What?* New York: Grosset and Dunlap.

Bruce, Stephen D. *Encyclopedia of Prewritten Job Descriptions.* Madison, CT: Business & Legal Reports, 1982.

Camden, Thomas and Polk, Karen T. *How to Get a Job in Washington: The Insiders Guide.* London: Surrey Books, 1990.

Editors of the Foreign Policy Association. *Guide to Careers in World Affairs.* New York.

Haldane, Bernard and Haldane, Jean. *The New Young Peoples' Job Power.* New York: Acropolis.

Irish, Richard K. *Go Hire Yourself an Employer.* 3rd edition. Garden City, NY: Doubleday, 1987.

Jackson, Tom. *Mastering the Hidden Job Market: How to Create New Job Opportunities in a World of Uncertainty and Change.* New York: Random House, 1992.

Jackson, Tom. *The Perfect Resume.* rev. ed. New York: Doubleday Press, 1990.

Jeffries, Francis. *The Total Guide to Careers in International Affairs.* Poolsville, MD: Jeffries and Associates, 1987.

Job Opportunities Bulletin. TransCentury Recruitment Center, 1901 N. Fort Myer Dr., Suite 1017, Arlington, VA 22209. Published bi-monthly, the Bulletin links international development organizations with individuals seeking international opportunities. The cost is $25 for a one-year subscription.

Joint Committee on Printing. *Congressional Directory.* Washington, DC: U.S. Government Printing Office.

Liebers, Arthur. *How to Get the Job You Want Overseas.* Revised. New York: Pilot Books, 1990.

Mann, Thomas E. *Career Alternatives for Political Scientists, A Guide for Faculty and Graduate Students.* Washington, DC: American Political Science Association.

Moore, Charles G. *The Career Game.* New York: National Institute of Career Planning, 1978.

Moskowitz, Milton, et al. *Everybody's Business: An Almanac.* New York: Harper & Row.

Payne, Richard A. *How to Get a Better Job Quick.* New York: NAL-Dutton, 1988.

Sanborn, Bob. *How to Get a Job in Europe: The Insider's Guide.* London: Surrey Books, 1991.

Schuman, Howard. *Making It Abroad: The International Job Hunting Guide.* New York: Wiley, 1988.

U.S. Government Manual. Washington, DC: Office of the Federal Register, General Services Administration.

Washington Information Directory. Washington, DC: Congressional Quarterly, Inc.

The Whole World Handbook: A Student Guide to Work, Study, and Travel Abroad. Council on International Educational Exchange, 205 East 42nd Street, New York, NY 10017.

Yearbook of International Organizations. Brussels, Belgium: Union for International Associations.

RESUMES

From College to Career: Entry Level Résumés for Any Major. Berkeley, CA: Ten Speed Press, 1992.

DIRECTORIES OF NONPROFIT ORGANIZATIONS

Alternatives to the Peace Corps: A Directory of Third World and U.S. Volunteer Opportunities. San Francisco: Food First, 1990.

Encyclopedia of Associations. Denise Akey, ed. Gale Research Co., 1980. Detailed information on 14,000 nonprofit organizations.

CODEL (Coordination in Development). 79 Madison Ave., New York, NY 10016. Acts as clearinghouse for church-related agencies operating in more than 80 countries.

Conservation Directory. Washington, DC: National Wildlife Federation. Annual list of organizations and agencies concerned with the conservation, management, and use of natural resources.

Directory of Organizations Concerned with Environmental Research. State University College at Fredonia. Geographic and subject listings of organizations (governmental, university, and private) throughout the world involved in environmental research.

Directory of Resources for Cultural and Educational Exchanges and International Communication. Washington, DC: U.S. International Communication Directory.

Encyclopedia of Associations: International Organizations. Detroit: Gale Research Incorporated, 1992. A guide to more than 11,000 international nonprofit membership organizations outside the United States, arranged by topic.

Foundation Directory. Stan Olson, ed. New York: The Foundation Center, Columbia University Press. 1992.

International Directory for Youth Internships. Council for Intercultural Studies and Programs, 777 U.N. Plaza, New York, NY.

Research Centers Directory. Detroit: Gale Research Company. A directory of 4,500 research institutes, centers, foundations, laboratories, bureaus, and other nonprofit research facilities in the United States and Canada. Information includes scope of research activities and names of publications.

Technical Assistance Programs of US Non-Profit Organizations. New York: American Council of Voluntary Agencies for Foreign Service. Separate volumes exist for Latin America, Africa, Near East–South Asia, and the Far East.

U.S. Non-Profit Organizatons in Development Assistance Abroad. New York: Technical Assistance Information Clearing House. Comprehensive directory of information on more than 400 nonprofit organizations, agencies, missions, and foundations and their work in 124 countries in Africa, East Asia, and the Pacific, Latin America, the Near East, and South Asia. The alphabetical listing gives programs and objectives, with cross-references by region, country, and organization. It can be consulted in library of American Council for Voluntary Action, New York.

U.S. Voluntary Organizations and World Affairs. New York: Center for War/Peace Studies. Listing of national and community organizations concerned with world affairs, explaining their purposes and activities, addresses, and staff sizes.

Voluntary Foreign Aid Programs — Report of American Voluntary Agencies Engaged in Overseas Relief and Development Registered with the Advisory Committee on Voluntary Foreign Aid. Washington, DC: Office of Private and Voluntary Cooperation, Agency for International Development.

Wilson, William K. *World Directory of Environmental Research Centers.* New York: Orix Press. Distributed by R. R. Bowker Co., New York.

DIRECTORIES OF BUSINESSES AND BANKS

General Directories

Fortune 500. An annual list of the top 500 U.S. corporations. Annual reports of individual corporations.

How to Find Information about Companies. Washington Researchers. This book is a good source of information about public and private companies, foreign and domestic. Updated frequently. 1991.

Middle Market Directory. New York: Dun and Bradstreet. Lists approximately 33,000 U.S. companies with a stated worth of $500,000 to $999,999.

Million Dollar Directory. New York: Dun and Bradstreet. Lists about 31,000 U.S. companies with a stated worth of $1 million or more. Gives officers, products (if any), approximate sales, and number of employees.

Moody's Manual. New York: Moody's Investment Service. Updated annually. Moody publishes manuals about securities and investments. Every other year.

Principal International Businesses. New York: Dun and Bradstreet. Has current information on approximately 55,000 companies in 133 countries worldwide. Updated annually.

Stafford, D. C. and Perkins, R. H. A. *Directory of Multinationals.* Basingstroke, Hants: Macmillan Publishers, 1989.

Standard and Poor's Register of Corporations, Directors, and Executives, 2 vols. New York: Standard and Poor's Corporation. Updated annually. Alphabetical list of approximately 34,000 U.S. and Canadian corporations, giving officers (names, titles, functions), products (if any), sales range, and number of employees.

Standards Directory of International Advertisers and Advertising Agencies. Wilmette, IL: National Register Publishing Company, 1985.

Standards Directory of World Marketing. Wilmette, IL: National Register Publishing Company, 1990.

Thomas Register of American Manufacturers. New York: Thomas Publishing Company. Eleven volumes updated annually. Volumes one to six list manufacturers by specific product. Volume seven is an alphabetical listing of companies and includes addresses, branch offices, subsidiaries, products, and estimated capitalization. Volume eight is the index to product categories and also contains a list of leading trade or brand names. Volumes nine to eleven contain catalogs of products.

Trade Directories of the World, compiled by U.H.E. Croner. New York: Croner Publications. This annotated list of businesses and trade directories is arranged by continent and by country. Includes an index to "trades and professions" and a country index.

Directories of American Companies with Foreign Subsidiaries

American Firms: Subsidiaries and Affiliates in Brazil. New York: Brazilian Government Trade Bureau.

Bureau of International Commerce, Trade Lists. U.S. Department of Commerce. Updated annually. Lists American firms, subsidiaries, and affiliates in each country with brief descriptions and addresses.

Directory of American Firms Operating in Foreign Countries. New York: Uniworld Business Publications. Lists companies alphabetically, giving name of officer in charge of foreign operations and countries of operation; also lists companies by country of operation.

Directory of U.S. Firms Operating in Latin America. Washington, DC: Pan American Union. This gives company lists, including the name of each manager, arranged by country.

Directory of United States Subsidiaries of British Companies. New York: British-American Chamber of Commerce, 1990.

Directories of Foreign Companies with American Subsidiaries

American Subsidiaries of German Firms. New York: German-American Chamber of Commerce.

Directory of Foreign Firms Operating in the United States. New York: Uniworld Business Publications.

Directory of Japanese Firms and Offices in the U.S. New York: Japan Trade Center.

Directories of Companies in Foreign Countries

Current European Directories. G. P. Henderson. Beckenham, Kent, England: CBD Research, Ltd. An annotated guide, arranged by country in Europe, to general directories of associations and research organizations.

Dun's Latin America's Top 25,000. Parsippany, NJ: Dun's Marketing Services, Incorporated, 1991. Businesses are listed geographically, by product classification, and alphabetically.

Europe's 15,000 Largest Companies. London: ELC Publishing Ltd., 1992. Distributed in the United States by Dun's Marketing Services (Parsippany, NJ). Companies and addresses are listed by country, sector, and alphabetically.

Jane's Major Companies of Europe. London: Jane's Yearbooks. Updated annually.

Major Companies of Europe. London: Graham and Trotman. Description of "Fortune 500" companies of Western Europe.

Principal International Business. New York: Dun and Bradstreet. Lists 55,000 leading enterprises in 140 countries by country, by product classification, and alphabetically.

Export-Import Companies

American Register of Exporters and Importers. New York: American Register of Exporters and Importers, Inc. Covers 30,000 manufacturers and distributors in export-import work. An especially important volume for those with both international and business qualifications, since export-import firms need both types of background.

Dun and Bradstreet Exporter's Encyclopedia, World Marketing Guide. New York: Dun and Bradstreet International. Updated annually.

Fortune 500: Top 50 Exporters. Annual list and information on top U.S. exporters.

Directories of Banking and Finance Industries

Banks of the World. Frankfurt am Main, Germany: Fritz Knopp Verlag.

Security Dealers of North America.

International Bankers Directory. Chicago: Rand-McNally.

Investment Companies. New York: Arthur Weisenberg and Co.

Money Market Directory. A directory of 6,000 institutional investors and their portfolio managers.

Moody's Bank and Finance Manual. New York: Moody's Investment Service, Inc. Two volumes updated annually.

Polk's Bank Directory.

Standard and Poor's Security Dealers of North America.

Who's Who in Banking: The Directory of the Banking Profession. New York: Business Press, Inc.

Banking Periodicals

The Banker
The Bankers Magazine
Bankers Monthly
Banking — The Journal of the American Bankers Association
Federal Reserve Bulletin
Journal of Commercial Bank Lending

Trade and Professional Associations

Directory of European Industrial and Trade Associations. Richard Leigh, ed. Detroit: Gale Research Company, 1986.

Directory of National Trade and Professional Associations of the United States. Washington, DC: Columbia Books. Alphabetical list of 4,300 national trade and professional associations. Gives chief officer, number of members, annual budget, and publications.

Encyclopedia of Associations. Detroit: Gale Research Co. Comprehensive list of national associations, with an alphabetical and key-word index. Gives name of chief officer, brief statement of activities, number of members, and publications.

Feingold, S. Norman and Nicholson, Avis. *The Professional and Trade Association Job Finder: A Directory of Employment Resources Offered by Associations and Other Organizations.* Garrett Park, MD: Garrett Park Press, 1983.

Corporation Records

Annual reports to shareholders are available in brokerage houses and in large business reference libraries. They can be obtained by phoning companies.
For companies traded over the counter, the Marvin Scudder Financial Collection is a valuable source of company history, annual reports, prospectuses, reorganization plans, and miscellaneous financial information.

Company Histories

American Economic and Business History: A Guide to Information Sources. Robert W. Lovett.
Studies in Enterprise: A Selected Bibliography of American and Canadian Company Histories and Biographies of Businessmen. Boston: Harvard University Graduate School of Business Administration.

BACKGROUND READING
ON MANAGEMENT CONSULTING

"Consultant's Corner, ACME Chief Personnel Managers Meeting." *MBA Executive,* March/April 1984, p. 5.
Consulting to Management. Larry E. Greiner and Robert O. Metzger. Englewood Cliffs, NJ: Prentice-Hall, 1983.
"The Future of Management Consulting," Carl Sloane. *Journal of Management Consulting,* Vol. 3, No. 1, 1986.
Management Consulting '89. Boston, MA: Harvard Business School Press.
"Management Consulting: A Game Without Chips." Thomas G. Cody. Fitzwilliam, NH: *Consultants News,* 1986.
Management Consulting: Annotated Bibliography of Selected Resource Materials. New York: Association of Management Consulting Firms (ACME).
Your Career in Management Consulting. New York: Association of Management Consulting Firms (ACME).

DIRECTORIES OF CONSULTANTS

Association of Management Consulting Firms — Directory of Members 1992/93. ACME (unit of Council of Consulting Organizations), 521 Fifth Ave., New York, NY 10175.

Bracus, Sam and Wilkinson, Joseph. *Handbook of Management Consulting Services.* New York: McGraw-Hill, 1986.

The Consultants and Consulting Organization Directory. Paul Wasserman and Janice McLean, eds. Detroit: Gale Research Co: 1991.

Directory of Consultant Members. New York: American Management Association. Annual.

Directory of Management Consultants and Industrial Services. Los Angeles Chamber of Commerce. Lists consulting firms and business and industrial services.

Directory of Membership and Services. Association of Consulting Management Engineers, 349 Madison Ave., New York, NY 10017. Annual.

Directory of Management Consultants. Kennedy and Kennedy, Inc., Templeton Rd., Fitzwilliam, NH 03447. Biennial.

Directory of Membership and Services. New York, NY: American Management Association.

Engineering Careers with Consulting Firms. Resource Publications. D.R. Goldenson and Company. Page profiles describing the activities of the firm, the nature of engineering services, and requirements for positions. Information arranged by specialty and geographic location.

Harvard Business School Guide, Management Consulting 1991–92. Sue March, ed. Cambridge, MA: Harvard Business School Press, 1991.

Industrial Research Laboratories of the U.S., rev. ed. William Buchanan, ed. Bowker Associates.

Management Consulting: A Game Without Chips. Kennedy Publishing Co., Fitzwilliam, NH 03447.

Management Consulting: A Guide to the Profession. 2nd edition. Geneva: International Labor Office, 1986.

Who's Who in Consulting: A Reference Guide to Professional Personnel Engaged in Consultation of Business, Industry and Government. Detroit: Gale Publishing Company.

A list of political consultants can be obtained from the American Association of Political Consultants, 320 North Larchmont Blvd., Los Angeles, CA 90004.

DIRECTORIES OF BOOK PUBLISHERS, NEWSPAPERS, PERIODICALS, AND BROADCASTING NETWORKS

Book Publishers

Editor and Publisher International Yearbook. New York: Editor and Publisher. Updated annually.

International Literary Market Place. Peter Found, ed. London and New York: R. R. Bowker. Updated annually. Contains facts on the worldwide publishing industry, minus the United States.

Literary Market Place with Names and Numbers. New York: R. R. Bowker. Updated annually. Contains facts on 22,000 firms and individuals in U.S. publishing, listing names, titles, addresses, and phone numbers.

Publisher's International Directory, R. R. Bowker Company. This directory gives names and addresses of 20,000 active publishers in 144 countries. New York: K. G. Saru. Distributed by Gale Research Company in Detroit.

Who's Who in Publishing, An International Biographical Guide. R. R. Bowker Company. Contains detailed biographical data of 3,500 leading persons in the publishing field.

Newspapers, Periodicals

Ayer's Directory. Philadelphia: N. W. Ayer & Son. Lists newspapers, magazines, and trade publications.

Ayer's Directory of Newspapers and Periodicals. Philadelphia: N. W. Ayer & Son.

Editor and Publisher International Yearbook. New York: Editor and Publisher. Encyclopedia of the newspaper industry. Directory of more than 8,000 U.S. and Canadian weekly and nondaily newspapers. Directory of newspapers in Latin America, Europe, Asia, Africa, and Australia.

Newspaper International. National Register Publishing Company. Lists newspapers and newsweeklies in more than 90 countries. Published annually in January, plus updated supplements.

Newspapers Career Directory. Hawthorne, NJ: Career Press Inc., 1990.

Standard Periodical Directory. Annual. A subject listing of 53,000 U.S. and Canadian periodicals giving addresses, scope, year founded, frequency, subscription rate, and circulation. Alphabetical index at end.

Broadcasting Networks

Broadcasting Yearbook. Washington, DC. Updated annually.

INDEX